Rediscovering Faithfulness

"This is among the most important, timely, and spiritually fruitful books I have read in decades. If you long for true faithfulness to God in the way and Spirit of Jesus—when so much of what is disguised as 'Christian' has little to do with him—I know of no better guide than Kenneth Wozniak's *Rediscovering Faithfulness*. Read it individually and in groups. Discuss, pray, and repent in it, for God's sake and for the world."

—**CHARLES W. BARKER**, retired campus minister, InterVarsity Christian Fellowship

"Throughout history, philosophers asked what constitutes a good person. From Aristotle to Kierkegaard, Kenneth Wozniak introduces their thoughts, comparing them with Scripture. Wozniak insightfully shows that faith in Christ leads us to faithfulness to Christ, that is, adopting his ethics and reflecting his character in our lives. Within these pages is a feast for the mind and heart, inspiring us to rise to the calling and privilege of being conformed to the image of Christ."

—**PATRICK KRAYER**, founder, Global Intercultural Mentoring

"Ethicist Kenneth Wozniak asks us to dig into Scripture not to find a list of 'dos and don'ts' but to discover the character of God. He challenges the church to abandon its syncretism and to choose to follow the kingdom-based social stance of Jesus. Providing interpretive tools and inspirational examples, Wozniak's writing is grounded in scholarship yet accessible to pastors and laypeople alike. His call to renewed faithfulness is a gift to us all."

—**GARY WATTS**, professor and dean emeritus, University of Jamestown

"This is an important book. Written with an ethicist's understanding and a prophet's perspective, Kenneth Wozniak has put his finger on a timely and important issue—many Christians' worldview urgently needs correcting. Wozniak has accurately seen through the mask of personal piety to the face of conformity with the world—a syncretistic worldview. Helpfully, Wozniak points us to a corrective—the early church and their 'all in' approach to following Jesus. He calls us to faithfulness!"

—**CHRISTOPHER SHORE**, chief development officer of economic empowerment, World Vision Inc.

Rediscovering Faithfulness

An Ethic after God's Own Heart

KENNETH W. M. WOZNIAK

WIPF & STOCK · Eugene, Oregon

REDISCOVERING FAITHFULNESS
An Ethic after God's Own Heart

Copyright © 2024 Kenneth W. M. Wozniak. All rights reserved. Except for brief quotations in critical publications or reviews, no part of this book may be reproduced in any manner without prior written permission from the publisher. Write: Permissions, Wipf and Stock Publishers, 199 W. 8th Ave., Suite 3, Eugene, OR 97401.

Wipf & Stock
An Imprint of Wipf and Stock Publishers
199 W. 8th Ave., Suite 3
Eugene, OR 97401

www.wipfandstock.com

PAPERBACK ISBN: 978-1-6667-5550-3
HARDCOVER ISBN: 978-1-6667-5551-0
EBOOK ISBN: 978-1-6667-5552-7

VERSION NUMBER 07/03/24

Scripture quotations, unless otherwise indicated, taken from The Holy Bible, *New International Version*®, NIV®. Copyright © 1973, 1978, 1984, 2011 by Biblica, Inc.® Used by permission. All rights reserved worldwide.

Scripture quotations from the Revised Standard Version (RSV) of the Bible are copyright © 1946, 1952, and 1971 National Council of the Churches of Christ in the United States of America. Used by permission. All rights reserved worldwide.

Excerpts taken from *The Moral Quest* by Stanley J. Grenz. Copyright (c) 1997 by Stanley J. Grenz. Used by permission of InterVarsity Press, P.O. Box 1400, Downers Grove, IL 60515, USA. www.ivpress.com

Used with permission of Pennsylvania State University Press: A Division of the Pennsylvania State University Libraries and Scholarly Communications, from *The Imago Dei as Human Identity: A Theological Interpretation*, Ryan S. Peterson, 2016; permission conveyed through Copyright Clearance Center, Inc.

Used with permission of Pilgrim Press, The United Church Press, from *Theology and Christian Ethics*, James M. Gustafson, 1974; permission conveyed through Copyright Clearance Center, Inc.

Used with permission of Trinity University Press, from *Character and the Christian Life: A Study in Theological Ethics*, Stanley Hauerwas, 1975; permission conveyed through Copyright Clearance Center, Inc.

To Brielle and Everleigh
Immeasurable gifts of God,
And treasures beyond expression

Contents

Preface | ix
Abbreviations | xiii

Introduction | 1

Part One: Faithfulness and the Social Milieu | 21

1   The Changing Understanding of Faithfulness | 23
2   The Early Christians | 27
3   The Social Milieu and the Kingdom of God | 39
4   Faithfulness and the Early Christians | 55
5   Returning to the Early Concept of Faithfulness | 68

Part Two: Faithfulness and Character | 73

6   The Notion of Character | 75
7   The Character of God | 85
8   Character Ethics | 103
9   Character Ethics in the Bible | 111
10   Character and the Image of God | 135

Part Three: Faithfulness and the Christian Life | 163

11   Faithfulness: Attitude and Intention | 165
12   Faithfulness: Commitment and Conduct | 197
13   Faithfulness, Love, and the Kingdom of God | 231

Conclusion: Rediscovering Forgotten Faithfulness | 256

Bibliography | 269

Preface

For the majority of Christians the notion of faithfulness is fundamental to their overall spiritual experience. Faithfulness is an expression, both outward and inward, of commitment and spirituality. As such it is tangible and substantial, but at the same time both ethereal and visceral. Like water passing between the fingers when one attempts to grasp it, faithfulness is a very real element of Christian maturity, yet challenges any attempt to grasp or even define it. The word has a definition, of course, but faithfulness is not a specific doctrine in the classic sense, like Christology, Soteriology, Ecclesiology, Eschatology, and the like, and so defies being studied in the way they can. However, is not faithfulness vitally important—experientially essential—for the one who aspires to live a mature Christian life? Just as commitment void of content is suggestive of shaky religiosity, so the Christian life lacking faithfulness is no Christian life at all.

What does it mean, from a moral sense, to be faithful? Addressing this perplexing question from a broad perspective is the burden of this book. Throughout its pages we will attempt to rediscover the actual meaning of faithfulness as we seek to construct an ethic of faithfulness—consistent living aligned with the heart of God.

One driver for writing this book is the conviction that Western Christianity has, in an expansive sense, abandoned what God has disclosed to be the core of faithfulness in favor of a comfortable blending of naïve piety and beneficial societal conventions. In short, the church and its constituents have adopted a syncretistic spirituality void of true faithfulness. Increasingly in many circles of the Western church the misguided adherents of such syncretism have gone so far as to affirm that the embraced elements of the secular society *are* Christianity. Whereas such syncretism is quite common among today's believers—generating legitimate concern over its core character of compromise—it is not the first time that Christian ethicists have been distressed about the phenomenon and subsequently given it exposure. In the "Translator's Introduction" to Søren Kierkegaard's 1847 work, *Purity of Heart Is to Will One Thing*, philosopher David V. Steere summarized Kierkegaard's concern over the dilution of Christian commitment in favor of a compromised, socially acceptable religiosity: "The comfortable Danish church in general he found to be blind to its compromises with bourgeois life which had reduced it to a low-pressure form of Christianity. This church stood out for him in sharpest contrast to the primitive Christian community."[1] The goal of this book is to rediscover what faithfulness meant to that "primitive Christian community" and to seek to benefit from that discovery.

The concern extends far back through the history of God's people. A thousand years before the birth of Jesus, King David—Israel's greatest king—lamented, "Help, Lord; for there is no longer any that is godly; for the faithful have vanished from among the sons of men."[2] David's social context in which he expressed his plea was "a time of universal moral corruption, and more particularly of prevailing faithlessness and boasting."[3] Some four hundred years later the prophet Ezekiel—capturing a similar concern—recorded this message of the Lord to Israel: "And you will know that I am the Lord, for you have not followed my decrees or kept my laws but have conformed to the standards of the nations around you."[4]

The problem, then, is not a new one; neither is concern over how it is to be addressed. In attempting to deal with it I stand in the tradition of many who have sought to call those who aspire to faithfulness to abandon their unreflective syncretism and align themselves with that which God has revealed concerning his moral expectations of his people.

---

1. Kierkegaard, *Purity of Heart*, 18.
2. Ps 12:1 RSV.
3. Keil and Delitzsch, *Commentary*, 5:192.
4. Ezek 11:12.

I write from the perspective of a Christian ethicist of orthodox faith. In doing so I approach faithfulness from a moral perspective, for faithfulness fundamentally concerns the life of the Christian and the Christian collective—the church—within a social context: the moral milieu of human experience. To challenge the prevailing moral assumptions and commitments—particularly among believers who think themselves to be living faithfully—is the ethicist's task and burden, just as it was for the prophets of old. As part of his earthly ministry Jesus assumed this prophetic role, and thus challenged the ethical miscalculations of the religious establishment of his day and context—miscalculations that all to often were defended vehemently by their adherents, generating significant and even forceful opposition. My desire in this writing is to remain true to the example of Jesus.

It is common—and desirable by many—when approaching ethics to view moral content as discrete answers to specific moral questions. I have taken a different approach, convinced that pursuit of faithfulness, and the ethic associated with it, is much greater—and entails something much more foundational—than the summation of individual answers to moral issues. Rather, an ethic of faithfulness finds its source in the moral excellence of the divine character. It is the moral character of God that underpins the ethic of faithfulness: that is why it is an ethic after God's own heart.

There are many to whom I am indebted for encouragement throughout this project. Chief among them is Mr. Matthew Wimer, managing editor at Wipf and Stock Publishers, and the entire Wipf and Stock staff. They have been a source of invaluable help with and throughout the process. It is because of them that the publishing experience has been both smooth and enjoyable. Dr. Stephen Davis of Claremont McKenna College has been a source of wise guidance from the inception of the project. I am thankful to him for his invaluable help throughout the writing. Rev. Jarrett Johnson has been an ongoing source of encouragement with his genuine interest in my work, for which I am continually grateful. I am deeply indebted to Dr. Ann Mulholland Wozniak, my dear wife and fellow ethicist, for her critical review of the text as well as many suggestions for improvement and clarification. Without her constant support throughout the years of this project, the book most certainly would not have been completed. Whereas the manifold gifts of these fellow pilgrims in the quest for faithfulness—as well as those of many others—have contributed beyond my ability to articulate, I alone bear responsibility for the book's content.

It is with great joy that I offer this volume to readers of all persuasions as an aid to their pursuit of faithfulness. In the words of nineteenth-century theologian and minister Thomas Verner Moore, "Should Christians be led to study the life of Jesus with a new interest, to draw out the less obvious facts of his wonderful history, and to investigate the inspired writings with more care and satisfaction, the labour bestowed on the preparation of these pages, itself a delightful pleasure, will be richly rewarded."[5]

Kenneth W. M. Wozniak
Carpinteria, California
April 2024

---

5. Moore, *Last Days of Jesus*, 6.

Abbreviations

ISBE   *International Standard Bible Encyclopedia.* 5 vols. Chicago: Howard-Severance, 1915.

TDNT   *Theological Dictionary of the New Testament.* 10 vols. Edited by Gerhard Kittel and Gerhard Friedrich. Translated by Geoffrey W. Bromiley. Grand Rapids: Eerdmans, 1964–76.

Introduction

FAITHFULNESS TO GOD IS a notion that nearly all Christians would affirm as a fundamental and essential element of the Christian life. One would be hard pressed to find a serious Christian who would argue that faithfulness is either optional or irrelevant. There is great diversity of opinion, however, concerning what faithfulness entails, both theologically and experientially.[1] Yet there is little disagreement among Christians that fidelity to God's expectations is at least part of what it means to be faithful.

The first, and most basic, expression of faithfulness—that is, the exercise of faith—is submission to the call to salvation, resulting in forgiveness and justification before God based upon the salvific work of Jesus Christ. In the New Testament the root meaning of faith "is no mere disposition of the human soul. Primarily, it is acceptance of the kerygma, i.e., subjection to the way of salvation ordained by God and opened up in Christ."[2] "Acknowledgment of Jesus as Lord is intrinsic to Christian faith along with acknowledgment of the miracle of His resurrection, i.e.,

---

1. For example, editors Wayne G. Boulton, Thomas D. Kennedy, and Allen Verhey, in the introduction of their collection of readings in Christian ethics, write, "each Christian is called by God to faithfulness to Christ. However, how different Christians understand that faithfulness may well vary depending upon how they understand the Bible, what their particular Christian traditions are, and upon their experiences as Christians and human beings." Boulton et al., *From Christ to the World*, 6.

2. Kittel and Friedrich, *TDNT*, 6:217.

acceptance of this miracle as true."[3] Faith entails belief. Very few Christians, if any, would disagree with this most fundamental understanding of the exercise of faith.

Subsequently, Christians are called to a life of ongoing faithfulness. It is at this point that perspectives regarding God's expectations start to diverge. Social contextual factors can color a person's understanding of faithfulness significantly. For modern Christians their personal or community's *Sitz im Leben* can influence their convictions regarding God's desires for his people—usually in ways of which they are not aware and, therefore, never question.

Many believers, particularly those in the West, have been led to understand that the faithful Christian is the one who commits herself or himself to finding and fulfilling God's call. Faithfulness is understood as something individual and specific. It has to do with a unique divine plan for each serious disciple of Jesus. Fidelity to the plan, according to this view, results in personal meaning, purpose, and fulfillment. Those results are the evidence of faithfulness on the part of the individual. In one pastor's blog we find, "It's encouraging to know that God has a plan and purpose for our lives. That means, He has a specific plan for your life individually."[4] He went on to justify his assertion by quoting Jer 29:11–13 in which God promised the exiled nation that there were divine plans for Israel, including a return to their homeland. The fact that the Jeremiah promise was intended for a collective—an entire nation—rather than an individual appears not to have influenced the author when he directly applied the passage to individuals. The promise, however, was not absolute; rather, it was contingent upon Israel's faithfulness to God. Verses 12–14a read, "'Then you will call on me and come and pray to me, and I will listen to you. You will seek me and find me when you seek me with all your heart. I will be found by you,' declares the Lord, 'and bring you back from captivity.'" Faithfulness and specific plans for prosperity, hope, and a bright future are linked in this incident from Israel's history. Unfortunately, much of current thought among Western Christians has substituted pursuit of the plan's results—prosperity and the like—as that which faithfulness entails, rather than the whole-heart seeking of God that the passage indicates.

---

3. Kittel and Friedrich, *TDNT*, 6:209.

4. Taylor, "7 Unique Callings of God," para. 1.

One psychologist reflected this focus on projected benefits when writing about how God interacts with his faithful people. She queried, "How do we gain awareness of our calling?," then answered with another question: "What things bring you pleasure, give you purpose, and ignite your passion?"[5] Rather than a focus on pursuing God according to passages such as the one in Jeremiah, the emphasis today appears to be on what pleasurable benefits the individual can realize from adherence to a surmised individual divine plan. This, it seems, is the predominant understanding of a faithful relationship with God.

The current notion of faithfulness as pursuit of, adherence to, and fulfillment of a specific divine plan for the individual—often resulting in the individual's pleasure and fulfillment as well as a sense of purpose and meaning—was not always what Christians understood God's expectations to be, nor is it true to the meaning of the word translated "faithful" in the New Testament. To understand accurately what it means to be faithful it will be beneficial to learn a bit about the Greek word *pístis* and its associated word group. Following that, an initial exposure to the earliest Christians' convictions regarding faithfulness will help launch the book.

THE NOTION OF FAITHFULNESS

In ancient Greek the word translated "faith" (Greek: *pístis*)—and the entire word group associate with *pístis*—does not convey any particular religious connotation.[6] When translated "faith" it carries the meaning of belief and trust. When pertaining to those who are faithful the word group has a distinct moral tone, the most fundamental element of which is obedience.[7] That notion of obedience carries through both the Old and New Testaments, and at times is even dominant.[8] In the Letter to the Hebrews the idea of obedience is especially strong in the eleventh chapter.[9]

The faithfulness of God is a major theme throughout the Scripture and serves as a model for the faithfulness of his people. Prior to the establishment of Israel, God showed his faithfulness to the Patriarchs, and

---

5. Hart, "5 Ways God Calls You!," paras. 7, 8.
6. Kittel and Friedrich, *TDNT*, 6:179.
7. Kittel and Friedrich, *TDNT*, 6:175.
8. Kittel and Friedrich, *TDNT*, 6:197.
9. Kittel and Friedrich, *TDNT*, 6:205.

continued to Moses and throughout Israel's Old Testament history.[10] One aspect of God's faithfulness is seen in his role as Father, in which "there is conveyed the idea of His faithfulness in loving and providing for His children."[11] Another goes beyond his relationship with the Patriarchs, Moses, and the rest of Israel, and explicitly refers to God's fulfillment of his promises to his chosen people: "the term is applied to the covenant-keeping Yahweh to express the truth that He is firm or constant, that is, faithful in regard to His covenant promises, and will surely fulfill them."[12] In this aspect we start to observe the moral nature of faithfulness. God loves, provides, and is veracious and honest. As such, God's faithfulness "is one of the characteristics of God's ethical nature. It denotes the firmness or constancy of God in His relations with men,[13] especially His people."[14]

The example of God keeping his promises continues throughout the New Testament, being captured most clearly in the Letter to the Hebrews, in which "this faithfulness of God in the sense of fidelity to His promises is set forth as the object of sure trust and hope."[15] It reflects a basic Greek concept in which faith is used to describe "a son who is bound by an oath, contract, pledge, etc., and who may thus be relied on."[16] Whereas in this regard the New Testament usage of the word group does not carry any unique or distinctive connotation compared with typical Greek usage,[17] in the New Testament faithfulness came to have a much broader sense than only promise-keeping based upon an oath or contract: it also included belief, obedience, trust, and hope.[18] As such, "it became the leading term of the relation of man to God,"[19] and thus was clearly a morally laden notion.

Recall that to exercise faith in God, according to the writings of the apostle Paul, fundamentally meant "acceptance of the kerygma, i.e.,

---

10. Orr, "Faithful, Faithfulness," para. 3.

11. Nixon, "Faith, Faithfulness," 483.

12. Orr, "Faithful, Faithfulness," para. 4.

13. This quote is from a source published in 1915. At that time use of the word "men" was intended to include both genders. Now it is generally recognized that use of a word that represents only one gender cannot properly be used to reference both.

14. Orr, "Faithful, Faithfulness," para. 2.

15. Orr, "Faithful, Faithfulness," para. 14.

16. Kittel and Friedrich, *TDNT*, 6:178.

17. Kittel and Friedrich, *TDNT*, 6:203.

18. Kittel and Friedrich, *TDNT*, 6:208.

19. Kittel and Friedrich, *TDNT*, 6:205. See footnote 13.

subjection to the way of salvation ordained by God and opened up in Christ."[20] Faith meant to acknowledge that Jesus is Lord, as well as to affirm the miracle of his resurrection.[21] Yet beyond acceptance of the *content* of the kerygma, to be a faithful one in relation to God meant to continue in the *way* of the kerygma; it meant an attitude of continuing to exercise faith, and "suggests not only intellectual credence, but also moral commitment to the person of Christ."[22] To be faithful in this sense reflects the meaning of the Hebrew words for faithfulness found in the Old Testament (*'emeth* and *'emunah*): being constant and firm, particularly fulfilling all obligations.[23] In the depiction of Jesus found in the Letter to the Hebrews he demonstrated faithfulness in this continuing, relational, and thus moral way: "Where Jesus is called a faithful high priest, the idea expressed is His fidelity to His obligations to God and to His saving work (Hebrews 2:17; 3:2, 6)."[24]

It is clear that faithfulness is far more than an initial exercise of faith—giving assent to certain content—or even continuing to affirm that content. Walking in the way of the kerygma is a constant and ongoing exercise in the moral realm of human existence. To be a believer "is not a static affair. It takes place in the flux of individual life. . . . Faith, then, is not exhausted by acceptance of the kerygma as though this were a mere declaration on joining a new religion. It has to establish itself continually against assaults as an attitude which controls all of life."[25] As such the faithful one, according to the Letter of James, is tested for steadfastness[26]—primarily by subjection to both temptation and persecution[27]—and will remain constant even to the point of death as did Antipas in the first century in the church of Pergamum.[28]

In the mid-nineteenth century Søren Kierkegaard captured this concept of constancy in faithfulness, referring to the faithful one as an Apostle, when he wrote, "Just as a man, sent into the town with a letter, has nothing to do with its contents, but has only to deliver it; just as a

20. Kittel and Friedrich, *TDNT*, 6:217.
21. Kittel and Friedrich, *TDNT*, 6:208.
22. Nixon, "Faith, Faithfulness," 485.
23. Orr, "Faithful, Faithfulness," para. 5.
24. Orr, "Faithful, Faithfulness," para. 17.
25. Kittel and Friedrich, *TDNT*, 6:218.
26. Nixon, "Faith, Faithfulness," 490.
27. Kittel and Friedrich, *TDNT*, 6:199.
28. See Rev 2:13.

minister who is sent to a foreign court is not responsible for the content of the message, but has only to convey it correctly: so, too, an Apostle has really only to be faithful in his service, and to carry out his task."[29]

At this point—even though this brief overview of the meaning of faithfulness has been far from exhaustive—there should be no confusion about the fundamental biblical notion of faithfulness, nor should there be any thought that it entails searching for and adhering to a specific divine plan for the individual, with the potential attendant benefits of purpose, meaning, pleasure, and fulfillment. Next, we will gain further clarity about the notion of faithfulness by looking at how the earliest Christians understood the concept.

THE EARLY CHRISTIANS

The earliest believers thought of faithfulness in much different terms from how it is understood by many Western Christians today. During the first centuries of the church those who aspired to faithfulness had a distinct view of what God's expectations of them entailed. For some of them it meant the ultimate sacrifice. The early Christian martyrs—at least those who died willingly—gave their lives rather than deny their faith. To them this kind of sacrifice was the clear and obvious implication of faithfulness to God.

> There are hundreds—thousands—of . . . martyrs from these years who endured the most terrible pain. But the strange thing is, the stories that come down to us about their deaths, even those few stories recorded by the Romans who killed them, tell us that most of these women, men, and children who were killed for their faith died with peaceful hearts, sometimes even singing hymns as they were burned or dragged by animals in front of the cheering crowds.[30]

What was it about these early Christians that led them to have this understanding of faithfulness, and how was it different from the common notion of many Christians today? Did the early Christians know something about God's expectations of the faithful that we have lost? If so, is it possible to recover those lost elements of faithfulness, and how are we to go about that task?

---

29. Kierkegaard, *Genius and an Apostle*, 106.
30. Loyola Press, "Early Christian Martyrs," para. 17.

Not all early Christians, of course, were martyrs. Most were not. Yet even those who did not end up being martyred had a quality to their commitment that seems not to have endured through subsequent generations. As far back as the fifteenth century German mystic Thomas à Kempis observed of the early Christians, "Behold the lively example of the holy fathers and blessed saints in whom flourished and shone all true perfection of life and all perfect religion, and you will see how little, almost nothing, we do nowadays in comparison with them."[31] Notice that Thomas referenced both their life action and their religious practice. It was their example of conduct that impressed him. He continued by citing the sufferings they endured in order to be faithful:

> Oh, what is our life when it is compared to theirs? They served our Lord in hunger and thirst, in heat, in cold, in nakedness, in labor and in weariness, in vigils and fastings, in prayer and in holy meditations, in persecutions and in many reproofs.
> Oh, how many and how grievous tribulations the apostles, martyrs, confessors, virgins, and other holy saints suffered who were willing to follow the steps of Christ.[32]

Following in the steps of Christ, as Thomas put it, appears to be at the core of these early sisters' and brothers' understanding of God's expectations of them, and what it means to be faithful to those expectations. It was a call they held in common, and the nature of it was the same for all of them. It even could be argued that God's desire was a collective one, applicable to all. Just as God's promise to restore exiled Israel was a collective promise to all, so God's expectations of Christians was directed not to specific people, but to the entire church community. What clearly is missing from their concept of God's expectations is individualism. God's call to faithfulness was something they shared, something in which they participated as members of their collective: the church as the followers of Jesus. It was not a set of individual plans God had for each of their lives, and faithfulness was not understood as "What does faithfulness mean for me?" It certainly did not entail finding a path that led to personal meaning, fulfillment, and pleasure.

---

31. Kempis, *Imitation of Christ*, 46–47.
32. Kempis, *Imitation of Christ*, 47.

JESUS' EXPECTATIONS OF PETER

What were the "steps of Christ" in which the early Christians walked? Who was the Jesus that these believers experienced? We get a glimpse in the post-resurrection encounter between Jesus and Peter.[33] Recall that Jesus had enabled the disciples to enjoy a huge haul of fish simply by instructing them to throw their net on the other side of the boat. He subsequently cooked them breakfast, then asked Peter three times, "Do you love me?" Apparently Jesus and Peter were walking alone at that point, separated from the others, for Peter turned and saw John following them. Jesus' instruction to Peter was simply "Follow me!" Whereas it may have been an instruction for Peter to continue walking with Jesus rather than be diverted by John, in the context in which it was said it also clearly referred to Peter's martyrdom after the manner of Jesus' death. The path Jesus walked had led to his crucifixion, and Peter was expected to follow him along that path.

How did Peter respond? Upon seeing John, Peter asked about the plan Jesus had for his fellow disciple. Rather than concentrate on the directive Jesus had just given, Peter started wondering about Jesus' expectations of another disciple, namely, John. Compared with the future martyrdom that Jesus had just revealed to Peter, Jesus' depiction of John's life—perhaps a very long one—was likely not well-received. So Jesus had to reiterate the directive to Peter, this time much more emphatically:[34] "Follow me!" Could it be that this notion of following Jesus is at the heart of what it means to be faithful? Irrespective of the specific outworking of the notion in the life of any particular individual, does faithfulness to God ultimately entail a focus only on one thing: following in the Jesus way? Regarding Jesus' emphatic directive to Peter, nearly a century ago theologian J. H. Bernard, provost of Trinity College Dublin, concluded, "This is the last precept of Jesus recorded in the last Gospel; and it is the final and essential precept of the Christian life."[35]

Kierkegaard, in his book appropriately entitled *Training in Christianity*, concurred with the notion that faithfulness to Christ fundamentally means following Jesus' life:

---

33. See John 21.

34. See Bernard, *Gospel According to St. John*, 2:771. Although the English translation "Follow me!" is the same in verses 19 and 22, the Greek used in verse 22 is much more emphatic than that of verse 19.

35. Bernard, *Gospel According to St. John*, 2:771.

> Christ constantly uses the expression "follower"; . . . when he uses the expression "disciples," He always so explains it that we can perceive that followers are meant, . . . not adherents of a doctrine but followers of a life . . .
>
> Christ came to the world for the purpose of saving the world, and at the same time . . . to be "the Pattern," to leave behind Him footsteps for those who would attach themselves to Him, who thus might become followers.[36]

In this selection Kierkegaard's description of Christ's expectations of his faithful ones clearly is the understanding he desires them to adopt and heed. It is Jesus' desire that they follow him, walk in his footsteps, emulate his life, and use the pattern he left as the model for their commitments and conduct. For the vast majority of Western Christians this understanding of faithfulness has been forgotten. Serious walking in Jesus' path is not something often observed in the lives of twenty-first century Christians.

Rediscovering the meaning of faithfulness to God is the burden of the following chapters. The book's goal is to demonstrate that such a rediscovery will lead many to greater fidelity to the Jesus they claim as Lord. Before beginning that quest, however, it will be helpful to consider some biblical passages that may point us in the right direction and think about what has led to the disparity between the early Christians' understanding of God's expectations of believers and the modern misconstrual of it.

THE CALL TO HOLINESS

In his masterful letter to the Roman Christians, the apostle Paul addressed them first as those who are "called to belong to Jesus Christ," then immediately referred to them as those who are "loved by God and called to be his holy people."[37] Elsewhere, in a letter to another congregation as well as one to a particular individual, he used this same or similar terminology.[38]

What is this call to which Paul referred? What did he mean when he asserted that Christians belong to Jesus Christ, and to what does a summons to holiness refer? Three lines of thought will help us understand what this calling means.

---

36. Kierkegaard, *Training in Christianity*, 215–16.
37. Rom 1:6, 7.
38. See, for example, 1 Cor 1:2 and 2 Tim 1:9.

First, the specific Greek term for *holy* (*hagios*) used by Paul when writing to various readers has, at its root, the notion of separation, particularly separation to God.[39] This notion was common throughout the early history of Israel, as reflected in the Hebrew word *qâdash*, and continued through the prophetic, post-exilic, and rabbinic periods.[40] It encompassed such elements of Jewish life as the temple, priests, sacrifices, feast days, the Sabbath, and the people of Israel themselves.[41] The separation to God, of necessity, entailed separation from the profane and common; and God, being the one to whom the holy was separated, was himself holy.

In the New Testament the meaning of *hagios* builds upon and expands the Old Testament understanding of *qâdash*. The fundamental meaning of separation remains, entailing dedication or consecration to God.[42] However, the notion quickly arises that holiness perhaps includes the moral realm: "that what is set apart from the world and to God, should separate itself from the world's defilements, and should share in God's purity; and in this way . . . speedily acquires a moral significance."[43] Moral *action*, however, is not what the notion of holiness included, and when thinking about what Paul had in mind when addressing his readers we must remember that "the reference of holiness is always to the static morality of innocence rather than to ethical action. . . . For this reason we should never translate [*hagios*] . . . as morality or moral."[44]

We are left in a bit of a quandary at this point, for if holiness includes an element of moral significance but is never to be translated "morality," how is it to be understood? The quandary is heightened when we realize that Jesus, to whom holiness is ascribed in both the Synoptics and the Gospel of John,[45] directed his followers to lives of purity as understood

---

39. See Trench, in which the meaning of *hagios* is explained: "Its fundamental idea is separation, and, so to speak, consecration and devotion to the service of Deity." Trench, *Synonyms of the New Testament*, 331.

40. For a much more detailed description of the concept of holiness during the Old Testament periods, see Kittel and Friedrich, *TDNT*, 1:89–100.

41. Kittel and Friedrich, *TDNT*, 1:97.

42. Bauer, *Greek-English Lexicon*, 9.

43. Trench, *Synonyms of the New Testament*, 332.

44. Kittel and Friedrich, *TDNT*, 1:109.

45. See, for example, Mark 1:24; Luke 1:35; John 6:69.

in the Sermon on the Mount: it entailed both character and conduct in the moral realm.[46]

If we understand the caution against equating holiness with morality to mean a warning against thinking about holiness as principally *conduct*, we correctly discern that the moral component of holiness references primarily *being* and *character*, patterned after the being and character of God. Morality commonly is viewed as obedience to *rules*, following a set of *principles*, or adherence to some sort of *code*. In this limited understanding of morality, the idea of being holy is distinctly separate from morality. However, if morality is understood more broadly to include *emulation* of a moral authority figure such as the earthly Jesus, *character formation* following the divine standard, and *response* to the exalted Jesus as pictured particularly in the Epistle to the Hebrews,[47] then holiness is, at its heart, a moral notion. In fact, the call to holiness as issued by Paul is an expectation of something that happens in the moral realm of human experience. It is not other-worldly or mystical. Rather, it is tangible in the life of the believer.

Second is the way interpreters of the relevant texts understand the meaning of the term in its written contexts. As was the case with the fundamental meaning of *hagios*, separation or consecration to God is generally agreed to be the root concept Paul was attempting to convey to his readers. Nineteenth-century Presbyterian theologian Charles Hodge argued that holiness in the Rom 1:7 passage refers to the vocation of the Christian, understood as "*clean, pure* morally, *consecrated.*"[48] Elsewhere he asserted that in the New Testament *hagios* "is commonly expressive of inward purity, or consecration of the soul to God."[49] In the context of the texts in which it is used, the word appears to mean more than simple separation from, or consecration to; it includes the pursuit of moral purity being the job of the Christian. Biblical expositor James Denney acknowledged that whereas the notion of holiness initially did not have a moral sense in that it did not refer to character, "it is assumed in scripture that the character of God's people will answer to their relation to Him."[50]

---

46. See Matt 5–7.

47. For a more complete articulation of this concept of ethics, see Wozniak, *Living as the Living Jesus*, 183–95.

48. Hodge, *Epistle to the Romans*, 23; italics original.

49. Hodge, *Exposition of 1 and 2 Corinthians*, 10.

50. Denney, *Epistle to the Romans*, 2:587.

Consistency between the One to whom the Christian is separated, and the character the Christian displays while separated to that One, is the unique and essential requirement of holiness. Of necessity, then, the call to be holy is the call to purity in the moral realm of human experience. At its heart this means that the expected character of the faithful Christian is to emulate the character of God.

Third, following the fundamental nature of holiness as moral and the expectation that the faithful will aspire to emulate the divine character, systematic theologians historically have understood holiness to entail a number of notions. In the early twentieth century theologian Augustus H. Strong pointed out that there was gradual development of the concept of holiness throughout Israel's history, indicating that the original meaning of separation later was overshadowed by the ideas of both physical purity and the rejection of moral evil.[51] To strengthen the assertion that the later understanding of holiness is to be preferred, Strong reminded his readers, "We must remember however that the proper meaning of a term is to be determined not by the earliest but by the latest usage."[52]

After affirming the fundamental meaning of both the Hebrew *qâdash* and the Greek *hagios*—that of separation—theologian Louis Berkhof of Calvin Theological Seminary argued that God's holiness is not fundamentally a moral attribute such as divine love, grace, or mercy. Rather, it is more ontological in that it imbues everything else that God is, and can be termed "majesty-holiness."[53] He went on, however, to assert that in the Scripture God's holiness includes a distinct ethical element. It is not completely distinct from majesty-holiness, but rather grows out of it:[54] "The fundamental idea of the ethical holiness of God is also that of separation, but in this case it is a separation from moral evil or sin. . . . [I]t also has a positive content, namely, that of moral excellence, or ethical perfection."[55] According to Berkhof, "*hagios* speedily acquired an ethical signification," and although it is not always used the same way throughout the New Testament, normally "it is employed in an ethical sense to describe the quality that is necessary to stand in close relation to God and to serve Him acceptably."[56]

---

51. Strong, *Systematic Theology*, 268.
52. Strong, *Systematic Theology*, 268.
53. Berkhof, *Systematic Theology*, 73.
54. Berkhof, *Systematic Theology*, 73.
55. Berkhof, *Systematic Theology*, 73.
56. Berkhof, *Systematic Theology*, 528.

That the holiness required of Israel consisted of not only a qualitative element before a holy God, but also a quantitative, tangible expression in everyday conduct was explained by theologian Stanley Grenz of Regent College at the turn of the twenty-first century: "Holiness involved obedience to the covenanting God as motivated by love and gratitude (Deut 6:5, 20)."[57] Grenz expanded this moral understanding of holiness by adding detail about the nature of holy conduct: "Holy living extended to all dimensions of human interaction, including aspects as diverse as family life and commerce. And holiness demanded concern for the less fortunate; it placed limits on vengeance (Deut 25:3); it even required proper care for animals (Deut 22:1–4)."[58] Strong pointed out that such holiness "received its full expression only in the New Testament revelation and especially in the life and work of Christ."[59]

The holiness expectation of Israel served as the basis for the life of holiness to which Paul called his readers. Grenz concluded, "The Christian ethical life is the life of holiness—the life of the people who are holy unto the Lord—in fulfillment of the Old Testament quest."[60] The apostle Peter, in his letter addressed to a host of Christians scattered throughout Asia Minor, warned against submitting to evil desires. He immediately went on to encourage his readers to be Godlike in conduct by leveraging God's expectation to Israel that they be holy:[61] "But just as he who called you is holy, so be holy in all you do; for it is written: 'Be holy, because I am holy.'"[62]

Berkhof summarized the relationship between the moral holiness of God and the holiness expected of believers: "This ethical holiness of God may be defined as *that perfection in God, in virtue of which He eternally wills and maintains His own moral excellence, abhors sin, and demands purity in his moral creatures.*"[63]

At this point it should be clear that the expectation of holiness is, at its heart, a *moral* one. It is a call to a life—including at a minimum attitudes, intentions, values, commitments, character, responses, judgments, and actions—that mimics the holiness of God. Moral Godlikeness is what

57. Grenz, *Moral Quest*, 98.
58. Grenz, *Moral Quest*, 99.
59. Strong, *Systematic Theology*, 268.
60. Grenz, *Moral Quest*, 128.
61. See Lev 20:26.
62. 1 Pet 1:15–16.
63. Berkhof, *Systematic Theology*, 74; italics original.

faithfulness to God entails. This, unfortunately—as we saw earlier—is not the focus of many Christians today when thinking about the meaning of faithfulness to God.

THE DEPARTURE FROM GODLIKENESS

If faithfulness to God means to be Godlike in holiness according to the pattern Jesus left, then why is the prevailing understanding of God's expectations so different? What has led the one who aspires to faithfulness to focus her or his efforts on a specific plan, fidelity to which yields fulfillment, meaning, contentment, and even pleasure, purpose, and passion? I suggest there are two significant social/theological/ethical realities that have led Western Christians off the path and into the ditch regarding God's expectations, both of which must be addressed if true faithfulness is to be rediscovered.

The first reality is that of the fall. The perfect, innocent creation was tainted by the fall, and part of the fullness of creation was lost. This, obviously, is not a recent occurrence, but dates from the dawn of human history itself. Yet its effects have continued through all recorded history, to this very day. The ideal of faithfulness can be seen in Gen 2 when God, perhaps following a habitual pattern, walked in the garden in the cool of the day enjoying fellowship with Adam and Eve. However, after the fall Adam and Eve did not meet with God, but instead hid because they were afraid. Hiding from God due to fear is not the divine ideal, yet it persists today. It is a result of the fall. Walking in harmony *with* God, as Adam and Eve did before the fall, is a habit that must be recovered following God's pattern of calling to them. In Jesus the pattern was not only reiterated and demonstrated during his life on earth, but left as the example for God's faithful.

Another way of looking at this reality is to think about the image of God. According to the creation story humans were made in God's image. The moral sense, I will argue later in the book, is a fundamental part of that image. Whereas the fall has not caused the image of God to be lost *de jure*, it most certainly is not apparent in its divine purity *de facto* in the lives of people, including most Christians. To be true to God—to follow in the Jesus way—is for the Christian somehow to move from being simply the image of God *de jure* to living a holy life in the moral realm that demonstrates the image of God *de facto*.

In his early 1940s writing, later simply entitled *Ethics*, German theologian and pastor Dietrich Bonhoeffer wrote concerning ethics and the effects of the fall, "The knowledge of good and evil seems to be the aim of all ethical reflection. The first task of Christian ethics is to invalidate this knowledge."[64] His reasoning was that prior to the fall humans knew God only in moral innocence. Subsequent to the fall, however, their knowledge was expanded to include both good and evil. The goal of human thought in the moral realm, he argued, should be to return to the state and experience of moral innocence in which people were created: Godlike, bearing the image of God. This is God's expectation, not only to be in God's image ontologically, but to express God's image as we live our lives. Determining how to approach that goal is a task I hope to outline in the following chapters.

The second reality is the syncretism that pervades much of Western Christianity. By that I mean Christianity has been blended with surrounding cultural elements such that a hybrid of affirmations, values, expectations, and commitments is formed—one that is not Christian according to what we find Jesus expects his followers to be. Such syncretism is, in fact, a pollution of Christianity, and those who embrace it have abandoned much of what the Christian life lived in the moral realm is supposed to entail, at least according to the New Testament's depiction thereof. Unfortunately, large expressions of Western Christianity have devolved into just such a syncretistic religion.

In his blog author Scott Bessenecker described what he has observed about American Christian syncretism. Seeing it as a religion in which cultural elements have supplanted the gospel, he noted that "the good news becomes obscured, bent into the shape of beliefs that aren't consistent with Jesus and his kingdom."[65] Another recent blog, the *Reverence Journal*, agreed, suggesting that "if a group of missionaries came right out of the New Testament and visited America they would think that we had created our own syncretistic folk-religion."[66]

To what are these authors referring when suggesting that American Christianity no longer is Christian, and what does syncretism have to do with God's desires? The *Reverence Journal* went on to suggest that American Evangelicalism actually is a mixture of Christianity and the American dream, or perhaps certain political ideologies, resulting in a kind of civil

64. Bonhoeffer, *Ethics*, 21.
65. Bessenecker, "Through My Lens," para. 3.
66. Rudd, "American Evangelical Syncretism," para. 3.

religion known as "Christian Nationalism."[67] Bessenecker asserted that both materialism and nationalism characterize this syncretistic religion, and the effect is not only "an obsession with luxury and comfort," but also a belief that "begins to fuse a secular state with the Christian faith."[68] In addition, he identified a focus on individualism as a key characteristic of American Christian syncretism, arguing that "we have contorted many of our faith practices and experiences to fit an individualist cultural form and lost something of the essence of our faith's communal orientation."[69]

Scientist, entrepreneur, and journalist Sumit Paul-Choudhury further explained the concept of syncretistic religion, noting that it is a "'pick and mix' approach of combining traditions and practices that often results from the mixing of cultures."[70] Assuming that one's basic needs are met, one is "more likely to be seeking fulfillment and meaning."[71] Sociology of religion professor Linda Woodhead, writing in the context of the United Kingdom, observed this individualistic, self-focused emphasis: "Religions do well, and always have done, when they are subjectively convincing—when you have the sense that God is working for you."[72] It is at this point that we begin to see how syncretism has influenced what many Christians view as faithfulness. Rather than understanding their Christian obligation to serve God in holiness, irrespective of individual circumstances, they focus on what they believe God's function to be: to serve the individual by devising a plan, or call, that is unique and distinct for each person. Fidelity to the plan is what faithfulness is about, with an expected return of personal meaning, purpose, and fulfillment. God will confirm that the individual has been faithful by blessing that person with material success.

This view of faithfulness appears to be much more aligned with the goals of the American dream than it does the collective expectation God has of all his followers as an entity, the church. That collective expectation—the one understood so clearly by the early Christians—has been forgotten by those who believe that relationship with God entails some sort of deal in which God devises a personal plan for individual delight and fulfillment, and the individual is faithful if he or she attempts to live

67. Rudd, "American Evangelical Syncretism," para. 4.
68. Bessenecker, "Through My Lens," paras. 7, 10.
69. Bessenecker, "Through My Lens," para. 9.
70. Paul-Choudhury, "Tomorrow's Gods," para. 29.
71. Paul-Choudhury, "Tomorrow's Gods," para. 27.
72. As quoted by Paul-Choudhury, "Tomorrow's Gods," para. 26.

according to the plan. Such an understanding could not be further from God's expectations of his faithful followers.

This book will focus on rediscovering the true nature of faithfulness to God, with the hope that those serious about Christian faithfulness will adopt it as a better way.

THE WAY FORWARD

In part 1 the notion of faithfulness within one's social milieu is introduced. The first chapter argues that believers' understanding of faithfulness has not remained static, but has changed since the time of the early Christians. A case is made to show how the church's understanding of faithfulness has changed dramatically through the centuries. It is suggested that there is great value in learning what faithfulness meant for the earliest Christians.

The remaining chapters in part 1 suggest that Christians in the first few centuries after Jesus' life on earth understood faithfulness to include many elements not often acknowledged by Christians today. Those elements—predominantly ethical ones—include obedience, emulation of Jesus, appropriation and reflection of the divine character, and responding to the exalted Jesus they worshiped. A picture is painted of the moral context that generated the first Christians' understanding of the nature of God's expectation of faithfulness as they engaged their surrounding society. It is asserted that the kingdom of God announced by Jesus was distinctly different and separate from the social milieu in which Christians found themselves, and thus faithfulness to God presented them with a significant social ethical challenge. Whereas the church has always been influenced by the changing social milieu, it is argued that a return to the original understanding of faithfulness by Jesus' earliest followers is required in order to approach faithfulness according to God's expectations.

In part 2 the relationship between faithfulness and character is explored from a moral perspective. It is argued that an element of the forgotten divine intention for the faithful is to become Godlike in character (and consequentially in commitment and conduct). The character of God is probed in an attempt to understand the ideal moral character. Character ethics as first expressed by Aristotle is investigated in order to understand the uniqueness of character ethics, and key instances of character ethics found in the Old and New Testaments—including that of the earliest Christians—is explored. Character in the life of Jesus as the archetype expression of the divine character is studied, including its paradigmatic role in the lives of those who desire to increase in faithfulness. In chapter 10 various understandings of the image of God are probed for their applicability to the notion of faithfulness, and an argument is made that a proper understanding of the image of God includes the human moral sense. Finally it is suggested that growing faithfulness includes reappropriation of the divine character—understood as the image of God—as humans experienced it prior to the fall. Such reappropriation entails becoming in our daily reality and experience the image of God not as *de jure* only, but *de facto* in our human experience.

Part 3 begins with chapter 11, which examines the extent and limits of Jesus' *emptiness* compared with his pre-incarnate state, using the kenosis passage as an initial basis for thought. Jesus' commitment to emptiness is viewed through the thought of subsequent interpreters of his life. His emptiness as displayed throughout his time on earth is presented, followed by a survey of instances where faithfulness after the pattern of Jesus necessitated self-emptying on the part of his followers. Examples of emptiness from the life of Jesus are compared with similar ones in the Old Testament, and it is proposed that emptiness can enhance Christians' faithfulness today.

Next, there occurs an exploration of the notion that an attitude of *obedience* is fundamental to faithfulness. It suggests that Western culture has abandoned this attitude, and that much of modern-day Christianity has accommodated itself to—or even embraced—this abandonment. A review of the Old Testament understanding of faithfulness as obedience is presented, followed by the parallel/contrasting notion that mere obedience is not sufficient fulfillment of God's expectations. The place of obedience in the life of Jesus is explored, and the assertion is made that a biblical understanding of obedience should serve as a model for Christians to follow.

The end of the chapter contemplates the notion of Jesus' *sufferings* as an expression of complete identification with the weaknesses and frailties of humanity as well as faithfulness to God. How Old Testament prophets were required to suffer is presented as an essential element of faithfulness. Consideration is given to the picture of the Suffering Servant of Isaiah as an ideal for God's faithful.

Chapter 12 is somewhat parallel to chapter 11, except that its focus is more on the external elements of faithfulness. It begins with a focus on *solidarity with the needy*, including the practice of generosity, and considers whether Jesus was biased in favor of the poor, asking if such bias is a normative component of faithfulness. Consideration is given to select incidents from the Old Testament, the teaching of the Psalms, Mary's Magnificat, the Sermon on the Mount, and other passages as evidence of God's attitude toward the poor and the requirement for his faithful to emulate that attitude.

Next an exploration is made of whether God's expectations include a disposition to pursue *peace* in everything, including a gracious disposition toward and seeking the best for one's enemies and abusers. This section probes whether passivity toward enemies—both personal ones and the enemies of the society in which one participates—is to be pursued, waiting for God to deal with them, or if a more aggressive stance should be adopted by the faithful. Consideration is given to whether there is a proper and appropriate use of force and violence by the faithful Christian, not only personally, but also with the broader society and between nations.

The end of the chapter investigates God's intention that the faithful not only *be* changed, but more importantly asks if the divine call includes an obligation to *foment change*. Whereas the theological notion of sanctification aims at achieving Christlikeness, the question is asked if, in the moral realm, the aim of the faithful follower should be to become an agent of change following the divine pattern that started with creation. Alternatively, the question is raised if a preservationist approach should be the ideal the Christian should pursue. The end of this section investigates how the notion of the rule of God should influence proper thinking in this arena.

In chapter 13 it is argued that the moral element of Godlikeness has its practical social and collective expression on earth as the kingdom of God that Jesus announced and brought. The kingdom of God, it is proposed, is the common glue that binds together all the disparate elements of faithfulness to God. The chapter shows that modern Christian thought errs by embracing a syncretistic model of faithfulness that blends societal norms and standards with Christian commitment. It considers classical Jesus vis-à-vis society notions to propose a normative faithfulness stance within society, particularly modern Western culture.

The conclusion draws upon the proposals, arguments, and learnings of the foregoing chapters to formulate a normative ethic by which faithfulness to God—understood more accurately and comprehensively than the dominant notion assumed by much of Western Christianity—can be approached. It is asserted that only by adopting such an ethic can both individual Christians and the Christian collective—the church—understand and respond appropriately to God, thus living faithfully within the social milieu in which they find themselves.

Let us begin our investigation of faithfulness, then, by considering the early Christians and the society in which they had to work out the meaning of faithfulness.

PART ONE

Faithfulness and the Social Milieu

MOST CHRISTIANS DO NOT live in social isolation. For them to express their faith without taking into consideration the environment in which they exist is an impossibility, since they are integrally involved in a social milieu that includes a physical setting, social norms and conventions, political realities, institutions, culture, religious networks, and the like. Living faithfully within such a context always has been a challenge for both Christians individually and the Christian collective, the church. Ethicist George W. Forell, in the preface to his collection of Christian social teachings, described this difficulty: "The most persistent and disturbing problem confronting the Christian community . . . has been and continues to be its relationship to the surrounding world."[1] During the two millennia since the establishment of the church there have been many attempts to outline the options Christians have for living faithfully vis-à-vis the society in which they find themselves, perhaps the most well-known of which in the last century was developed by Yale Christian ethicist H. Richard Niebuhr in his 1951 book *Christ and Culture*.[2] Niebuhr developed five alternative attitudes the Christian can take toward culture, from complete endorsement to total rejection. Hinting that discovering the meaning of faithfulness in a social context has been an ever-present obligation, Forell went on to assert that "Christian thought had always to deal with the

1. Forell, *Christian Social Teachings*, ix.
2. See H. Richard Niebuhr's *Christ and Culture*.

relationship of the Christian community and the individual Christian with the social and political environment."[3] The notion of how that was to be approached faithfully has changed considerably since the first century.

---

3. Forell, *Christian Social Teachings*, ix.

1

The Changing Understanding of Faithfulness

THE COMMON WAY WESTERN Christians in the twenty-first century have decided to understand faithfulness is one of several particular approaches, others of which have characterized the thinking of Christians in past ages. For many modern believers faithfulness is *individual*; yet it also is specific *for* the individual. Faithfulness entails adherence to a specific, unique divine plan intended to result in a sense of purpose, fulfillment, and most of all meaning. Theologian William Placher noted this common yearning among many Christians: "*there is something . . . God has called me to do with my life, and my life has meaning and purpose at least in part because I am fulfilling my calling.*"[1] In this view faithfulness to God can be measured and even validated by the degree to which the individual enjoys pleasurable benefits from what is surmised to be adherence to the specific divine plan. Assuming one's basic needs are met, the purpose of Christian living is the quest for fulfillment and meaning.

In addition, Western Christians have adopted a syncretistic stance toward societal involvement that includes populist Christianity, civil religion with its inherent political ideologies, nationalism, materialism, luxury, and comfort. Those who are successful reassure themselves that

---

1. Placher, *Callings*, 2; italics original.

they are living faithful lives, and that God indeed is working for them. Unfortunately their thinking has substituted pursuit of the desired results for the pursuit of faithfulness itself. As mentioned in the introduction, American Christianity is no longer Christian, and neither is that which passes for Christianity in many other parts of the world.

What, then, should faithfulness entail, if not pursuit of a specific divine plan for the individual's fulfillment? Recall Kierkegaard's simple notion of following in the footsteps of Jesus. This is the root of faithfulness, and includes emulation of Jesus' life, commitments, and conduct. The faithful life is one lived in the moral realm of human experience, encompassing the entire scope of attitudes, intentions, values, character, responses, judgments, and actions displayed by Jesus. Such an understanding is not the focus of many Christians today. It was not always so, however. If we look back past the modern era we will see that the notion of faithfulness, including the specific concept of calling, has evolved through the millennia since Jesus walked the earth.

Placher laid out this evolution by publishing a collection of writings from Christians through the ages; they are generally associated with the authors' convictions regarding what it meant to be called as a Christian. Placher argued quite convincingly that prior to the modern era Christian thought fell chronologically into three major understandings of calling. Although the concept of "call" is only the initial element of the overall notion of faithfulness, reviewing Placher's high-level argument will serve us well in our effort to rediscover the meaning of faithfulness.

The Protestant Reformation generated a distinct notion of what calling for the Christian meant. It included two distinct elements: joining the people of God through the initial act of faithfulness—acceptance of salvation by grace through the death of Christ—and fidelity to a particular work, be it a job or a role or station in life.[2] Over time the notion, for some Protestants, began to narrow by focusing on employment or a job, with the attendant confirmation of faithfulness via economic success.[3] The chief characteristic of this view of faithfulness, however, was that *all* Christians are called.[4] Calling was not limited to a select few, each with a special purpose. Whereas the focus of many current Christians' understanding of being called is finding and fulfilling God's individual specific plan—be it through a job or anything else—as long as it results

---

2. Placher, *Callings*, 206–7.
3. Placher, *Callings*, 210.
4. Placher, *Callings*, 206.

in purpose and meaning, the uniqueness of Christian calling during and after the Reformation was that it was all-inclusive; all Christians were called by God both to salvation and to work, and thus lived out their faithfulness on a common plane of moral experience.

During the thousand years or so prior to the Reformation the common understanding of call was distinctly different from what it was after the Reformation. "The standard medieval social division was among those who pray (priests, nuns, and monks), those who fight (the nobles), and those who work (mostly peasants in the fields)."[5] Whereas members of the monarchy and nobility were committed to fighting, war—though not necessarily understood as always sinful—was viewed as being at odds with spiritual efforts and pursuits;[6] thus the social distinction between those who fought and those who prayed. The Christian understanding of calling during this period was exclusive: one was called to the religious life of monk, nun, friar, or priest, or one was not. "Calling" generally referred to the religious life, except for perhaps the generalized calling to family commitment. The notion of calling entailing a job or a specific plan that would result in meaning was not an element of the calling concept.[7]

In the medieval era the exclusivity of calling, being uniquely characteristic of clerics and members of religious orders, served to maintain social distinctions. All were not on the same plane in the moral milieu in which they lived. Unlike the leveling effect of the Reformation's understanding of calling, which applied the notion to all and thus put all in a common moral realm, the exclusivity of medieval clerics and those of religious orders yielded various concepts of faithfulness for the different social levels. As we will see, this was a significant change from the notion of faithfulness that characterized the earliest Christians during the first few centuries.

From the dawn of the church and continuing for several centuries the fundamental understanding of a call from God was that of a summons to become a Christian, a follower in the way of Jesus. A divine calling had no unique elements tailored for the individual and intended for personal meaning, success, fulfillment, and the like. Its primary focus was not one's particular work, be it a job for earning an income or some other investment of one's time and energy. The option of choosing a profession or job was not available to most people in the first few centuries

---

5. Placher, *Callings*, 107.
6. Placher, *Callings*, 112.
7. Placher, *Callings*, 113.

of the church. Rather, for the most part work for the ancients was predetermined to be what their parents had done before them.[8]

As was the notion after the Reformation, the early Christian's concept of that to which they were called was a common one: it applied equally to all. The concept of a divine calling being only to and for certain ones who would dedicate themselves to religious work was not part of the early Christians' perception of that to which people were called. For the first Christians the questions surrounding faithfulness to God's call concerned whether "'to be conformed to this world' (Rom. 12:2), or to commit themselves to this new community of 'aliens and exiles' (1 Pet. 2:11) that followed Christ."[9] Personal salvation was not properly thought of as a distinct first step which subsequently may or may not be augmented with a commitment to follow in the Jesus way (although the recipients of the Epistle to the Hebrews made the mistake of attempting to be Christians, but only barely so for fear of persecution). For the early Christians the call of God was a summons to join with the community of God's faithful. As such they enjoyed both the forgiveness of sin and eternal life through the gracious salvific work of Christ, and committed themselves to walk in the way of Jesus. For them, to continue to walk in the Jesus way, irrespective of the consequences they might face, was what faithfulness meant.

Placher posed a very helpful question when thinking about the earliest Christians and the situation of Christians today when he asked how the early Christians' lives of faithfulness to God's call might connect with what faithfulness should mean today.[10] He observed that the social situation faced by today's Christians is more like that of the early Christians than any other believers from the start of the medieval period through the modern era. "Our situation is more like those first few centuries: many of our neighbors follow another faith or none at all. Many of the values and beliefs common in our culture challenge our faith. Our beliefs may seem quite peculiar to many of our neighbors.... [Q]uestions, asked long ago, confront Christians once again."[11] I contend that learning from our earliest forbearers in the faith about what faithfulness was and what it required of them is the most profitable way to know what it means for believers today. It is to that task we now turn.

---

8. Placher, *Callings*, 23.
9. Placher, *Callings*, 23–24.
10. Placher, Callings, 24.
11. Placher, *Callings*, 24–25.

2

The Early Christians

UNDERSTANDING THE EARLY CHRISTIANS

WE CAN LEARN CONSIDERABLY from the earliest believers who dealt with the challenge of determining what it meant to be faithful in the social and political environment in which they found themselves, particularly since they were the closest chronologically to Christianity's founder, Jesus Christ. They were the first conveyors and interpreters of his message, and they lived within the same general social/temporal milieu in which Jesus lived. They also were the first Christians to confront the question of what it meant to be faithful in the social context in which they found themselves. Resolution of the Christians' dilemma, unfortunately, could not be found simply by resorting to an academic exercise. They could not rely on either the classical ethical alternatives found in Greco-Roman culture or Judaism (much of which had been significantly Hellenized by the first century) to provide them with the answer. Rather, in order to understand what faithfulness meant to the early Christians in their context we have to determine how they dealt with the various elements of their social milieu itself. According to early Christianity scholar Wayne A. Meeks, "We must ask about their social forms. Where did they stand within the world of the cities of the Roman empire? What were their relationships with the other groups and movements in Judea and Galilee? With the Jewish communities of the Diaspora?"[1]

In addition to delving into the early Christians' approach to living faithfully in their social context, it will be helpful to our investigation into their notion of faithfulness to consider their consciousness regarding life itself. To that end there is one striking difference that stands out between their thinking and that typical of both their pagan peers and those who live in the West in the twenty-first century: their attitude toward death. This is a subject that those of modern society and the social milieu in which most Western Christians live go to great lengths to avoid. For the Christians of the first few centuries, however, it was different. A current scholar of early Christianity, Brad Kirkegaard, noted this difference:

> In a cultural context such as the United States in the twenty-first century, where a significant majority self-identify as Christians, . . . [the] failure to fully connect death to our daily lives is puzzling. . . . [T]he preoccupation with death in the ancient world offers an interesting curative to our this-worldly cultural focus. Early Christians not only cared for the dead, they incorporated the dead into their lives. The stories of the martyrs and their bloody deaths lovingly told offered a measure by which one tried to live life.[2]

Could it be that maintaining a mental and emotional connection to the deaths of other Christians, particularly those who suffered and were martyred, colored the way those of the first centuries thought about faithfulness? Did their understanding of the death of Jesus on their behalf drive them to a kind of faithfulness that we in the twenty-first century have lost? Was their ever-present conviction that upon death they immediately would be joined to Christ an influence on their conviction about how to be faithful while still alive? Is it possible that modern society's intentional disconnect from death has significantly shaped the perspective about faithfulness shared by the vast majority of Christians in their current Western social milieu, and that in a negative way? Learning more about what motivated the early Christians' social stance, driven by their understanding of that which faithfulness required of them, may help in our quest to establish an ethic of faithfulness appropriate for Christians today. Although an exhaustive review of the social/political/religious

---

1. Meeks, *Moral World*, 95–96.
2. Kirkegaard, "Placing Early Christianity," para. 14.

milieu of the early Christians is beyond the scope of our investigation, highlighting some of the more influential elements will suffice to sensitize us to the challenge confronted by our earliest sisters and brothers in the faith. To do that, let us consider the observations and assertions of several scholars who have applied their expertise to understanding the social milieu in which Christians of the first few centuries lived.

THE SOCIAL MILIEU OF THE EARLY CHRISTIANS

Christians in the first few decades after the resurrection and ascension of Jesus were small in numbers. They were a minority in the societies in which they lived, originally viewed as a sect of Judaism before taking on their own distinct identity. Even when they had spread beyond Jerusalem through the Roman Empire, they remained small in numbers compared with the general population and did not enjoy any significant social or political power with which to exercise influence within the social milieu in which they found themselves. Rather, they lived "on the margins."[3] As such, they had to learn to fit in with the dominant society while developing a practical faithfulness that yielded an assurance and even a psychological certitude that they were not compromising their commitment to God.

What characterized the social environment in which the earliest Christians sought to work out their faith? Clearly their Jewish background and religious setting was a key component of the milieu of the first Christians to the point that they did not think of themselves as anything other than Jewish. Meeks asserted, "The meaningful world in which those earliest Christians lived—the world which lived in their heads as well as that which was all around them—was a Jewish world. But the Jewish world was part of the Greco-Roman world."[4]

Christian Identity and Greco-Roman Society

Christian identity as distinctly Jewish did not last. Not only were gentiles becoming Christians, particularly as Christianity spread outside of Palestine through the missionary activities of Paul and others, but many Jews increasingly rejected Christians as merely a sect within Judaism. Increasingly new Christians were not from Jewish backgrounds, and the

3. Kirkegaard, "Placing Early Christianity," para. 3.
4. Meeks, *Moral World*, 97.

common identity of those who sought to be faithful to Jesus became distinct both from Judaism and the Greco-Roman culture in which more and more Christians found themselves. That culture was centered largely in the cities, wherein upright human conduct was worked out in the polis among one's neighbors.[5] According to Meeks, "the colonists of heaven had to rub elbows and do business with citizens and fellow residents of Ephesus and Alexandria and Corinth.[6]"

Although living in the cities of the empire and necessarily engaging with the society in which they found themselves, early Christians did not wholeheartedly embrace the values and practices of Greco-Roman culture, and they certainly did not accept the pagan religious customs that surrounded them. Such a stance attracted both suspicion and criticism, and thus the life of the Christians was anything but settled and comfortable. At times they could accommodate themselves to the dominant society, and at other times they could not. It was into this mid–first-century social setting that Paul wrote the letters he sent to the nascent Christian communities he had established, letters which we will soon see influenced their thinking regarding faithfulness in the social milieu.

Religion in first-century Rome did not present much of a challenge to most of the population since it demanded little. Christianity was different, and therein lies the difficulty Christians faced. Meeks observed, "For the most part . . . cults, including that of the Jews and, after them, that of the Christians, found ways to adapt to the ethos of the imperial city . . . There were occasions, however, when conflicts between ultimate loyalties could not be avoided."[7] It was those ultimate loyalties that caused great consternation for those who sought to live faithfully while coexisting with the general population in Greco-Roman society. They had no Christian guidebook to turn to for insight; yet compromising their faith was not a notion readily embraced by those who only recently had committed themselves to Jesus as Lord.

Placher referenced the thought of first-century Roman philosopher Pliny the Elder when pointing out:

> Most religions in the Roman Empire were not so challenging. Roman religion was primarily a matter of performing the proper sacrifices in hopes of getting appropriate rewards or at

---

5. Meeks, *Origins*, 12–13.
6. Meeks, *Origins*, 13.
7. Meeks, *Moral World*, 22.

least avoiding divine retribution. Taking no chances, a sophisticated Roman might seek initiation in any number of different religious cults, with none of them involving any expectation of ethical transformation. "Chance" or "Luck" was the most popular deity of the time.[8]

For Christians, however, joining several cults as a means to increase their luck or sacrificing to various deities in order to win their favor constituted betrayal of their primary affirmation, "Jesus is Lord!" In addition to the temptation to compromise religiously, the early Christians faced another risk. Whereas in the Jewish context of Palestine there was an element of tolerance that allowed for local exercise of religion, similar to the experience of present-day Western Christians who generally can practice their faith without risk of government retaliation, "the first-century Roman context was different. In Rome, only Caesar was lord. . . . Annually at tax time, the denizens of a city would make their way to the local temple, pay their tax, and proclaim 'Caesar is lord.' If they didn't make this declaration, they could be executed for treason. Christians knew this, and they took their chances."[9]

Paul and the Early Church

In many respects Christians were able to accommodate themselves to the standards and conventions of society without compromising their faith. Even if they could not enthusiastically endorse these societal elements, their expectation of Jesus' soon, triumphant return enabled them to endure the society during what they believed to be a short period of time before Jesus appeared in triumph. In his first letter to the Corinthian Christians Paul sought to accommodate, rather than confront, the dominant society, suggesting that one not seek to change his or her social situation.[10] The important question is whether Paul consistently maintained that position, irrespective of the social context, or did his instructions to the nascent Christian communities vary with the environment in which the Christians found themselves? While acknowledging that circumstances colored how the church related to the government,[11]

---

8. Placher, *Callings*, 31.
9. O'Brien, "Commitments of the Early Church," para. 3.
10. See 1 Cor 7:17–24.
11. Bainton, *Christendom*, 55.

twentieth-century church historian Roland Bainton appears to have had in mind a time frame that covered several centuries, not just the first. Regarding Paul's instructions about Christian involvement in the social milieu, Bainton argued that Paul consistently took a qualified accommodating social stance: "Paul took a median position, asserting that government was instituted by God and entrusted with the sword to protect the good and punish the bad. He instructed Christians to obey the laws and pay taxes out of conscience rather than from fear. In other words, Paul endorsed the power of the state."[12]

Is it true that Paul consistently advocated a mediating, accommodating position that defined Christian faithfulness within the social milieu? Over one hundred years ago German theologian Ernst Troeltsch contended that "Paul's ideas were quite distinct from the ideals of the Gospel"[13] in that "austere radicalism has already given way to compromise, with the necessity for being on terms of understanding with the general life of the world.... In reality the Pauline world church... did not merely recognize the State as permitted by God, but prized it as an institution which at least cared for justice, order, and external morality."[14] He went on to assert that "the radical endeavour to apply the Sermon on the Mount naturally recedes into the background."[15]

Troeltsch acknowledged that Paul's conservative social thought included bits of radicalism, but relegated these bits to the personal spiritual realm.[16] He thus dismissed any non-conservative teaching as applicable to the social sphere, and concluded that Christianity "will always have a conservative trait of adaptation and submission towards the existing social order and social institutions, the conditions of power and their variations."[17]

It appears that Meeks agreed with Troeltsch that Paul's social instruction aligned with the broader norms of the Roman social milieu, but also contained a spiritual stance distinct from the general society. Referencing Paul's first letter to the Thessalonian Christians, Meeks observed, "We see, then, a certain paradox in this letter. The specific moral expectations that Paul expresses, of the sort that one could state as moral rules,

12. Bainton, *Christendom*, 55.
13. Troeltsch, *Social Teachings*, 80.
14. Troeltsch, *Social Teachings*, 80.
15. Troeltsch, *Social Teachings*, 81.
16. See Troeltsch, *Social Teachings*, 84.
17. Troeltsch, *Social Teachings*, 85.

are hardly different from those widely accepted as 'decent' in Greco-Roman society . . . Yet the overlaid theological warrants tend to emphasize distinctiveness and separation from the dominant society. 'Holiness' is synonymous with 'purity,' and the metaphor implies separation."[18]

Is it actually true that Paul's instructions concerning Christian involvement in society was conservative, endorsing the prevailing norms, values, and standards? Whereas it is incontrovertible that in his letter to the Christians in Rome Paul endorsed the place of the secular government in maintaining order in that particular society,[19] it is also clear that general accommodation to the social milieu was not to be without limits. In the section prior to the one dealing with the secular government, Paul's clear instructions to his readers were that they were not to conform to the pattern of their society, but rather were to be transformed into something distinct from it.[20] The word Paul chose to express his understanding of the Christian's appropriate stance within the social milieu, "transformed" (*metamorphoō*), does not denote changing from one type into a related or similar type, but rather changing into something totally different[21] or a complete change of form.[22] It need not be an outer, visible change, but rather can be an inner one, and is not limited to spiritual experience. Moral change that results in distinct, different conduct, can be included in such transformation.

Paul wrote two letters to the Corinthian Christians that have survived and eventually became part of the New Testament. In both he instructed them that their conduct within the society was to be distinctly different from the prevailing norms. Regarding the use of the secular courts to resolve disputes between Christians, Paul clearly condemned such conduct. In fact, he went so far as to instruct the Corinthian Christians to choose to be wronged or cheated rather than engage in the standard societal practice of conflict resolution through the use of lawsuits decided by secular courts.[23] In his second letter to the Corinthians Paul directly addressed the matter of Christians engaging in close social relationships with unbelievers, and condemned such associations.[24] They were to avoid

18. Meeks, *Moral World*, 128–29.
19. See Rom 13.
20. See Rom 12:2.
21. Trench, *Synonyms of the New Testament*, 263.
22. Kittel and Friedrich, *TDNT*, 4:755.
23. See 1 Cor 6:1–7.
24. See 2 Cor 6:14–18.

any sort of arrangement or engagement in which they were tied closely to the secular society, choosing rather to "come out from them and be separate . . . Touch no unclean thing." Paul allowed for no linking whatsoever between what he termed "righteousness and wickedness . . . light and darkness." For the Christian there was to be no accommodation to the conventions of society and commerce; syncretism was to have no place in the life of the Christian. That such separation from society—or as Paul expressed it, purification from contamination—is not only spiritual but also physical is made clear in verse 7:1. Forell summarized Paul's position regarding the social milieu by commenting on Rom 13 as well as Eph 5 and 6: "the dialectic relationship of the Christian to the world whose rulers are accepted as agents of God but which nevertheless is seen under the domination of the evil powers which must be opposed."[25]

These are but a few examples of Paul's teaching in which Christians were forbidden from compromising their values and commitments when engaging with their social milieu, even though the benefits of the secular government's overseeing of a peaceful society were to be embraced. His position was not a mediating one, nor did he wholeheartedly endorse the prevailing social and political institutions, and social radicalism was not relegated to the spiritual sphere in Paul's thought. Yet Paul did not teach the nascent churches to establish a social order wholly distinct from, and in conflict with, Greco-Roman society. Whereas he expected Christians to avoid syncretism, he did not call them to open conflict with the secular powers. How did it come about, then, that Christians in the first few centuries were targeted and persecuted by Rome? What influenced their convictions about faithfulness, such that they willingly endured and sometimes even welcomed martyrdom? What empowered them to oppose, to the death, the pressures and demands of the social milieu in which they found themselves?

The Rise of Persecution

During the early years of the first century, unity throughout the vast Roman Empire was essential. Although geographically based religions were tolerated,[26] these religions themselves could not unify the empire;

25. Forell, *Christian Social Teachings*, 22.

26. See Bainton: "The Roman government made a distinction between recognized and unrecognized religions, *religiones licitae* and *illicitae*. All the religions in the Empire were tolerated in the lands of their origin; and the government intervened only

the proliferation of religions, several of which could be endorsed by any particular individual, did not form a common base for the society. Yet the need for unity was paramount. According to Bainton, "the need was acutely felt for one common religion that, in addition to all local cults, would be practiced throughout the Empire and thus act as a cohesive force. This common religion was found in the cult of the deified ruler."[27] The fact that Christianity was not a legitimate religion, however, immediately made it subject to suspicion not only by the government but also the wider society. In this environment the early Christians had to work out how to establish themselves, being faithful without compromise while simultaneously not creating offense to the point of drawing the society's anger. Kirkegaard expressed this quandary by observing that "the dominant culture of the day was Greco-Roman, and it is within this milieu that Christianity found its place . . . Early Christianity can in its entirety be thought of as a social movement, with every practice that set Christians apart from the rest of Greco-Roman society a critique and challenge built upon their particular perspectives. The practices that set Christians apart, however, do not necessarily match up with what we might expect."[28] He continued by articulating what those distinctives entailed:

> So what social differences actually did set early Christians apart? They clearly were distinctive, so much so that despite their small numbers Christians start appearing in Greco-Roman sources from the period even while they are still a very small minority. . . . [W]e find Christians noted particularly for their sharing of possessions, extremes of self-restraint, disregard for death, treatment of one another as brothers and sisters, and care for the poor.[29]

None of these distinctives, though perhaps appearing strange to the broader society, would have generated outright persecution of the Christians. They would, however, have generated curiosity. How could it be that death, for them, was disregarded as something extremely important, even paramount? That, coupled with the general society's misunderstanding of the Lord's Supper as being a cannibalistic ritual, put the Christians in a

---

to suppress criminal rites . . . [I]f Christianity was to be considered a new religion, it would have to be numbered among the *religiones illicitae*." Bainton, *Christendom*, 53; italics original.

27. Bainton, *Christendom*, 53.
28. Kirkegaard, "Placing Early Christianity," para. 4.
29. Kirkegaard, "Placing Early Christianity," para. 7.

difficult social position. In addition, their unique attitude toward death—disregard and lack of fear—led them to a unique understanding of how to express their faithfulness: refusal to compromise their fundamental commitment to Jesus by acknowledging Caesar as lord. Theologian Brandon J. O'Brien noted, "Christians could care for the plagued and refuse to hail Caesar because they didn't fear death. This set them apart from their pagan neighbors, to be sure. And it motivated their conduct in the empire."[30] It is not surprising that Christian uniqueness, including refusal to engage in the empire's unifying religion, not only made them an easy target, it also fomented persecution.

From shortly after the time Paul was writing his letters to the churches in the 50s through the early part of the fourth century a number of the Roman emperors conducted persecutions of the Christians. Persecution was not continuous during these centuries, but it did exist in varied and significant forms, and for various reasons. The persecution under Nero was motivated by his desire to shift blame for the fire in Rome from himself to others;[31] he chose the Christians. Later in the first century Domitian targeted the Christians not only because they refused to worship him, but due to his general dread of anyone or anything that posed a challenge to his authority.[32] In the early second century Trajan conducted a somewhat moderated persecution, if such a thing exists. The governor Pliny wrote Trajan, describing his approach to punishing Christians even while disclosing his lack of complete understanding of the Christians' situation.[33] In his response to Pliny, Trajan directed, "They are not to be hunted out. [Although] any who are accused and convicted should be punished, with the proviso that if a man says he is not a Christian and makes it obvious by his actual conduct—namely, by worshiping our gods—then, however suspect he may have been with regard to the past, he should gain pardon from his repentance."[34]

The persecutions continued and grew both in intensity and geographical dispersion. Marcus Aurelius persecuted Christians for philosophical reasons, believing Christianity was both immoral and revolutionary. At the turn of the third century Septimius Severus banned

30. O'Brien, "Commitments of the Early Church," para. 11.
31. See Galli, "Persecution in the Early Church"; and Wells, "Persecution."
32. See Galli, "Persecution in the Early Church"; and Wells, "Persecution."
33. For the full text of Pliny's writing, see Bainton, *Christendom*, 57. Bainton quoted from Pliny's *Epistulae* 96, and also translated the quote.
34. Galli, "Persecution in the Early Church," para. 19.

conversions to both Judaism and Christianity and made baptism a crime; in the middle of the third century Decius, fearing the potential political threat of expanding Christianity, demanded that Christians engage in pagan religious practice. Those who refused to do so were executed. Valerian asserted that the Christians were to blame for the empire's vast civil unrest and external military attacks. His persecution included not only execution, but also confiscation of property. Finally, at the beginning of the fourth century, Diocletian sought to extinguish Christianity because he viewed it as an impediment to his goal of restructuring the empire. He expanded persecution to include prohibition of Christian worship, destruction of churches and Christian literature, and arresting of clergy who refused to engage in pagan worship.[35] Pastor John Stott, long-time rector of All-Souls Church in London, summarized the plight of the early Christians like this:

> The early Christians faced a continuing conflict between Christ and Caesar. During the first century the emperors manifested an ever-increasing megalomania. They had temples erected in their honour, and demanded divine homage from their subjects. These claims came into direct collision with the lordship of Christ, whom Christians honoured as king, indeed as "the ruler of the kings of the earth".... But how could believers say "Caesar is Lord" when they had confessed that "Jesus is Lord"? They went to prison and death rather than deny the lordship of Christ.[36]

We have seen that in places in Paul's letters he advocated a type of accommodation to the surrounding social milieu in which the Christians found themselves, although this accommodation had its limits. Yet accommodation for the purpose of self-preservation indeed would have been a strong temptation to Christians who found themselves in an environment of increasing persecution. Placher noted, "For Christians at the time . . . persecution must have seemed a terror. It might start up again at any point, stirred up by anyone from local neighborhoods to a new emperor, and the forms of torture Christians faced were horrible indeed. They could easily enough become 'martyrs' . . . A call to follow Christ only rarely ended in martyrdom, but the [possibility] was something any Christian had at least to consider."[37] There were those who succumbed to

---

35. See Galli, "Persecution in the Early Church"; and Wells, "Persecution." For more details on Diocletian's persecution, see Bainton, *Christendom*, 89–90.

36. Stott, *Contemporary Christian*, 96.

37. Placher, *Callings*, 26.

the pressure and recanted. Yet others did not and maintained an uncompromising—even defiant—position vis-à-vis the social milieu, to the point of welcoming the resultant death sentence. What was it that caused them to adopt such a position, when even Paul allowed for certain endorsements of societal standards? From where did their strong convictions come regarding how to express their faithfulness within their society?

3

The Social Milieu and the Kingdom of God

THE RECIPIENTS OF THE Epistle to the Hebrews—written not by Paul but by an unknown author likely trained in classical philosophy in Alexandria—had adopted an approach to their new Christian faith that could be characterized as barely Christian. Their faith confession, in fact, had nothing particularly Christian about it, enabling them to maintain the outward impression that they were traditional Jews while convincing themselves that they had adopted Christianity. Immaturity and marginal faithfulness, at best, were the result. In all likelihood they took this social stance in order to avoid persecution, even martyrdom.[1] It was the threatening social milieu in which they found themselves that drove their understanding of what it meant to be a Christian, including their stance within their society. The need to address this misunderstanding motivated the author of the Epistle to the Hebrews to write to the spiritually immature Jewish converts with a corrective.

---

1. For a fuller explanation of the stance adopted by the recipients of the Epistle to the Hebrews see Lane, *Hebrews*, 88–89; and Hagner, *Encountering the Book of Hebrews*, 86.

PAUL, THE SOCIAL MILIEU, AND THE KINGDOM OF GOD

The early Christians throughout the Roman Empire similarly struggled with how to establish themselves vis-à-vis their social milieu. Being recipients of the letters of Paul, written during the 50s and perhaps into the very early 60s, their thinking was influenced by the social content included in those letters. As was the case a decade later with the recipients of the Epistle to the Hebrews, they found themselves in a threatening environment, sometimes extending as far as the specter of persecution. In spite of Paul's clear teaching that Christians are to be morally distinct from society, several elements of Paul's teaching, selectively emphasized by those early converts, as well as their experience would have tempted them to settle on a social stance that assured the greatest possible stability and protection—their Christian social distinctives notwithstanding. Those elements and experience included Paul's mediating position regarding support for the government and delineation of moral expectations that in many cases did not stray from those of the general social order. It also included the Christians' acceptance of many of the broader environment's social conventions, and their ability to adapt to social pressures.

Just as the writer of the Epistle to the Hebrews assumed that his audience had the traditional and common understanding of the kingdom of God as found in the Old Testament, so Paul made the same assumption. He did not treat the subject in a systematic manner anywhere, although he mentioned it a few times. Most of his comments had to do with kingdom *qualifications*, such as living a life worthy of the kingdom and avoiding a sinful life of greed, idolatry, rage, immorality, drunkenness, etc.[2] There are two places, however, in which Paul *characterized* the kingdom. In Rom 14:17 he wrote, "For the kingdom of God is not a matter of eating and drinking, but of righteousness, peace and joy in the Holy Spirit," and in 1 Cor 4:20 he stated, "For the kingdom of God is not a matter of talk but of power." Although helpful, these two references are nebulous at best, and do little to paint a detailed picture of the nature of the kingdom of God or its social expectations of those who participate in the kingdom. Whatever Paul assumed concerning his readers' understanding of the kingdom it was an Old Testament understanding; he did not enhance their understanding by instructing them regarding the nature of the kingdom.

---

2. See, for example, 1 Cor 6:9–10, Gal 5:21, Eph 5:5, and 1 Thess 2:12.

It has been argued by some that the lack of kingdom references throughout Paul's letters do not suggest that he neglected teaching about the kingdom.³ Rather, Paul perhaps used substitute language, such as references to the work of the Spirit or specific teaching about the resurrected Jesus, to teach about the kingdom. Often this approach asserts that Paul did not have to go into detail characterizing the kingdom of God since his readers were quite familiar with it from what they knew of the life of Jesus.⁴ Whereas neither proving nor disproving such arguments is our focus, at best they appear to be *assumptions* about what Paul's readers knew about the kingdom, and may even be attempts to defend Paul to show he most certainly had not neglected a subject so explicit and central to the life and teaching of Jesus, even though he barely mentioned it in his letters to new Christians.

Anyone interested in understanding Paul better should investigate and consider this perspective. However, another view may account better for the actual facts of Paul's writing. What is clear is that the readers of Paul's letters had the content of some of those letters (although none of Paul's early converts had the content of all the letters), and they had whatever oral traditions about the life of Jesus that had reached their respective locations in the Roman Empire, however incomplete they may have been. Readers of a Jewish background likely also had something of an understanding of the kingdom as expressed in the Old Testament. They did not, however, have the Synoptic Gospels or an oral expression of the Synoptics, for the Synoptics had not yet been written at the time Paul wrote his letters. It would be overly presumptive to assert they had a clear understanding of the kingdom of God as depicted in the Synoptics. In addition, they likely did not have the Acts of the Apostles, for it was written just after the last of Paul's letters to the churches. Even though in Acts there are several references to Paul's preaching of the kingdom of God,⁵ the only possible indication of the content of that preaching is in 28:23, which states that Paul preached from the Old Testament ("from

---

3. See, for example, Bredenhof, "Kingdom of God in Jesus and Paul"; and Vlach, "Kingdom of God in Paul's Epistles."

4. For example, see Vlach, who wrote, "When Paul uses the term 'kingdom' he does not define it, indicating that his audiences probably had prior knowledge about its meaning." Vlach, "Kingdom of God in Paul's Epistles," 59. Bredenhof mentioned "the concept of the Kingdom appears to be well known among Paul's readers. . . . [T]he Kingdom had been well-exposited, beginning with Jesus and continuing with his apostles." Bredenhof, "Kingdom of God in Jesus and Paul," 18–19.

5. See, for example Acts 19:8, 20:25, 28:23, and 28:31.

the Law of Moses and from the Prophets"). The lack of any significant kingdom teaching in Paul's letters strongly suggests that his readers did not have a clear understanding of its nature, except perhaps an Old Testament understanding.

What, then, did the early Christians—particularly those dispersed through the Roman Empire who had come to Christian faith through the ministry and letters of Paul—likely understand about the kingdom of God? The challenge for those Christians was that the picture of the kingdom in the Old Testament was less than fully developed in detail, and as more gentiles became Christians their lack of a background in Judaism would have left them with very little concept of the kingdom. To the extent that they were familiar with it, however, they would have understood the kingdom as depicted in the Old Testament, entailing a few concepts.

THE KINGDOM OF GOD IN THE OLD TESTAMENT

The most fundamental point to understand about the kingdom of God in the Old Testament is that, whereas the term is not explicitly used, the notion permeates the whole story of God's working as told in the Bible. "As Creator, he is committed to caring for and sustaining all of his creation. He governs and rules wisely over all his creatures and works."[6] "The basic notion is of the active rule of Yahweh as King over the whole world."[7] Yet the kingdom extends beyond just the created world, to include all of creation as well as non-created realities: "he is the King, and the entire universe is his kingdom. This truth is illustrated by Psalm 103:19: 'The LORD has established his throne in the heavens, and his kingdom rules over all' (cf. Ps 47:8; cf. Dan 4:34–35)."[8]

Beyond the overarching notion of God's sovereign reign throughout all of reality, there are social elements that characterize the kingdom. Nineteenth-century New England theologian F. B. Denio clarified this perspective of the kingdom in the Old Testament in two articles he wrote in 1886. "The general idea of the kingdom of God is that of a state of society where the will of God is supreme. There his commands are known and loyally obeyed in all the departments of human activity. The subjects

---

6. Gentry and Wellum, *God's Kingdom*, 207.
7. Marshall, "Kingdom of God, of Heaven," 801.
8. Gentry and Wellum, *God's Kingdom*, 244.

THE SOCIAL MILIEU AND THE KINGDOM OF GOD   43

in this kingdom are in intimate fellowship with their ruler."[9] The first example of the kingdom in society is found at the beginning of humanity, prior to the fall, in Gen 2 "which depicts Adam and Eve placed in a garden sanctuary. Only as they spend time in the presence of God will they be equipped to implement his rule in the world in the way in which God himself would relate to his creation."[10] The kingdom was formalized, however, not in Eden but with the Abrahamic covenant.[11] Selection of Israel as God's own—to the exclusion of all others—with the expectant distinct and holy behavior, has continued and never abated.[12] It was an unexplained exclusiveness based upon the relationship between God and Israel, intended to maintain that relationship.[13]

Not only was the kingdom characterized by an exclusiveness—God's selection of Israel alone—but it also was fundamentally distinct from and in opposition to the rest of society. Denio explained, "From a very early period the Old Testament had contrasted the people of God with other peoples. It first appears in Gen. IV. and V. In Gen. X.8 seq. this contrast heightens into a distinction between God's people and a world-kingdom, which is a distinction that never disappears."[14] However, distinction from, and contrast to, the surrounding society was not the extent of the difference between the kingdom of God and the worldly kingdom; rather, the difference extended to actual antagonism between the two: "An underlying thought of Old Testament prophecy is the antagonism between the society of men[15] by whom the true God is served and worshiped, and the societies of men which constitute world-kingdoms."[16] This is a key point that we will see later in the ministry of Jesus: the kingdom of God is in outright conflict with the kingdom of the world. There can be no compromise between the two.

---

9. Denio, "Kingdom of God in the Old Testament," 55.
10. Gentry and Wellum, *God's Kingdom*, 216.
11. Denio, "Kingdom of God in the Old Testament," 57.
12. Denio, "Kingdom of God in the Old Testament II," 71.
13. Denio, "Kingdom of God in the Old Testament II," 71.
14. Denio, "Kingdom of God in the Old Testament II," 71.
15. Denio's use of "men" was not intended to exclude women and children. Rather, Denio was employing the unfortunate convention of his day, using "men" to refer to all people. Other referenced authors use this same approach. I have pointed out the most blatant examples in footnotes.
16. Denio, "Kingdom of God in the Old Testament II," 75.

In time Israel demanded an earthly king, like its surrounding nations. Saul, the first king, was replaced by Israel's greatest king, King David. This move to a human king fundamentally changed the national consciousness of Israel, establishing it with an earthly identity parallel to other worldly kingdoms. The uniqueness of the kingdom of Israel was to be its righteousness, distinct from that which characterized other kingdoms. "With this development of the national consciousness came a development of the kingdom of God. David as the theocratic king recognized as never before the nature of the kingdom and of the proper human kingship (2 Sam. XXIII.3). It was seen that righteousness was the fundamental law of this kingdom, whoever might administer it."[17] The difficulty with the approach of an earthly kingdom with a human king was that it could not approach the divine ideal of the kingdom of God. The result was that the notion of a real, in-time kingdom of God on earth began to fade. "Each century after David saw the actual kingdom receding more and more from the ideal even of its songs. The heightening ideal of the prophets did not raise the people. At last a change in the situation was accepted by the prophetic order, the past was flung away, the present development was accepted as transitory, and the establishment of the kingdom of God came to be regarded as possible only by a complete renovation of society then existing."[18]

Renovating the current society was something judged far too extensive for Israel to accomplish, even through the end of the Old Testament age. "The present constitution of things was accepted as totally inadequate, and the kingdom of God was regarded as belonging to the future rather than the present."[19] The result was that "for Israel at the close of Old Testament history the kingdom of God has a past and a future, but no present."[20] It was this view of the kingdom of God that the early Christians to which Paul wrote were accustomed. They had a very limited understanding of the kingdom of God, at best, viewing it as pictured in the Old Testament with its expressions in the past and future, but not in the present. This understanding colored their mindset when reading Paul's letters and was at least partly responsible for their misunderstanding and misapplication of Paul's social teaching.

17. Denio, "Kingdom of God in the Old Testament II," 73.
18. Denio, "Kingdom of God in the Old Testament II," 74.
19. Denio, "Kingdom of God in the Old Testament II," 75.
20. Denio, "Kingdom of God in the Old Testament II," 76.

The social teaching found in Paul's letters, when correctly understood, needed no correction. The early Christians, however, being both limited in their knowledge of the faith,[21] and threatened by their Greco-Roman social milieu, had selectively misinterpreted and misused Paul (perhaps unintentionally or subconsciously) in order to decrease the societal threat to their well-being. The result was social accommodation and even syncretism. It was the misperception of Paul and the limited understanding of the kingdom that needed correcting. The Synoptic Gospels, not written for those specific purposes, nevertheless providentially provided the corrective through their central focus on the kingdom of God, including its present reality, as taught and demonstrated by Jesus.

JESUS AND THE KINGDOM OF GOD IN THE SOCIAL MILIEU

The gospel accounts of the life of Jesus, particularly those of the Synoptic Gospels, have played a fundamental role in understanding the nature and expectations of Christianity since they were written in the first century. It is a mistake, however, to assume that the first Christians, particularly those converted under the ministry of Paul and dispersed through the Roman Empire, had a clear understanding of the Synoptics. Whereas the events of Jesus' life occurred prior to the writing of Paul's letters, the content of Jesus' life as recorded in the Synoptics was not known to Christians until after they were written and distributed. The earliest of the Synoptics, Mark, was written around AD 67; the other two—Matthew and Luke—in the 70s. John's gospel was not written until the mid-80s at the earliest. This distinction—between the time of the occurrence of the events of Jesus' life and the time the early Christians became aware of those events by means of the Synoptic Gospels—is not clearly perceived by many Western Christians. They have unreflectingly assumed that *awareness* of the life and teaching of Jesus by the early Christians corresponded to the *timing* of Jesus' life. It did not. The distinction is crucial

---

21. This limitation of understanding was not unusual for early Christians. See, for example, Acts 18:24–26, in which the learned Christian Apollos, although having a thorough knowledge of the Old Testament and teaching about Jesus accurately, was limited in his Christian understanding and required further instruction from Priscilla and Aquila. Also see Acts 19:2, in which Paul encountered some Christians in Ephesus who had not heard of the Holy Spirit.

for understanding how the early Christians' approach to faithfulness in their social milieu developed.

If we consider the sequence of understanding that the early Christians—not the initial converts in Jerusalem but rather the converts of Paul's missionary journeys and similar converts throughout the Roman Empire—had of the writings of Paul and the Gospels, it quickly becomes clear that they first had Paul's letters and later the Gospels.[22] Prior to the written Gospels they also encountered the oral tradition of the life of Jesus, likely in various versions.[23] This tradition was quite accurate but also incomplete. It was the Synoptic Gospels that painted a fuller picture of Jesus' life and teachings[24]—a picture that dramatically altered the Christians' convictions regarding what it meant to be faithful within their social milieu.

What was it in the Synoptics that changed, or perhaps more accurately provided a corrective to, the early Christians' convictions concerning a faithful social stance within their context in Greco-Roman society? Quite simply, it was Jesus' teaching about the kingdom of God. We are not attempting to articulate the whole of that teaching here, for to do so is beyond our current focus and scope. Many books have been written on that subject and are readily available. Rather, we will concentrate

---

22. See Boyd: "Our earliest 'snap shot' of what the original followers of Jesus believed comes from Paul, not the Gospels." Boyd, "How Reliable," para. 10.

23. Oral tradition in the first century was significantly more influential and pervasive than it is among twenty-first-century Western Christians, if for no other reason than the relatively high illiteracy rate among the population of the Roman Empire. Not only was the oral tradition highly accurate, but the church took great care to preserve and reenact the tradition through recitations and performances. For our purposes the point is not that the oral tradition was influential, pervasive, or accurate; rather our focus is that it was *incomplete*, particularly regarding the social implications of the kingdom of God. For more on the oral tradition see Boyd, "How Reliable"; Horsley, "Oral and Written Aspects"; and Tusculum University, "Early Christian Oral Transmission."

24. Mark, the first of the Synoptics, includes about fifteen references to the kingdom of God, and thus is significant for understanding Jesus' teaching regarding the kingdom. John's Gospel mentions the kingdom only four times, twice in chapter 3 and twice in chapter 18, and thus records little of what Jesus said about the kingdom. Matthew and Luke—the other two Synoptics—contain the overwhelming majority of references to the kingdom from Jesus' teaching. They also were developed from multiple sources that included Mark, another source they had in common, and one or more additional sources unique to each of them. It is from Matthew and Luke, then, when coupled with Mark, that Jesus' kingdom teaching becomes clear in its most full-orbed depiction. This picture of the kingdom was not available to the early Christians until at least a decade after Paul's letters, and subsequent to their encounters with the accurate, albeit incomplete and varied, oral tradition.

on the *character* of the kingdom as taught and demonstrated by Jesus. That character influenced early Christian thinking about faithful societal engagement, and ultimately led Christians to migrate from the social accommodation and syncretism that they had read into and derived from Paul's letters, to resolute defiance of Rome—even to the point of persecution and martyrdom.

THE EVER-PRESENT KINGDOM

The first thing to realize about the kingdom of God in the teaching and conduct of Jesus is that it was all-pervasive. The kingdom was not one among many of the elements of Jesus' ministry; rather, it formed the heart of his message and the focus of his actions. Swiss theologian Urs Eigenmann expressed this over-arching nature of the kingdom as follows:

> The kingdom of God . . . was Jesus' primary concern. At the beginning of his public life he said: "The time is fulfilled, and the kingdom of God is at hand; repent, and believe in the gospel" (Mk 1,14f.)! In the Sermon on the Mount he exhorted his disciples: "But seek first his . . . kingdom and his justice, and all these things shall be yours as well." (Mt 6,33). . . . The kingdom of God . . . is therefore not just one of many subjects and not just a locally restricted factor, but a universally deciding one.[25]

Another theologian, G. Richard Wheatcroft, echoed the same perspective, noting also that the kingdom was Jesus' focus from the outset of his ministry: "The first words Jesus spoke when he began his mission and ministry in Galilee were, 'The time has come: the Kingdom of God is upon you; repent and believe the Gospel.' (Mk. 1:14 NEB) The consensus of biblical scholarship is that the Kingdom of God is the central focus of the message and ministry of Jesus."[26] Forell pointed out that the kingdom was not something ethereal, of a different realm from the human one, or just a future eschatological reality. Realizing that Jesus' announcement of the presence of the kingdom would henceforth characterize and constrain the moral realm of human experience, he wrote, "The whole of New Testament ethics is implicit in this proclamation. It is the ethics resulting from repentance and faith in the light of the realization that the

---

25. Eigenmann, "Social Contract," para. 2.
26. Wheatcroft, "Kingdom of God," para. 1.

kairós has come, the time is fulfilled, the kingdom of God is at hand."[27] When the early Christians understood that the kingdom of God was a present reality, they realized it would alter their understanding of faithfulness. Precisely how that understanding would be altered depended upon Jesus' kingdom teaching.

Having declared that the kingdom was present, Jesus had to convince his audience that it was not present in the form they expected: God ruling supremely over all of creation and society, with an exclusivity enjoyed by his chosen people, Israel. Rather, the present kingdom primarily entailed the incarnation of God in Jesus. It was not God's demonstration of *power* that characterized the present kingdom, but rather his *presence with humanity* and their responsive emulation of his example. Eigenmann expressed the concept of the kingdom present, without losing sight of the kingdom future, when he wrote, "The kingdom of God is already dawning and come near in Jesus himself. It is universally present, fragmentally, wherever people act in the spirit of Jesus; . . . It is necessary to adhere to both these aspects at the same time; to the fact that the kingdom of God is present now in fragments, and to the fact that it is the eschatologically utopian horizon of all our efforts."[28]

Ethicists Glen Stassen and David Gushee captured the dilemma Jesus confronted when seeking to teach his listeners the nature of the kingdom—not fundamentally God's power on display but rather his reigning presence in the lives of people: "God's salvation is the kingdom of God, and it means that—at last—God has acted to deliver humanity and now reigns over all of life, and is present to and with us, and will be in the future."[29] They went on to point out Jesus' key kingdom virtues. One that would influence the early Christians' convictions regarding faithfulness is the eighth Beatitude: "Matthew 5:10 says, 'Blessed are those who are persecuted for righteousness' sake, for theirs is the kingdom of heaven.'"[30] When Jesus linked the present kingdom to the endurance of persecution by kingdom participants, he was conveying that God's presence among his faithful does not mean that their sufferings will cease; rather, they will increase.

---

27. Forell, *Christian Social Teachings*, 13; italics original.
28. Eigenmann, "Social Contract," para. 15.
29. Stassen and Gushee, *Kingdom Ethics*, 28–29.
30. Stassen and Gushee, *Kingdom Ethics*, 45.

THE KINGDOM OF GOD AND FAITHFULNESS

This leads us to the concept of faithfulness within the context of the kingdom, understood as the abiding and ubiquitous presence of God. As participants in God's present kingdom, how are his people to demonstrate their faithfulness? Emulation of Jesus—the one whose presence effects the arrival of the kingdom—is to be the fundamental characteristic of faithful kingdom members. "Because Christ placed his mission and his teachings within the context of the kingdom of God, we must do likewise, and because Christ embodied his teaching in the way he treated people, we must do the same."[31]

Faithfulness and the kingdom of God are intertwined throughout the Synoptic Gospels, "like the interlocking strands of a DNA molecule"[32] according to Loveday Alexander, emeritus professor of biblical studies at the University of Sheffield. As such, the faithfulness of emulation entails taking on the role of an apprentice of Jesus and learning through imitation in order to become both a witness to and an agent of the kingdom.[33] Stassen and Gushee expressed this notion by asserting, "Ethics as incarnational discipleship points to the *incarnate Jesus, who taught the Sermon on the Mount and the kingdom of God, in the tradition of the prophets of Israel, embodied it in his practices and called us to embody it in our practices of discipleship*."[34] Kingdom faithfulness, then, primarily entails not adherence to laws, principles, or rituals, but rather immersion into the kingdom of God as it was played out in the life of Jesus. For the early Christians this idea would have altered completely their understanding of how to establish themselves within their social milieu. It was a calling, in fact, to establish themselves as Jesus had when he became God incarnate and brought the kingdom of God into the human social reality of the first century.

THE KINGDOM OF GOD AND SOCIETY

What was it that Jesus brought to human society when he brought the kingdom of God? If we were actually to see the kingdom in Jesus, what would we observe? In Matt 4:17 and Mark 1:15 we learn of the *fact* of

31. Stassen and Gushee, *Kingdom Ethics*, 97.
32. Alexander, "Gospels and Acts," 10.
33. Alexander, "Gospels and Acts," 12, 14.
34. Stassen and Gushee, *Kingdom Ethics*, 58–59; italics original.

the kingdom when Jesus announced its presence. In Luke 4:18–19, however, Jesus—standing in the Nazareth synagogue on the Sabbath—quoted from Isa 61 to depict the *social nature* of the kingdom present among his human peers. It is noteworthy that in Luke's presentation of the gospel he positioned Jesus' Isaiah quotation after both Mary's Magnificat[35] and the description of the ministry of Jesus' forerunner, John the Baptist.[36] Both of those statements are clear proclamations of *social upheaval* as a result of Jesus' arrival in the world. When Jesus quoted Isaiah he was building upon both Mary and John, declaring that what he brought was a *new social order*, particularly for the suffering of society: the poor, prisoners, the blind, and the oppressed. A few verses later Jesus declared that the new order was fulfilled that very day in the presence of his audience.[37] There is no doubt that Jesus was proclaiming the kingdom of God as a present social reality—but a reality vastly different from the one to which his audience was accustomed. John Howard Yoder described the social transformation associated with this event from Jesus' life as a "new regime":

> In the ordinary sense of his words Jesus, like Mary and like John, was announcing the imminent *entrée en vigueur* of a new regime whose marks would be that rich would give to the poor, the captives would be freed, and men[38] would have a new mentality (*metanoia*), if they believed this news.... [W]hat the event was supposed to be is clear: it is a visible socio-political, economic restructuring of relations among the people of God, achieved by his intervention in the person of Jesus as the one Anointed and endued with the Spirit.[39]

It should not surprise us that introduction of a new regime would be viewed later by Rome as a threat to the status quo.

The drastic change in social relationships associated with the present kingdom would have political implications that affected Jesus' followers.[40] They, as Jesus' apprentices, witnesses, and agents were to be as

35. See Luke 1:46–55.

36. See Luke 3:4–6.

37. See Luke 4:21.

38. Here is another example of an author using male language. Yoder's use of an exclusively male term does not indicate that he was referring only to men. Rather, he was using an outdated convention to convey both genders—an unfortunate use of language.

39. Yoder, *Politics of Jesus*, 39.

40. See Yoder: "Jesus was, in his divinely mandated (i.e. promised, anointed, messianic) prophethood, priesthood, and kingship, the bearer of a new possibility of human, social, and therefore political relationships. His baptism is the inauguration and his

enmeshed in the present reality of the kingdom as was he. Both Matthew and Luke included another incident from Jesus' life that pictures the kingdom in a different way.[41] Matthew described it as a wedding feast; Luke termed it a great banquet. In both recordings it is cited as a description of the kingdom. How, though, can it be said that the kingdom is not only social, but political, particularly when describing it by painting a verbal picture of a banquet? In what ways did the proclamation of good news for the poor, oppressed, sick, and outcast affect the political realities of the Roman Empire? Eigenmann viewed the parable of the banquet as *subversive*, and thus politically threatening:

> The richest metaphor for the kingdom of God is that of the wedding feast . . . This illustrates what Jesus thought . . . the kingdom of God as a reversal of the social order . . . The guests whom the host causes to be called are, according to Luke, "the poor and maimed and blind and lame," together with others from the country roads (Lk 14,21–23) and according to Matthew "bad and good" (Mt 22,10) . . . "one could, in such a situation, have classes, sexes, and ranks all mixed up together. . . . [W]hat a social nightmare that would be." . . . The social challenge of such equal or egalitarian commensality is the parable's most fundamental danger and most radical threat . . . The Kingdom of God . . . clashes fundamentally with honour and shame, those basic values of ancient Mediterranean culture and society.[42]

In the banquet parable we see how good news to disadvantaged individuals began to threaten the social order, and thus became political. When announcing the kingdom present in society Jesus was not merely bringing help to individuals who needed it; he was doing so in a way that challenged the social conventions as established by Greco-Roman society and enforced politically throughout the Roman Empire. This announcement, indeed, constituted a threat to Rome. "Since Jesus used the metaphor Kingdom of God in the context of the 'domination order' of the kingdom of Caesar, Herod and Caiaphas, it has political connotations. It would evoke a vision of a political order where God ruled, not Caesar, Herod and Caiaphas. . . . Obviously, Jesus' vision of the Kingdom of God

---

cross is the culmination of that new regime in which his disciples are called to share." Yoder, *Politics of Jesus*, 62–63.

41. See Matt 22:1–14 and Luke 14:15–24.
42. Eigenmann, "Social Contract," para. 9.

would be seen by Caesar, Herod and Caiaphas as a potential threat to their power."[43]

The centrality of the kingdom of God in the ministry of Jesus—particularly the kingdom's social and political realities—altered significantly the early Christians' understanding and convictions concerning God's expectations of the faithful. When they came in contact with the written Gospels the nature of the present kingdom—mentioned so little in the Pauline epistles with which they were familiar—served as a corrective to their misunderstanding of Paul and the conclusions they had erroneously derived from his letters regarding how they were to establish themselves within their social milieu. That corrective necessitated that they conduct themselves in an entirely different way in society from that with which they were accustomed, including their response to the demands of Rome. Yoder pointed out the kingdom's clash with the broader society by commenting on the series of Jesus' teachings in the temple toward the end of his earthly ministry, as recorded by Luke:

> Every pericope in the section 19:47—22:2 reflects in some way the confrontation of two social systems and Jesus' rejection of the status quo. The trap question about the denarius (20:20–25) is the most openly political, but differs from the others only in that this meaning is more transparent. . . . In the context of his answer "the things that are God's" most normally would not mean "spiritual things"; the attribution "to Caesar Caesar's things and to God God's things" points rather to demands or prerogatives which somehow overlap or compete, needing to be disentangled. What is Caesar's and what is God's are not on different levels, so as never to clash; they are in the same arena.[44]

It is noteworthy that at the end of the gospel section referenced by Yoder, Luke mentioned that the religious authorities, the chief priests, and the teachers of the law were looking for a way to get rid of Jesus.[45] When the early Christians perceived this reality about their Lord they understood that if they were faithful emulators of Jesus the leaders would seek to get rid of them as well.

---

43. Wheatcroft, "Kingdom of God," para. 9.
44. Yoder, *Politics of Jesus*, 52–53.
45. See Luke 22:2.

THE KINGDOM OF GOD AND CONFLICT

Meeks commented on another gospel incident involving the conflict between Jesus' kingdom and the kingdom of Caesar; the occasion of Jesus' trial before the Roman governor Pilate.[46] Jesus had indicated that his kingdom is not of this world, not meaning it is ethereal or intangible, but rather that it both has a different source from human kingdoms and the way of his kingdom is not the violent way of human kingdoms (John 18:36). He was pointing out an irreconcilable conflict between the kingdom of God and Caesar's kingdom, particularly as demonstrated through the conduct of his followers. "In other places, the two realms are seen as unalterably antagonistic, and one must choose between God or Christ and Caesar. . . . the most poignant irony in this gospel comes when the Jews who refuse Jesus as their king are made to say . . . 'We have no king but Caesar' (John 19:15)."[47] This incident would have made it clear to the early Christians that there was no middle ground by which they could be faithful to their affirmation "Jesus is Lord!" and also endorse the values and political realities of their social milieu. Their Christian commitment necessarily entailed alignment with the kingdom of God and rejection of the demands of Rome; unwillingness to embrace this necessity entailed rejection of Jesus and the kingdom of God. Syncretism was not an option.

Yoder, using Luke's incident in which Jesus characterized the extreme requirements of the faithful,[48] summarized the expectation Jesus had of his followers: "Jesus is here calling into being a community of *voluntary* commitment, willing for the sake of its calling to take upon itself the hostility of the given society. . . . What matters is the quality of the life to which the disciple is called. The answer is that to be a disciple is to share in the style of life of which the cross is the culmination."[49]

The kingdom message of the Gospels transformed the perception the early Christians had of faithful participation in their social milieu, from compromising accommodation and even syncretism to open defiance when pressured by Rome. Although the kingdom of God did not entail aggression against Rome, it necessarily was in outright conflict with the political power structure. There was no limit to the extent that Jesus' followers were to remain faithful when in conflict with the kingdom of

46. See John 18:28—19:16.
47. Meeks, *Origins*, 168.
48. See Luke 14:25–27.
49. Yoder, *Politics of Jesus*, 45.

Caesar, even to the point of death. Such rigid defiance was deemed intolerable by Rome, and so the Christians became subject to persecution.

4

Faithfulness and the Early Christians

WE HAVE SEEN THAT there were a few elements of the kingdom of God that the early Christians understood accurately prior to their exposure to Jesus' kingdom teaching in the Synoptic Gospels. They knew that faithfulness meant distinction from the broader society—a distinction that never disappeared. That distinction played out in routine life as antagonism between the people of God and the other people of the social milieu in which the faithful found themselves. They also knew that God did not tolerate compromise in loyalty, values, commitment, practices, or character, for the kingdom's social essence was God's rule over all. His will was supreme.

This rigid and broad understanding of the kingdom had led believers to the conviction that the kingdom had both a past and a future in society, but not a present reality. God's people, it was thought, could participate in the all-encompassing kingdom, but not until the eschatological future.

Jesus' kingdom teaching changed the view the early Christians had of both the kingdom's scope and its influence on the meaning of faithfulness. When they were exposed to the Synoptic Gospels their worldview was dramatically altered, as was their view of how God expected the faithful to establish themselves within their social milieu. For Jesus the kingdom was—from the outset of his earthly ministry—the central focus of his message. Fundamental to that message was that God not only reigns over all but also is present with his people. That presence, however, did not mean that suffering would end; rather, just as Jesus' life was characterized by increasing suffering, so would be the lives of the faithful if they emulated Jesus.

The early Christians saw in Jesus' kingdom teaching that faithfulness at its root did not entail following a set of rules or adherence to a moral code. Rather, the primary characteristic of the faithful was emulation of Jesus, particularly in suffering. This is the concept Peter—who spent three years in the presence of Jesus learning from and observing him—captured in his first letter, written after the letters of Paul. In the context of the suffering slave, Peter wrote, "Christ suffered for you, leaving you an example, that you should follow in his steps.... [H]e entrusted himself to him who judges justly."[1]

Imitation of Jesus and becoming his apprentice—including suffering as Jesus suffered—was the kingdom call to those who sought to be God's faithful. When the early Christians learned that faithfulness meant being immersed into the kingdom just as it had played out in the life of Jesus, their concept of how to live in their social milieu became clear: they were to live as Jesus had lived, following in his footsteps. One reality of such emulation of Jesus was that the faithful—just like Jesus—would encounter a society in which those with power would seek to get rid of them.

What specifically was the social character of the kingdom taught and lived by Jesus? If the faithful were to conduct themselves in the society as Jesus had done, what would we expect to see when observing them? Earlier we learned that in Luke's recording of Jesus' declaration of his purpose—in which he quoted from Isa 61:1–2—it was made clear that he was introducing a new social order that favored the suffering of society. In this new regime the existing social conventions were overturned through the inbreaking of the kingdom of God: the poor finally received good news; those incarcerated were freed; anyone who could not see was given sight; and the oppressed were freed from their oppression. Jesus' statement of purpose built upon Mary's song of social upheaval, as well as John the Baptist's declaration of God's salvation in which the impossible was finally made a reality through the Lord's arrival in society.

In the parable of the great banquet Jesus further showed the social character of the kingdom. Rank and class distinctions were obliterated,

---

1. See 1 Pet 2:18–23.

along with the honor and shame that necessarily accompanied various levels within the society. All were one and equal at the feast of the kingdom of God. This social leveling, along with the upheaval and new order proclaimed by Jesus, naturally would be viewed as a significant threat by the political hierarchy of the Greco-Roman milieu in which the early Christians lived. However, emulation of Jesus and walking in his way required that the faithful align themselves with the new social ethical reality of the kingdom of God. The faithful, living as did Jesus in the kingdom of God present, would do away with harmful social distinctions among people. They would favor the unfavorable of society and thus ensure the surrounding Greco-Roman culture with its oppressive treatment of the lowly was exposed as being opposed to God's moral expectations. They would advocate for a new regime in which God alone ruled over all, thus clashing directly with the power of Rome. They would not compromise their declaration that Jesus is Lord, irrespective of what it cost them, and they would walk in the way of Jesus even if it meant following him in death.

Did early Christians actually live this way? Did they demonstrate their faithfulness by living in the present reality of God's kingdom, as had Jesus? To what extent did they walk in the Jesus way, and to what extent did they remain faithful in suffering? The investigative work of several scholars can give us insight into the answers to these questions.

VALUES AND TRAITS OF THE FAITHFUL

To understand how the early Christians lived out faithfulness it will be helpful to consider two elements of their fidelity: their values and their traits. Learning how these two drove their participation in their social milieu will give us a solid picture of the way they were influenced by the gospel depictions of the life of Jesus and his kingdom teaching, as well as the other writings that eventually made up the New Testament.

Values of the Faithful

Conduct and convictions regarding their stance in their social milieu were driven by the Christians' values—values that were shaped by the life of Jesus, his teaching about the present kingdom of God, and the teachings of Paul when writing to nascent Christians communities in the Roman Empire. The most fundamental among those values was the faithfulness of God. Such faithfulness served as the basis and prototype for the faithfulness of the early Christians. Meeks noted, "The stability of God's promises provides the necessary context for moral action, particularly when the action is itself defined as faithful, that is, action befitting the pattern of God's action, which may defy the customary and commonsensical."[2] Note that the possibility of conduct counter to the societal norm is introduced in this depiction of faithfulness as being patterned after the action of God. For the early Christians faithfulness to God did not necessitate conformity with the value expectations of society.

Meeks took faithfulness one step further when he pointed out that "the fundamental exemplar of God's fidelity," for the early Christians, "was the story of Jesus Christ, particularly of his death and resurrection. . . . Jesus' faith or faithfulness is identical with his obedience and his self-sacrifice."[3] The early Christians affirmed that God's foundational faithfulness was demonstrated ideally by the suffering life of Jesus, to the point of death, and that they were to follow that ideal even if it required them to be misaligned with the norms of Greco-Roman society.

Following naturally and closely upon the value of faithfulness was the early Christians' value of aligning themselves with Jesus. Their identity was that of being Jesus followers. "To be called a Christian was far more than a demographic designation or a reflection of family heritage; it was one's identity. The name represented allegiance to Christ in the whole of one's life, and allegiance to Christ was demonstrated by living a certain sort of life, one characterized by faithfulness and virtue."[4] In addition to living a life patterned after that of Jesus, they also adopted his name. They not only were to walk *in* the Jesus way, they were to walk *with* the living Jesus.

Specific values followed the general ones of Godlike faithfulness and whole-life identification and alignment with Jesus. Walking with Jesus entailed adopting the moral life of Jesus. Troeltsch wrote, "The ethic of the Gospel is marked by emphasis on purity of intention . . . without any allowance for conflicting motives or for expediency. Above all, it connects this moral conduct with its supreme object—a personal relation with God,"[5] then added these specifics: "Christ requires men to be indiffer-

2. Meeks, *Origins*, 159–60.
3. Meeks, *Origins*, 160.
4. Klein and Steiner, *What Is My Calling?*, 43.
5. Troeltsch, *Social Teachings*, 52.

ent to material happiness and to money, to practice sexual self-restraint, to have a mind that values the unseen and eternal more than the seen and temporal . . . Here the Gospel is extremely radical. It is not ascetic, but it is very severe."[6] Such values transformed the thinking of the early Christians, to the point that the moral milieu of the faithful would have differed drastically from that of their social environment. Withdrawal from society was not what their adopted Jesus values required of them, but rather social immersion as individuals and a believing community morally distinct from their social and political surroundings.

At this point it is easy to see how the early Christians would have viewed the world as consisting of two moral realities within one social milieu. They were motivated by the faithfulness of God, even to the point of defying the expectations of society. Their example for conduct was the life of Jesus, whom they were to emulate and with whom they were to walk. The moral purity of Jesus was their life standard, as opposed to materialism or self-indulgence, and their minds were to be focused on the eternal rather than the temporal. They were morally distinct from their dominant society. It is not surprising to learn that they adopted a dualistic understanding of the moral world that their Jewish predecessors had embraced: God's world, on the one hand, and Satan's on the other.[7] The distinction was emphasized by the early Christians "to dramatize the separation from one life and one society and the joining of another."[8] Conversion necessarily included "a transfer of loyalty and sense of belonging from one set of social relations to another, quite different set."[9]

The rejection of societal moral norms mentioned by Meeks took practical form in a number of values embraced by the early Christians. Prime among these was rejection of official participation in government-sanctioned work. As an example, Forell quoted third-century Christian father Origen of Alexandria, who defended Christianity against the anti-Christian second-century Greek philosopher Celsus: "But we recognize in each state the existence of another national organization, founded by the Word of God, and we exhort those who are mighty in word and of blameless life to rule over churches . . . that they may reserve themselves for a diviner and more necessary service in the church of God—for the

---

6. Troeltsch, *Social Teachings*, 54.
7. Meeks, *Moral World*, 100–101.
8. Meeks, *Origins*, 12.
9. Meeks, *Origins*, 31.

salvation of men."[10] One way of living out their conviction that there were two distinct moral realities in their society, one good and one evil, was to refuse to participate in government work so that they could focus on leadership of the church.

A similar value was repudiation of government-sanctioned killing, for the early Christians felt it to be a violation of God's moral standards. Such killing was "rejected by Christians on ethical grounds. . . . Any shedding of blood (*effusio sanguinis*) was abhorrent even in civil justice. The Christian could not assume the office of a judge who would have to pass sentence of death."[11] This repudiation extended to support of, and participation in, war on behalf of the state: "The taking of life in war was unanimously condemned by all Christian writers of the period prior to Constantine . . . war was incompatible with the injunction of the Lord to love one's enemies. . . . Tertullian of Carthage . . . took the legalistic stand that Christ, when he told Peter to put up his sword, had thereby disarmed every soldier."[12] Tertullian's attendant lack of concern over the results if the state were to adopt his position needs to be emphasized, for it points to an important reality of the early Christians' value system. They viewed their values as appropriate for them only as members of God's good society, as opposed to the evil social milieu that surrounded them. The rejoinder to their refusal to embrace and conduct themselves according to the values of the Greco-Roman world—that society would collapse if all were to adopt the values of the Christians—was irrelevant to them, for their values were only for those who participated in the present kingdom of God.

There was one more practical value that both solidified the early Christians' convictions and cemented their moral distinction from their surrounding society. It motivated them and drove their conduct. The martyrs served as archetypes of faithfulness for the early believers. Kirkegaard wrote, "Martyrs provided another ideal, and truly were the heroes of the early church to which Christians looked in admiration and whom pagans regarded with bafflement."[13] We will review several of these martyr stories later in the chapter, but at this point we turn to some of the traits that the early Christians' values engendered.

10. Forell, *Christian Social Teachings*, 58–59.
11. Bainton, *Christendom*, 60.
12. Bainton, *Christendom*, 60.
13. Kirkegaard, "Placing Early Christianity," para. 8.

Traits of the Faithful

Not all early Christians held the identical view of society and their participation in it, even though they held similar values. Whereas it would be a mistake to assert that there were radical differences among the faithful, their respective views of the degree to which they could embrace certain cultural elements of the dominant society varied somewhat. Second-century church father Irenaeus, for example, appealed to Paul's writing in Rom 13 to argue for the legitimacy of secular government to the extent that it maintains justice and order. He also maintained, however, that secular governments would perish under the judgment of God for any conduct that was unjust, impious, or tyrannical.[14] Another second-century church father, Tertullian, had a different emphasis from Irenaeus. Forell wrote of Tertullian that his view was "complete and disdainful separation from the 'world.'"[15] Several factors likely contributed to variations among early Christians; for example, Irenaeus was raised in Christianity, whereas Tertullian was from a pagan, militaristic household. Be that as it may, there are some general traits that characterized the early Christians.

First, the influence of sin upon the society was evident to the early Christians, even though the secular government had a role to play in establishing and maintaining order. Their mindset affirmed that sin had corrupted the whole of creation and darkened what formerly reflected divine light. Forell described this trait as follows: "Into this darkness caused by human sin shines the light and it creates a new society dialectically related to the world, opposing and permeating it simultaneously like leaven or salt."[16] The faithful were characterized by a perspective that saw two societies: the sinful one that had corrupted the whole world, and the new one created by God to oppose worldly society and influence it for good. Faithfulness included separation from the sinful of society while prodding that same society with its need to yield to God.

The Revelation to St. John, written late in the first century, came to influence the early Christian's attitude toward their social milieu, particularly since it was written specifically with the evil of the Roman Empire in mind. "The thirteenth chapter here given is the counterpart of Romans 13. There is a limit to the acceptance of the authority of the rulers of

---

14. See Forell, *Christian Social Teachings*, 39–40, in which he quoted Irenaeus's writing, *Against Heresies*.
15. Forell, *Christian Social Teachings*, 41.
16. Forell, *Christian Social Teachings*, 13.

this world."[17] A misunderstanding of Paul had caused some to adopt a syncretistic approach to societal engagement. The written gospels, with their overwhelming emphasis on the kingdom of God, rectified that misunderstanding—establishing clearly the kingdom of God as distinct and opposed to the kingdom of the world—and Revelation solidified the evil nature of secular society and the requirement that the faithful resist it even to death. This mindset, very much different from the current one of Western Christianity, typified the Christians of the first few centuries.

A second trait of the early Christians was that they were followers of Jesus. They saw him as their teacher and sought to learn from him. This learning included not only objective content, but also practice in walking in the way of Jesus. They were Jesus' apprentices, trying to do what he did and act as he acted. Becoming a faithful Christian meant engaging in an unending process of whole-life education, learning everything there was to learn from the teacher, Jesus.[18] Alexander characterized this trait with the following:

> Being a disciple meant personal choice and commitment: it often meant leaving home to live and travel with one's teacher. And it was never primarily about book-learning: being a disciple meant above all paying close attention to your teacher, to their character, actions and lifestyle as much as to their words. Ideally, it meant being formed into the likeness of the teacher, passing on the tradition, modelling your practice and lifestyle on theirs. It meant internalizing the teachings and lifestyle (the *bios*) of the teacher, becoming part of a chain of transmission so that their teachings and lifestyle could be passed on to the next generation.[19]

That being the case, it was not possible for the early Christians to be half-hearted in their faithfulness. They could not choose to be partly like Jesus, and partly not; being a half-Christian was tantamount to being a hypocrite. What characterized the early followers of Jesus was that they were just that—followers of Jesus wholeheartedly, completely, and without compromise with the surrounding society or surrender to the threats of the secular government.

The third trait of the early Christians was that they were willing to sacrifice and suffer. This follows from the second trait, walking in the path of Jesus and being like him in every way. Inherent in the incarnation

---

17. Forell, *Christian Social Teachings*, 29.
18. See Alexander, "Gospels and Acts," 8.
19. Alexander, "Gospels and Acts," 8.

was Jesus' inevitable social isolation, loneliness, ostracism, mistreatment, temptation to compromise, being misunderstood and attacked, and ultimately being killed. Believers in the first few centuries understood that faithfulness meant they were being called to the same experience. Placher characterized this trait of the early Christians when he wrote:

> It was not easy to be a Christian during the first several centuries of the church's existence. Christianity began as an obscure cult out on the eastern edge of the Roman Empire, and most of those living in the empire heard of it first in wild rumors: Christians engaged in orgies; they wanted the world to end; when they met together, they ate flesh and drank blood.... Since they would not sacrifice to the divine emperor, they must be traitors. After all, this Jesus they worshipped had been executed by a Roman governor.
>
> Becoming a Christian thus often meant isolation from family and friends. Christians didn't fit in; if they fell victim to persecution they could break their parents' hearts and put their children at risk. Persecution was only occasional, but it carried the risk of torture and death. Yet more and more people kept joining the church. It was as if the blood of the martyrs watered its growth.[20]

This trait—*willingness* to endure sacrifice and suffering—was not something the Christians tried to hide; rather it was evident to those who made the effort to observe them. One highly influential example was the second-century philosopher Justin Martyr, who later converted to Christianity and himself was martyred. In describing Justin's observation of Christianity Meeks wrote, "he had heard the Christians slandered, but when he saw their fearlessness in the face of death and other threats, he recognized that the slanders must be false. For no 'pleasure lover or dissolute person or cannibal' ever showed such indifference to death (2 *Apol.* 12.1)."[21]

Sacrifice and suffering—even to the point of dying as Jesus had done—was not something from which the early Christians recoiled, as did those of the Greco-Roman social milieu in which they found themselves. It was a trait that puzzled any who observed it, for it was not normal for that society, just as it is not normal in Western society today. Rather, it was a distinguishing trait that, along with the others, was

---

20. Placher, *Callings*, 23.
21. Meeks, *Origins*, 20.

a hallmark of faithfulness among the first believers to walk consistently and completely in the way of Jesus.

The final trait of the early faithful has been suggested a number of times thus far, but it now warrants specific identification: they lived their lives in the context of Christian communities. They were not isolated Christians. For example, Paul wrote many of his letters to *communities* of Christians. Adoption of the values of Jesus meant they were immersed in their society—even while holding to values radically different from those of the society—as believing and witnessing *communities*. A new Christian separated from his or her old life and its society but joined a new *community* as a Christian brother or sister. Christians lived under a moral imperative to choose between the "worldly society" and a *community* of disciples, not isolated discipleship. Under the threat of persecution increasing numbers of people joined the church, the *community* of the faithful; they did not defy Rome only as individuals.

In the next section we will review the stories of several martyrs and observe that for all of them the Christian community was vital, even as their unwavering faithfulness led to death.

EARLY CHRISTIAN FAITHFUL

Not all early Christians were equally mature, and their expressions of faithfulness varied widely. Some, under governmental threat and pressure, became apostates and abandoned their faith altogether; others initially affirmed the deity of the emperor in order to save their lives, only later to repent of that affirmation and seek reinstatement into the Christian community. There were some who had the means to purchase a *libellus*—an official document vouching for their loyalty to Rome—and thus buy their way out of persecution. Still others, though, refused to compromise their commitment to the lordship of Christ, even in the face of the threat of torture and death. The ones who survived were known as confessors; the ones who remained faithful unto death were known as martyrs.

We have conducted a brief overview of the social milieu in which the believers of the first few centuries found themselves, including the social pressures and expectations to which they were subject. The influence of the writings of Paul upon their social thinking, as well as the correcting life example and kingdom teaching of Jesus, were very strong and formed the fundamental commitments of the believers vis-à-vis their political and social environment. In the moral realm in which they lived such commitments took the form of values and traits that directed the lives of the early Christians. What, however, characterized their outlook and mindset such that certain ones remained steadfast in their faithfulness, even through threat, torture, punishment, and finally death? If we look at the last days of the lives of a few martyrs it should help us appreciate what ultimate faithfulness—faithfulness in the extreme—meant viscerally for those who had the opportunity to save their lives, but steadfastly refused to do so.

Recall that the early Christians had a view of death quite different from that of most Western Christians today. They incorporated death into their daily lives, both caring directly for the dying and being inspired by the deaths of those who had gone before them, including those who had died as a result of their unwavering faithfulness. The primary example was the death of the first martyr, Stephen,[22] whom many Christians in the first few centuries viewed as an example of faithfulness and from whom they took inspiration.

Bishop Ignatius of Antioch was one of the early martyrs in the second century. While being transported to Rome to face his death he was greeted by another bishop, Polycarp of Smyrna. That encounter resulted in Ignatius writing to several churches, including the church at Rome.[23] His plea to his fellow Christians—the Christian community in the city where he was to be martyred—was that they not intervene on his behalf to prevent his martyrdom,[24] but rather "just pray that I may have strength of soul and body so that I may not only talk (about martyrdom), but really want it. It is not that I want merely to be called a Christian, but actually to be one. Yes, if I prove to be one, then I can have the name. Then, too, I shall be a convincing Christian only when the world sees me no more. . . . I am voluntarily dying for God—if, that is, you do not interfere."[25] He went on to indicate that his discipleship was about to begin, for by dying as had Jesus he finally would be with Jesus.[26]

Some forty years after Ignatius's martyrdom Polycarp himself was also martyred, around AD 156. His congregation—the Christian community of which he had been a part—recorded the events of Polycarp's

---

22. See Acts 6:8—8:1.
23. Wright, "Ignatius," 498.
24. Placher, *Callings*, 33.
25. Placher, *Callings*, 34.
26. Placher, *Callings*, 35.

death in a letter specifically addressed to the church in Philomelium, but also to all Christian churches worldwide. It depicted Polycarp's understanding of faithfulness in a way similar to Ignatius's in that Polycarp was an imitator of Christ.[27] Yet at his trial his own words—when he was urged several times by the Roman proconsul to curse Christ and affirm Caesar—indicate that for him faithfulness entailed unwavering loyalty to Christ irrespective of the cost. This was because Polycarp was moved deeply that throughout his long life Christ had been loyal to him without fail: "I have served him eighty-six years, and he has done me no wrong; how can I blaspheme the king who saved me?"[28]

It wasn't only church leaders who endured faithfully, even to death. About two decades after the death of Polycarp—in AD 177—a young slave named Blandina was also martyred. The occasion was a holiday in Lyons, Gaul, to celebrate the emperor and Rome. Festivities were part of the celebration, and the governor decided to torture Christians to entertain the crowd.[29] The not-uncommon accusations of cannibalism and other perversions had been leveled at these Christians, sparking Blandina's response, "I am a Christian and there is nothing vile done by us."[30] She, along with the rest of her small Christian community about to be martyred, was tortured mercilessly, and finally executed. Blandina was the last to die. "She had encouraged many others and saw them go on before her to Jesus. Now she was ready to hasten after them. She faced death rejoicing—as if being called to a marriage feast rather than wild beasts."[31] Her focus was not the fear of death or the pain of torture. These appear to have been quite insignificant to her in light of her imminent joining with Jesus and the others of her group who had just died. For Blandina there was a strong sense of solidarity with her fellow Christians. Her faith was strong, and she was unwavering in her commitment. Yet she was not a Christian in isolation; in fact, the prospect of once again joining her faithful friends seems to have bolstered her even as she was tortured to death.

One of the most well-known martyr stories is that of Perpetua, a young mother of twenty-two who was still nursing her baby. Perpetua

27. Wright, "Polycarp," 791.
28. See Bainton, *Christendom*, 63, in which Bainton quoted Polycarp.
29. Severance, "Blandina," para. 4.
30. Severance, "Blandina," para. 1.
31. Severance, "Blandina," para. 9.

was of noble birth,[32] with a respectable family and background living in North Africa. She, along with four others, was arrested in AD 203. Even when under family pressure to save herself she would not recant, holding steadfastly to her identity as a Christian.[33] On the day of their execution, "they marched from the prison to the amphitheater joyfully as though they were going to heaven, with calm faces, trembling, if at all, with joy rather than fear. Perpetua went along with shining countenance and calm step, as the beloved of God, as a wife of Christ."[34] After being severely injured while facing the animals, they eventually were killed by gladiators. Like Blandina, Perpetua and her fellow Christians were martyred in solidarity, encouraging and being encouraged by each other.[35] She faced death with joy, looking forward to being wedded to Christ.

Ignatius was eager to die, for death would join him to Christ. Polycarp faced his martyrdom viewing it as an opportunity both to imitate Jesus and also be faithful as God had always been faithful to him. Blandina, in solidarity with her fellow martyrs, viewed death as the means by which she would join in the great banquet with Jesus; and Perpetua gave up even her infant child in order to die and thus be wedded to Christ. It is notable that the mindset of these four was not primarily focused on theological arguments or biblical content, vital and essential as those are. Intense relationship with Christ, and the opportunity to enhance that relationship, seems to have been at the heart of faithfulness for these martyrs. Not all early Christians were martyrs, and there were many who remained faithful in the extreme without being martyred; for all, however, continual enhancing of their personal relationship with Christ—as believing individuals and also as believing communities—was at least a large part of the essence of their faithfulness.

---

32. Wright, "Perpetua," 765.
33. Placher, *Callings*, 39.
34. Placher, *Callings*, 45.
35. For a more extensive depiction of the absolute necessity and vital role of community in the Christian life and martyrdom of Perpetua, see Gonzalez, "Early Christians in the Roman Empire."

5

Returning to the Early Concept of Faithfulness

EARLIER IT WAS SUGGESTED that the most profitable way for believers today to discover what faithfulness means is to learn what it meant for the Christians of the first few centuries. Why is this? Recall that Placher argued our social situation is closer to that of the early Christians than at any time since the early medieval period. He wrote, "Our situation is more like those first few centuries: many of our neighbors follow another faith or none at all. Many of the values and beliefs common in our culture challenge our faith. Our beliefs may seem quite peculiar to many of our neighbors. . . . [Q]uestions, asked long ago, confront Christians once again."[1] To learn about faithfulness from the early Christians, then, is to learn from those who not only were closer to the earthly ministry of Jesus than any believers since, but the social situation they confronted was closer to ours than that of any other time. We have much to learn from how they worked out the meaning of faithfulness in a social milieu similar to ours.

Much of the rest of the book deals with the ideal character of the faithful, the way they are to display their faithfulness in the society, and the relationship between faithfulness and the kingdom of God. Before

---

1. Placher, *Callings*, 24–25.

approaching those subjects, however, it will be helpful to our understanding of the nature of faithfulness to review the approach taken by one group of modern Christians—a believing community in one village—less than one hundred years ago whose experience parallels closely that of the early Christians. Their challenge was how to remain faithful to God while undergoing extreme pressure to capitulate to the government under which they lived—to submit, conform, and engage in blatant evil. To that end, let us consider the story of what happened in the mountain village of Le Chambon-sur-Lignon in southern France during the Nazi regime of the 1940s. The events were captured by ethicist Philip Hallie in his 1979 book *Lest Innocent Blood Be Shed: The Story of the Village of Le Chambon and How Goodness Happened There*.

The population of Le Chambon consisted primarily of French Protestants. André Trocmé, of Huguenot background, became their pastor in 1934. His sermons focused on Jesus' teaching in the Sermon on the Mount, particularly love of God and neighbor.[2] When the Nazis took power in France during World War II, Trocmé preached "a forceful sermon to his congregation in which he urged them to uphold their religious values and to resist all actions that betrayed the teachings of the Gospel."[3] During the next several years the village, under the leadership of Trocmé, his wife Magda, pastor Edouard Theis, Trocmé's cousin Daniel, and schoolteacher Roger Darcissac, harbored and cared for some 3,500 Jews, including many children. Through the pacifistic resistance network they developed, the people of Le Chambon along with those of the surrounding farms saved about 5,000 lives.

What motivated Trocmé to take such a defiant approach, in direct opposition to the government under which he lived—risking his very life—yet without resorting to violence against it? It appears to have been love for both Jesus and his teachings, as well as his desire to emulate Jesus.[4] Hallie wrote:

> Trocmé had a desire (as he put it in his notebooks) "not to be separated from Jesus." What this meant to him was that God had shown mankind how precious man[5] was to Him by taking

---

2. *Read the Spirit*, "André Trocmé (1901–1971)," para. 2.
3. *Jewish Foundation for the Righteous*, "Pastor André Trocmé," para. 4.
4. Challies, Review, paras. 4 and 7.
5. This use of male language was not intended by Hallie to refer only to adult males; rather, it is an example of the unfortunate convention of the time in which male language was employed to refer to both genders as well as adults and children.

the form of a human being and coming down to help human beings find their deepest happiness. Trocmé believed also that Jesus had demonstrated that love for mankind by dying for us on the cross. . . . In short, Jesus was for Trocmé the embodied forgiveness of sins, and staying close to Jesus meant always being ready to forgive your enemies instead of torturing and killing them. Trocmé could not bear to separate himself from Jesus by ignoring the precious quality of human life that God had demonstrated in the birth, the life, and the crucifixion of His son.[6]

The bold stance of Trocmé and the people of Le Chambon did not come without a cost, for the Vichy government knew what was going on in the village, and the Gestapo intended to kill the leaders. "Daniel was arrested along with the children he had been hiding and taken to the Majdanek concentration camp. He was gassed and incinerated in 1944."[7] Trocmé did not back down when governmental pressure increased. "In February 1943 Trocmé and two colleagues . . . were arrested and interned at the Saint-Paul d'Ejyeaux camp near Limoge. . . . [T]he commander of the camp tried to persuade Trocmé to sign a commitment to cease his lifesaving activities and comply with the Vichy orders, but he declined."[8]

The story of Trocmé, the other leaders, Le Chambon, and the surrounding area is a story of uncompromising faithfulness in the face of intense pressure to recant and conform. It cost some of the faithful their lives. Yet for that community syncretism and compromise with the values of the Nazi regime were not an option; rather, faithfulness to Jesus and emulation of his example were the moral standard of those at Le Chambon, and they pursued it irrespective of the cost.

Such faithfulness is indeed rare today, particularly in the West, and the story of *Lest Innocent Blood Be Shed* can help all of us see how a community of modern Christians did the same thing that the early Christians did when working out how to be faithful in the social milieu in which they found themselves. One person, reflecting on this story, commented, "What you'll have a much harder time doing is imagining a town behaving like this now."[9] Indeed, we will; and imagining a local Christian congregation—or even individual Christians—following the example of

6. Hallie, *Lest Innocent Blood*, 34.
7. Hammond, "Heroes of the Faith," para. 13.
8. Eurnekian and Tenembaum, "Pastor André Trocmé," para. 7.
9. Kornbluth, Review, para. 12.

the Christians of the first few centuries and the people of Le Chambon during the Nazi regime is quite difficult as well.

We have reviewed the challenge faced by early Christians when confronted with a social milieu and governmental authority that expected them—and even took severe steps to coerce them—to compromise their faithfulness to Christ. Their example of how they dealt with their situation while maintaining their commitment should continue to serve as a standard for Christians today. The faithful community of Le Chambon teaches us how modern believers can emulate the early Christians. What, however, are the elements and characteristics of faithfulness, and how can Christians today reflect them? It is to that question we now turn.

PART TWO

Faithfulness and Character

THE EARLY CHRISTIANS, as well as believers such as those of the Le Chambon community who followed in the early Christians' path of faithfulness, had within themselves a certain something that propelled them on their moral journey in spite of all the threats and opposition they faced. Their inner resolve and convictions as well as outward devotion and actions emerged from some source so deep within their being as to be indistinguishable from it. Solomon, in describing the way of wisdom, expressed this reality of the inner self when he wrote: "Above all else, guard your heart, for everything you do flows from it."[1] What was that source of conduct—that "heart," as Solomon described it—and how does it relate to faithfulness?

One common understanding of the nature of faithfulness is that it entails specific commitments and consistent conduct. Such a notion of faithfulness could include adherence to a set of rules or laws, working to achieve certain predefined ends, or fidelity to community standards or conventions. In any particular decision-making situation involving a conflict between rules, desirable ends, or standards, the individual may engage in reasoning, reflection, calculation, analysis of alternatives, consideration of likely consequences, and the like prior to acting, but in the end the faithful one will—unsurprisingly—endorse and sustain the moral expectation predetermined by the rules, desirable ends, or standards.

1. Prov 4:23.

What is it that drives this unsurprising moral action? Why is the outcome predictable? How is it that those who share the same commitments inevitably and predictably work out those commitments similarly when faced with similar situations? What accounts for the moral consistency among both the early martyrs and the members of the Le Chambon community?

When seeking to understand this phenomenon we soon find ourselves dealing with ontological questions, specifically the nature of God. Recall from the introduction that God's holiness imbues all that God is, and includes the ethical. Faithfulness to God, in its most fundamental understanding, entails moral Godlikeness, for (as we saw in the first epistle of Peter), the faithful are commanded, "just as he who called you is holy, so be holy in all you do; for it is written: 'Be holy, because I am holy.'"[2] The moral component of holiness primarily references being and character—as opposed to actions such as adherence to rules or fidelity to standards—patterned after the being and character of God. The nature of our being is fundamental to—and a precursor to—cognition, conviction, and conduct. At the heart of what we are is our *character*, and that character influences our functioning in the moral realm—assuming we understand morality to include character formation. What we need to know is from where each of us gets that character, and can that character—while imbuing all of the human self—change in some fashion without forfeiting our shared fundamental humanity? The 1 Peter passage, being a command to followers of Jesus, suggests that it can, in that the pursuit of faithfulness includes the quest to become and be holy as God is holy.

Our objective in this part is to explore the relationship between faithfulness and character, with the notion of character itself being our starting place. Our exploration will include investigating the character of God and how it may be possible for humans to share in the divine character. We will look into character and faithfulness as found in the Bible while seeking to determine if there is a character norm for the faithful that distinguished the early believers and perhaps can be reappropriated by Christians today. The relationship between divine character and the image of God in which humanity was created will be investigated, including the effects of the fall on that image. Faithfulness understood as living out that image *de facto* will then be probed. Let us begin with the idea of character itself.

2. 1 Pet 1:15–16.

6

The Notion of Character

MANY MODERN BELIEVERS STRUGGLE conceptualizing the whole area of ethics, since they have been conditioned to hold that ethics focuses on commands or rules. To them the moral life is delimited by obedience to rules as well as decisions and judgments that reflect adherence to what has been commanded. As such they view ethics as an external realm, even if it includes thoughts: it is not a matter of one's essential being. Ethicist J. Philip Wogaman pointed out the shortcoming of this approach, arguing that Christian ethics must not be limited to matters of moral decision-making, but also must include our nature, our being. "The problem with exclusive preoccupation with judgments and decisions is that we may lose track of the *being* of the Christian, and it is this *being* that is presupposed whenever we ask what kinds of judgments and decisions Christians should make."[1]

The idea that ethics fundamentally entails our being—who we are—is not new. It goes back to Aristotle's thought in the fourth century BC, and also was supported by such formative thinkers as Plato, Augustine, and Aquinas.[2] Thus the concept has a history not only in Greek philosophy, but also in Christian thought. This notion—that ethics at its heart involves our being—arises from the realization that human

1. Wogaman, *Christian Ethics*, 278–79.
2. Timpe, "Moral Character," para. 1.

experience in the moral realm is more—as well as more fundamental—than the summation of discrete experiences of moral judgment, obedience to commands, and adherence to moral principles. The moral life is part of who we are and a continuous, constituent element of what it means to be human. We label this core part of ourselves "character."

The Theology of Work Project—a research organization dedicated to producing biblically based materials focused on non-church work environments—viewed character, understood as part of our being, as a precursor to moral conduct. It asks, "Could it be that many of the ethical choices we make are already substantially decided before we make the decision? That our character automatically shapes much of what we decide to do? And because of this, our ethical decisions are largely determined by who we are (the type of character and values we've embodied)."[3] Expressed another way, New Testament professor Robert L. Brawley wrote, "It is as if essence does precede existence, or at least that essence and existence are intimate companions. The wager is that what we do is a matter of living out who we are."[4]

It is important to clarify that the concept of character—as something inherent to our being—is not the only understanding of character. There is a view of character that has to do with personal qualities that enable the production of excellent *performance*. That is not the notion of character we are investigating. Rather, we are exploring character as it exists in the moral realm of human experience, and—at its best—ultimately results in excellent *ethics*.[5] Beyond that, circumscribing moral character is anything but straightforward. However, it "is arguably the most important determinant of the overall impressions people form of others."[6] As an example, recall the early Christians, particularly the martyrs. The Romans' impression of the Christians was formed not merely by their conduct and unwavering commitment in the face of sure torture and death, but by the character that drove them—something the Romans simply could not comprehend, because they did not understand the Christians' underlying character.

This brings us to the question of the source of character. If it is part of who we are, does it follow that for each of us character is what it is—immutable—and that from our formation it is inalterably fixed?

---

3. Theology of Work Project, "Character Approach," para. 4.

4. Brawley, *Character Ethics*, ix.

5. Park et al., "Tripartite Taxonomy," 17.

6. Park et al., "Tripartite Taxonomy," 17.

If such were true our experience in the moral realm would be much less complex than it actually is. Character however—while not fickle—most certainly is malleable. This fact yields immeasurable complexity to our moral experience and makes the notion of character much broader than can be described in a few words. It also burdens each of us with responsibility for our character, for we can play a significant role in forming our character—something that renders ethics far more extensive than making discrete decisions or following rules. The key question in this regard is, "'What type of person should I become?' . . . If a person develops good character, he or she is more likely to do the right/good thing . . . It is more an ethics of becoming than of doing."[7] The follow-on challenge is how each of us is to assume responsibility for our character formation. How are we to seize our character, rather than allowing it to be molded by something external? Ethicist James Gustafson provided a hint when he asserted, "It is persons who discern . . . Some have developed characters on the basis of critical evaluations of past experiences and of the exercise of their initiative in becoming what they are throughout their personal moral histories."[8] Later we will explore *how* the faithful Christian can develop and grow character intentionally, but at this juncture it is sufficient to understand that character is not fixed, but somehow is developed.

DEFINING CHARACTER

Before determining how, in an attempt to be faithful, we can develop our character, it will help to investigate what character actually is. If moral character could be defined, what would that definition be? It should not come as a surprise that discovering a simple definition of character ultimately defies our efforts so to do. Ethicist Stanley Hauerwas suggested, "No one-sentence description can do justice to the complexity of a concept such as character."[9] There are those, however, who have proposed definitions. The Character Lab, for example, defined character as "everything we do to help other people as well as ourselves,"[10] and thus holds that character is external *actions* rather than something linked to our *being*. A different approach assumes that "what kind of person one

---

7. Theology of Work Project, "Character Approach," para. 1.
8. Gustafson, *Moral Discernment*, 31.
9. Hauerwas, *Community*, 271.
10. *Character Lab*, "Character," para. 2.

is is constituted by one's character,"[11] then indicates that an individual's character can be understood "as primarily a function of whether she has or lacks various moral virtues and vices."[12] Moral *traits*, in this example, give definition to one's character.

Just after the turn of the twentieth century Strong wrote, "We speak of voluntary affections, and may with equal propriety speak of voluntary opinions. These permanent voluntary states we denominate character.... The use of the word in morals implies that every thought and act is chiseling itself into the imperishable substance of the soul ... Character ... is the man's true self."[13] Thus Strong advocated a more internal view of character, entailing an individual's very being itself.

In the nineteenth century Kierkegaard engaged the challenge to define character when he asserted, "Character is that which is engraved ... but the sand and the sea have no character and neither has abstract intelligence, for character is really inwardness."[14] Although Kierkegaard's concept of inwardness defies a simple definition (as we might suspect, since he equated inwardness with character), it at least refers to the subjective element of one's being. Of note is that Kierkegaard held that character is something which is "engraved" on a person. The challenge is to determine the identity of the engraver, and how the engraving takes place. Hauerwas quantified the notion of character, writing "the idea of character in its broadest sense is used most appropriately to identify individuality or distinctiveness."[15] Philosopher Kevin Timpe appeared to agree with this idea of distinctiveness when he described the early meaning of the Greek word *charaktêr* as "any distinctive feature by which one thing is distinguished from others," then extrapolated that idea to the present: "In contemporary usage character often refers to a set of qualities or characteristics that can be used to differentiate between persons."[16]

Adding to this understanding is the suggestion that character refers to *dispositions*, specifically "dispositions to act, think, and feel in ways that benefit the individual and society."[17] Timpe agreed, suggesting "the virtues and vices that comprise one's moral character are typically

---

11. Timpe, "Moral Character," para. 3.
12. Timpe, "Moral Character," para. 3.
13. Strong, *Systematic Theology*, 506.
14. Kierkegaard, *Present Age*, 43.
15. Hauerwas, *Character*, 11.
16. Timpe, "Moral Character," para. 6.
17. Park et al., "Tripartite Taxonomy," 17.

understood as dispositions to behave in certain ways in certain sorts of circumstances."[18] In this regard conservative political writer David Brooks quoted Yale law professor Anthony T. Kronman's definition of character: "an ensemble of settled dispositions—of habitual feelings and desires."[19] Yet these dispositions are not necessarily passive. They can exert influence on one's moral life, even though they may not be determinative. Hauerwas believed "character is best understood as a direction or orientation rather than a compelling force . . . Character is directing, but it is not compelling in the sense that it represents an external force over which we have no control. Character, however, may be thought of as compelling in the sense that it may direct our life in a rather definite and limited fashion."[20]

At this point it is clear that a simple definition of character—one on which the majority of ethicists agree—simply is not possible; at least it has not been put forward heretofore. Whereas this may be frustrating in that it does not yield a simple help to those seeking to be faithful, attempts at defining character can be of benefit. Although still vague, most definitions avoid the concept of actions, and see character as more tied to our being, and may actually be something *engraved* on our being. This linking may include moral traits or something distinctive that distinguishes one thing from another and differentiates between persons. It also may entail some sort of force, or active disposition that exercises influence to direct our moral life.

More can be done to clarify our understanding of character, not by additional efforts at *definition*, but through observation and *describing* that which is observed. To that task we now turn.

DESCRIBING CHARACTER

It is often asserted that character, whereas generally stable, is not rigid; it can be formed.[21] Yet there is no agreement on how this is done.[22] Further-

---

18. Timpe, "Moral Character," para. 4.
19. Brooks, *Road to Character*, 57.
20. Hauerwas, *Character*, 123.
21. See, for example, Park: "While relatively stable in the absence of exogenous forces, character is malleable." Park et al., "Tripartite Taxonomy," 16.
22. See, for example, the Character Lab, which asserts: "Although character strengths are malleable, surprisingly little is known about how to cultivate them intentionally." *Character Lab*, "Character," para. 8.

more, some argue that character formation happens slowly, over time.[23] One analysis claims that character is not monolithic, but consists of various parts or aspects, including interpersonal, intellectual, and intrapersonal elements.[24]

We can glean a great deal about the nature of character by reviewing the work of Hauerwas. Fundamentally he held that "character cannot be thought of as a kind of outer manifestation that leaves a more fundamental self hidden; it is the very reality of who we are as self-determining agents."[25] The exercise of our being, then, is enacted through the bestirring of our character.

Hauerwas supported the idea that character can be acquired, even to the point that our natural self can be overcome: "The idea of character in its most paradigmatic usage indicates what a man[26] can decide to be as opposed to what a man is naturally. We assume that a man chooses to have a kind of character."[27] As such, an individual exercises control over her or his disposition, and character development includes the active involvement of the individual rather than yielding acquiescence to some external force or influence. Hauerwas advocated that "our character *should* be formed by our own effort rather than as a passive response to our particular environment. This normative commitment, however, depends on being able to show how men can determine themselves beyond their cultural conditioning; or, perhaps better, that they can give a particular order to the elements of their desires and choices."[28] Brooks concurred, using more populist language: "Character is not innate or automatic. You have to build it with effort and artistry. You can't be the

---

23. See, for example, Timpe: "According to the Stability Claim, moral character traits are relatively stable over time. The Stability Claim doesn't preclude the possibility of an individual changing his moral character over time. Rather, it holds that such changes take time." Timpe, "Moral Character," para. 30.

24. See Park: "Exploratory factor analyses yielded a three-factor structure consisting of interpersonal (interpersonal self-control, gratitude, social intelligence), intellectual (zest, curiosity), and intrapersonal (academic self-control, grit) factors of character." Park et al., "Tripartite Taxonomy," 16.

25. Hauerwas, *Character*, 115.

26. The use of male language by Hauerwas is unfortunate. Likely his intent was not to reference something associated with male persons, but rather to reference persons of both genders. Perhaps the reader will overlook this use of language and appreciate the valuable contributions Hauerwas has made to our understanding of character.

27. Hauerwas, *Character*, 12.

28. Hauerwas, *Character*, 17–18.

good person you want to be unless you wage this campaign."[29] The means by which a person "can determine themselves beyond their cultural conditioning" will be explored later as part of our effort to establish a means to faithfulness; at this point it is sufficient to acknowledge that faithful character formation involves our active, intentional participation—a campaign each of us must wage.

In opposition to the common understanding that ethics is an external thing, focused on rules, principles, and the like, Hauerwas held that the core of our moral experience is internal, and focused on the individual's character: "The problem of character is an attempt to stress the importance of our subjectivity for the moral direction of our lives. It is concerned with how that direction becomes embodied in our selves through our beliefs, intentions, and actions."[30] This concentration on how that which we affirm intellectually and intend volitionally forms our inner moral self comprises the initial effort each person—as a responsible moral *agent*—pursues in developing and forming his or her character in the direction he or she has previously chosen. The degree to which an individual maintains that effort to fruition dictates the degree to which she or he may be said to have strong character. Hauerwas leaned upon the thought of early twentieth-century German philosopher Nicolai Hartmann to express this notion of self-formed character strength: "We talk of the strength or weakness of character as a way of indicating whether a man may be relied upon and trusted even under duress. Character in this sense is what Hartman calls moral strength, which is the capacity of 'the person to speak for himself, to determine beforehand his future conduct not yet under his control, therefore to guarantee himself beyond the present moment.'"[31] Fundamental to this intentionally formed character, then, is consistent and predictable reliability and trustworthiness.

When considering the idea of character we soon encounter the notion of virtues, and the question of how virtues relate to character. Are they the same thing? Is one external and the other internal? Does one precede the other, or is one dependent upon—or perhaps an outgrowth from—the other? Whereas character cannot simply be said to be the sum of one's virtues, there is a close relationship between the two. Hauerwas held that the interconnectedness of a person's suite of virtues, or maybe

---

29. Brooks, *Road to Character*, 12.
30. Hauerwas, *Character*, 33.
31. Hauerwas, *Character*, 15.

the interrelatedness of virtues, is driven by one's character.[32] Moreover, he distinguished between a person's character, and "having character." For Hauerwas the notion of character could be tied rather closely to a set of virtues, though not equated with them completely. To "have character," on the other hand, means much more of what I have been describing as our moral being, our internal and subjective self, that which we can form intentionally and which is informed by our adopted beliefs and commitments. It is this understanding of character—or rather "having character"—that is more fundamental than a set of virtues, and helps form them.

> When we think of a person's character, a distinguishing trait such as honesty or kindness is usually what we have in mind; but when we speak of a man as "having character," we are more apt to be thinking of something like integrity, incorruptibility, or consistency. The former denoted more the common meaning of the "virtues," while the latter indicates a more inclusive concept than virtue. The virtues, like the idea of character, require effort on the part of the agent. The idea of character, however, not only denotes a more general orientation than the virtues, but having character is a more basic moral determination of the self. The various virtues receive their particular form through the agent's character.[33]

It is this concept of character—particularly when understood as the intentional fruit of the individual acting as a responsible moral agent—that is expressed through select virtues.

A bit more needs to be said about the relationship between character formation and the moral agency we exercise as responsible individuals. As active, intentional moral agents we influence and control—perhaps even determine—the development of our character. The conduct of an individual as a moral agent is constrained by that person's predetermined and pre-acquired beliefs. They act as guardrails to steer moral conduct. When such conduct is repeated and becomes habitual, character is formed. Character, then, is the outgrowth of a moral agent's ongoing

---

32. See Hauerwas: "Character cannot be equated with the simple sum of all the recommended good qualities in their individual specification that we may feel a person should have. It may, however, be thought of in terms of the particular 'mix' or connection between the various virtues characteristic of any one person's life pattern." Hauerwas, *Character*, 75–76.

33. Hauerwas, *Character*, 15–16.

conduct, driven by the agent's beliefs. Hauerwas stated this dependency of conduct on active moral agency as follows:

> Character is the qualification or determination of our self-agency, formed by our having certain intentions (and beliefs) rather than others. Once it is clear that character is but the concrete determination of our agency we can understand why no ultimate distinction can be made between acquiring character and having character. Character in its particular manifestation cannot be a static possession men have once and for all. Since it is born in intentional behavior it exists only as a qualification of that continuing behavior.[34]

Character is not only malleable and formed through the habitual conduct of an individual acting as a moral agent—consistent with her or his beliefs. It also can be augmented—or maybe even improved—over time as the agent continues in the moral path on which she or he started, perhaps adjusting beliefs through learning and thus adjusting the conduct that forms character. Hauerwas tagged this sort of character one's "orientation": "The idea of character, therefore, involves in the most fundamental way the relation between thought and action. . . . Our character is thus the qualification of our self-agency through our beliefs, intentions, and actions through which we acquire an ongoing orientation."[35]

This concept of character development through the active exercise of moral agency, guided by one's beliefs, is an expression in ethical terms of what Christians mean by the doctrine of sanctification. In simple terms, growth in sanctification is one way of understanding the goal of faithfulness. Development of character by continual action of the moral agent in the direction of one's beliefs is active faithfulness at work. For the Christian the "beliefs" referred to as the guardrails that constrain the conduct of a moral agent are the agent's convictions about Jesus Christ as depicted in the Bible (not only the Gospels, but also other writings such as the Epistle to the Hebrews). Hauerwas expressed this truth when he concluded:

> The idea of character can be used ethically to interpret the doctrine of sanctification as it provides the means to articulate how sanctification involves the basic determination of the self and the requisite unity of the Christian agent. The sanctification of

---

34. Hauerwas, *Character*, 115.
35. Hauerwas, *Character*, 230.

the Christian moral life is the continuous unifying of the Christian's intentions through the central image of Jesus Christ. This is not a matter of one "good work" added to another, but rather the Christian's growth in the significance of the central image that dominates the orientation of his character. The idea of character therefore provides the means of explicating the nature of the Christian life without separating that life from its source.[36]

It behooves us as those seeking to be faithful—as well as seeking to determine what it was about the early Christians that drove their faithfulness even in the face of extreme persecution—to understand the Jesus of the Bible. How is it that the Bible's depiction of Jesus can drive development of our character as a means to increased faithfulness? To answer that, we must first understand something of the character of God, for character ethics "is about how the character of God is shaping our own characters—about whether we are becoming more holy, just and loving people, to name three prominent character traits in the Bible."[37]

---

36. Hauerwas, *Character*, 231.
37. Theology of Work Project, "Character Approach," para. 2.

7

The Character of God

To this point I have been arguing that character is not fixed or rigid, but rather is malleable. In addition, it appears to be something that an individual can direct, form, and evolve through active conduct in a particular, predetermined direction in accord with acquired beliefs and affirmations—the individual acting as a responsible moral agent to form his or her character over time. When this is done in the moral realm by an individual with Christian beliefs it parallels the doctrine of sanctification in the theological realm and constitutes at least a portion of what it means to live an increasingly faithful life. What, however, does it mean for God to have character? Does God have a particular set of beliefs that guide divine character development? Can God's character be developed at all? Is it malleable, as is the character of a human being? Assuming that God's immutability yields a "no" answer to questions regarding the changeableness of the part of God's being associated with character, how can it be said that God *has* character? How does the divine character compare with that which a responsible human moral agent can build?

DEFINING GOD'S CHARACTER

Many scholars have attempted to define the character of God. Reviewing just a few of those will enable us to circumscribe the whole subject of the divine character before we attempt to depict it in a way that is helpful to our goal of determining how God's character can help God's people become more faithful.

One approach to understanding God's character is to view it through the lens of creation. For example, J. Burke wrote, "Genesis 1–3 reveal to us the character of God, and the way in which He wishes us to be personally involved with His plan and purpose."[1] He continued by attempting to link human character with select external traits of God: "The very first aspect of God's character to which we are introduced, is His ability and desire to create. . . . [This is] something we can all identify with—the desire to make something,"[2] and then "we share something with a being who sees chaos, and seeks order, who finds disorder and seeks structure."[3] Burke concluded with a summary of the divine character:

> From the first three chapters of Genesis, we have seen the character of God described in the following way:
>
> - He is a creative being
> - He is an interpersonal being
> - He is a loving father[4]

For Burke, then, God's character is revealed in what we observe of creation: the desire to create in an orderly, structured fashion; a linking of the divine creative desire communicated within the Godhead with something similar implanted in the humans he created; and conveyance of love through the creative process of human character development after the pattern of the divine character.

In the mid-twentieth century theologian Henry Thiessen conveyed this same notion of God's character linked with concern for his created human beings when he asserted, "He is a personal, almighty, holy, and loving God. If God is all this, we would expect Him to have a longing concern for His creatures and come to their help. That He has such a concern and does come to man's help is evident from His provision for man's material and temporal needs."[5]

---

1. Burke, "In the Beginning," para. 1.
2. Burke, "In the Beginning," para. 3.
3. Burke, "In the Beginning," para. 6.
4. Burke, "In the Beginning," para. 47.
5. Thiessen, *Systematic Theology*, 108.

Stott expanded the idea of God's character revealed in his physical care for created humans to include God's redemptive care as well. In support of his argument that physical and spiritual concern should be seen as one, Stott began with the divine character itself:

> First, there is *the character of God*. The God of the biblical revelation, being both Creator and Redeemer, is a God who cares about the total well-being (spiritual and material) of all the human beings he has made. Having created them in his own image, he longs that they will discover their true humanness in their relationships to him and to each other. . . . On the other hand, God cares for the poor and the hungry, the alien, the widow and the orphan. He denounces oppressions and tyranny, and calls for justice. He tells his people to be the voice of the voiceless and the defender of the powerless, and so to express their love for them.[6]

Stott's approach to depicting God's character does not mention any traits of God at all, but only his functions as creator and redeemer. Yet similar to others his focus is on humans. It is a relational focus, including both the divine/human relationship and relationships among humans as reflective of God's character. Those relationships can be fostered well and consistently through adherence to that which God has revealed. He argued, for example, "The law and the prophets thus reflect the character of God. What he is, his people must be also, sharing and reflecting his concerns. In particular there is no dualism in the thinking of God."[7]

Another approach to understanding God's character does not primarily have in view God's creative work, although humans are included. Rather, it seeks to specify the divine character in terms of God's being, particularly God as love. Berkhof saw God's love as the divine character when it is experienced by God's creatures. When God communicates himself to humans, his loving character is being conveyed to them. He wrote, "When the goodness of God is exercised towards His rational creatures, it assumes the higher character of love, and this love may again be distinguished according to the objects on which it terminates. In distinction from the goodness of God in general, it may be defined as *that perfection of God by which He is eternally moved to self-communication.*"[8]

---

6. Stott, *Contemporary Christian*, 343; italics original.
7. Stott, *Contemporary Christian*, 344.
8. Berkhof, *Systematic Theology*, 71; italics original.

Divine love, however, is not only God's character directed toward a human being. It exists within the Trinity itself, understood as communication among the three. In his classic work *The Doctrine of Divine Love; or Outlines of the Moral Theology of the Evangelical Church*, nineteenth-century German orthodox Lutheran theologian Ernst Wilhelm Christian Sartorius argued, "In the higher and divine sense of the word, love is the oneness of union of distinct persons, and this is, in the highest and most complete sense, the triune God, the Father, the Son, and the Holy Spirit, Love."[9] Avoiding the temptation to break down divine love into a distinct set of features, Sartorius continued his argument that love is not an expression of God, or an external depiction, but instead is at the heart of God's being. "The attributes of the divine nature, knowledge, and will are explained and combined in too poor and human a relation of reflection, if they are not perceived to be one in all-comprehending love, which, as free as necessary in its action, is not so much an attribute which God *has*, as the nature which he is; for God *is* Love."[10] Such love, however, is not *restricted* to the Trinity; in fact it can be conveyed to and experienced by humans. In this way the character of God can be communicated and perhaps appropriated—in some way we have not yet considered—by those seeking to be God's faithful people.

> All the propositions concerning the nature and attributes of God usually explained after long preliminary discussions in theological manuals, with abstract and often merely negative prolixity, are summed up by the apostle in the great saying, *God is love*, in one living, all-comprising, all-producing idea by which every one who has known and experienced anything of the living power of love—and what human being has not?—may know God, and know not only that He is, but also what He is (1 John iv.7).[11]

GOD'S CHARACTER, HOLINESS, AND LOVE

Even though Strong argued that character is more ontological than did those who advocated a traits-based or conduct-based approach to describing God's character, he did not agree with those who view that God—in his essential being—is love. Rather, when it comes to the moral

---

9. Sartorius, *Divine Love*, 4–5.
10. Sartorius, *Divine Love*, 8; italics original.
11. Sartorius, *Divine Love*, 3; italics original.

aspect of God he argued that the attribute of holiness, not love, is more fundamental to God's *being*; love, however important, is not fundamental to God's being but instead is one of many divine moral *attributes*.

> The moral attributes of truth, love, holiness, are worthy of higher reverence from men, and they are more jealously guarded by God, than the natural attributes of omnipresence, omniscience, and omnipotence. And yet even among the moral attributes one stands as supreme. Of this and of its supremacy we now proceed to speak....
>
> [W]hen God acts, he manifests not one attribute alone, but his total moral excellence. Yet holiness, as an attribute of God, has rights peculiar to itself; it determines the attitude of the affections; it more than any other faculty constitutes God's moral being.[12]

Why is it that Strong, while affirming the fundamental nature of God's being as moral, held that holiness is central to that being, rather than love? In part he was reacting to the thought of theologian William Newton Clarke. Clarke wrote in the late nineteenth century that "God would not be holy if he were not love, and could not be love if he were not holy. Love is an element in holiness. If this were lacking, there would be no perfect character as principle of his own action or as standard for us."[13] He went on to explain his thinking:

> Holiness requires God to act as love, for holiness is God's self-consistency. Love is the desire to impart holiness. Holiness makes God's character the standard for his creatures; but love, desiring to impart the best good does the same. All work of love is work of holiness, and all work of holiness is work of love. Conflict of attributes is impossible, because holiness always includes love, and love always expresses holiness. They never need reconciliation with each other.[14]

Strong generally was supportive of Clarke's thinking, but found it too vague. For Strong there had to be a clear delineation between God's holiness and God's love. Regarding Clarke's view Strong stated:

---

12. Strong, *Systematic Theology*, 295.

13. See Strong, *Systematic Theology*, 295, in which Strong quoted from Clarke's 1899 book *Outline of Christian Theology*.

14. Strong, *Systematic Theology*, 295, in which Strong quoted Clarke.

> The general correctness of the foregoing statement is impaired by the vagueness of its conception of holiness. The Scriptures do not regard holiness as including love, or make all the acts of holiness to be acts of love. Self-affirmation does not include self-impartation, and sin necessitates an exercise of holiness which is not also an exercise of love. But for the Cross, and God's suffering for sin of which the Cross is the expression, there would be conflict between holiness and love. The wisdom of God is most shown, not in reconciling man and God, but in reconciling the holy God with the loving God.[15]

Why was it that Strong had a need to establish a clear delineation between divine holiness and divine love? Nearly a century after Strong made his assertion Grenz offered an insightful idea to explain not only Strong, but other theologians of his era, and their proclivity toward God's holiness as more foundational to God's being than love. Grenz saw that the motivator for those who argue for the foundational character of holiness as opposed to love was their desire to affirm strongly the way God deals with sin. Grenz wrote:

> In the twentieth century, many theologians asserted that holiness, which includes God's resolute disposition against sin—and not merely love—must be ranked among the fundamental moral attributes of God. . . . [T]he great Baptist thinker Augustus Hopkins Strong elevated holiness to "the fundamental attribute in God."
>
> In part this magnifying of holiness as a central divine attribute is motivated by the desire to protect God's prerogative in condemning unrepentant sinners and in turn to make palatable the doctrine of hell. Properly understood, however, love includes within it what this concern seeks to preserve. Simply stated, the presence of sin transforms the experience of the divine love from the bliss intended by God into wrath.
>
> The possibility of experiencing love as wrath arises out of the nature of love itself. Bound up with love is a protective jealousy.[16]

The explanation that wrath is, if you will, the other side of the love coin, may strike us as odd, for the common understanding is that love and wrath are opposites, not the same thing expressed in different ways depending upon human conduct before God. It is the jealousy aspect of

---

15. Strong, *Systematic Theology*, 295–96.
16. Grenz, *Theology*, 73.

God's nature, however, that holds the key to appreciating the point Grenz made. He went on to explain his assertion about wrath:

> Genuine love, therefore, is positively jealous. It is protective, for the true lover seeks to maintain, even defend, the love relationship whenever it is threatened by disruption, destruction, or outside intrusion. Whenever another seeks to injure or undermine the love relationship, he or she experiences love's jealousy, which we call "wrath." When this dimension is lacking, love degenerates into mere sentimentality.
>
> It is in this way that we can understand that the Loving One is a jealous, wrathful God. Those who would undermine the love God pours forth for the world experience his love in the form of wrath.[17]

Although it takes some reorientation of thinking to embrace the argument Grenz made about love and wrath, it helps us understand better what is meant when love is affirmed as God's fundamental moral being.

THE FUNDAMENTAL NATURE OF LOVE

This brings us to the question of how love works within God as the most basic element of his moral being and what it means for us as we seek to rediscover what God requires—his character—of his faithful followers. Grenz accurately expanded on the notion that God is love by addressing six aspects of that love. First, he defined God's essence, but augmented that definition by viewing it through the continuous interaction within the Trinity. He wrote, "As the apostolic writer indicates, the essence of God is love. The doctrine of the Trinity indicates how this is the case. Throughout all eternity the divine life—the life of the Father, Son, and Spirit—is best characterized by our word 'love.' Love, therefore, that is, the reciprocal self-dedication of the trinitarian members, builds the unity of the one God."[18] It is love, defined as the reciprocal self-dedication between and among all three members of the Godhead, that constitutes the eternal life they all share.

Second, love among the members of the Trinity describes the inner life they share, distinct and separate from anything outside of themselves—including creation. It is the interrelatedness of the Trinity that

---

17. Grenz, *Theology*, 73.
18. Grenz, *Theology*, 71–72.

allows their essence to be love, for love is a relational concept. Within the triune Godhead there is both love's subject as well as its object.[19]

Third, love is more fundamental to who God is than anything else. We have seen that Grenz asserted, "Love is the eternal essence of the one God."[20] He went on to explain, however, what he meant: "Trinitarian love is not merely one attribute of God among many. Rather, love is the fundamental 'attribute' of God. 'God is love' is the foundational ontological statement we can declare concerning the divine essence."[21] In fact, what God is and what God wills are identical. "Ultimately the divine disposition and the divine being coalesce.... God's essence and God's character are both love. Consequently, there is no dichotomy between God's own being and God's will, for God wills what God is. God wills what is right, and the 'right' that God wills is nothing else but what characterizes God's own being as the Triune One."[22] Yet God's being, essence, and will consisting of love does not exhaust what it means to say that God is love.

Grenz's fourth aspect of love is seen when God interacts with and responds to creation; he can only do so in a manner consistent with the divine essence, love. "'Love,' therefore, is not only the description of the eternal God in himself, it is likewise the fundamental characteristic of God in relationship with creation. With profound theological insight, therefore, John bursts forth, 'For God so loved the world that he gave . . .' (John 3:16)."[23] We see for the first time that divine love is expansive enough not to be limited to the relational aspect of the Trinity; it also encompasses and characterizes the relationship between creator and creation.

Fifth, expanding the notion of God's love as describing the active relationship between God as Creator and the world as God's creation, Grenz extended the concept to include the moral realm of human experience. Foundational to God's moral attributes is God's character as love. Humans experience this love ethic as God's goodness to them. It

---

19. See Grenz: "When viewed in terms of its role in the doctrine of the Trinity, the term 'love' offers a window on the profundity of the reality of God as understood by the Christian tradition. Trinitarian 'love' describes God's inner life—God as God throughout eternity apart from any references to creation. The explanation as to how love can be the essence of God lies in the triune nature of God as Father, Son, and Spirit. Love is a relational term, requiring both subject and object . . . because God is triune, the divine reality already comprehends both love's subject and object." Grenz, *Theology*, 72.

20. Grenz, *Theology*, 72.
21. Grenz, *Theology*, 72.
22. Grenz, *Theology*, 95.
23. Grenz, *Theology*, 72.

takes such forms as grace, mercy, and long-suffering, but these terms are merely attempts to describe God's moral essence: his character of love.[24] "Because God is love, God is good—that is, gracious, merciful, and long-suffering—in all he does. Above all, because God loves, he seeks the salvation and renewal of fallen creation."[25] It is that divine character, conveyed to humans through a number of attributes that describe God's love, that impinges upon them as the core experiential affirmation by which an individual can begin to form her or his own character after the character of God.

Finally, God's love is the moral standard for all humans. It is what God expects of his creation: emulation of God's love character. Such emulation is what it means to be faithful. Grenz wrote, "Not only is God morally perfect, he is the standard for morality. . . . God's disposition toward creation is the standard by which we will be judged and we are to judge all human conduct."[26] He then leveraged 1 John 3:16 to argue that God's character and our conduct are integrally connected, and that our obligation as God's faithful is to emulate God's demonstration of his love. Our moral obligation is to act toward each other as Jesus did for each of us on the cross: "This is how we know what love is: Jesus Christ laid down his life for us. And we ought to lay down our lives for our brothers."[27]

GOD'S CHARACTER TRAITS

We have seen that God's moral character, being, and essence are love—defined as reciprocal self-dedication between and among all three members of the Godhead—and that such love is perceived by humans as what appears to be a number of attributes or traits of God that we experience. Yet not all that we perceive of God's moral character is completely communicable to us as his creation. Since our moral obligation as God's faithful is to emulate God's moral character, it behooves us to know in what ways we can copy God, and what aspects of the divine character that we perceive are reserved for God alone.

---

24. Grenz, *Theology*, 74.
25. Grenz, *Theology*, 74.
26. Grenz, *Theology*, 95.
27. 1 John 3:16.

God's Self-Disclosure

This brings us to the question of character, integrally entwined with being, and its relationship to conduct. The two are closely connected, as Strong asserted: "We cannot study character apart from conduct, nor conduct apart from character. But this does not prevent us from recognizing that character is the fundamental thing and that conduct is only the expression of it."[28] He went on to point out the linking between human conduct and God's character by quoting from eighteenth-century Cambridge University theologian William Law to argue that even though conduct is outwardly observable, it actually is internally driven. Law wrote, "Ethics are not external but internal. The essence of a moral act does not lie in its result, but in the motive from which it springs. And that again is good or bad, according as it conforms to the character of God."[29]

Yet how does one make the jump from character to conduct? In the case of God it is through the divine attributes, for it is through the attributes that God's character is revealed to us in tangible form.[30] Berkhof was quick to point out that certain divine attributes are not superior to others, for there is a oneness, equality, and harmony among them.[31] The all-important fact about the divine attributes is that they are revealed to humans through God's self-disclosure—a divine act that establishes our fundamental understanding of the attributes themselves. Berkhof continued, "It is commonly said in theology that God's attributes are God Himself, as He has revealed Himself to us."[32] Through general revelation—particularly the created order—the special revelation of the Scripture, and the revelation of God in the incarnation and life of Jesus we learn of the divine attributes. Shortly we shall see that some theologians hold that the descriptions of the attributes are objective statements of God's unalterable nature intertwined with the divine being—not just human expressions of our perception of God. Others hold that human statements describing the divine attributes—even those in the didactic

---

28. Strong, *Systematic Theology*, 303.

29. Strong, *Systematic Theology*, 303.

30. See Berkhof: "[Some theologians] prefer to consider the Being of God in connection with His attributes in view of the fact that it is in these that He has revealed Himself." Berkhof, *Systematic Theology*, 41.

31. See Berkhof: "Scripture does not exalt one attribute of God at the expense of the others, but represents them as existing in perfect harmony in the Divine Being." Berkhof, *Systematic Theology*, 42.

32. Berkhof, *Systematic Theology*, 45.

portions of Scripture—are doxological, not objective statements of a static divine reality but rather expressions of praise arising from the God/human relationship. In actuality there is no need to decide between the two, for both can be said of God's attributes and both are of value as we pursue greater faithfulness. The basic truth is not objective reality versus doxological expression, but rather God's self-disclosure of the divine nature—including but not limited to the divine attributes—through all of the forms of revelation God employed. Berkhof captured both of these perspectives. First, concerning the objective reality of the attributes and our means to learn of them, "the only proper way to obtain perfectly reliable knowledge of the divine attributes is by the study of God's self-revelation in Scripture."[33] Second, as outgrowths of the relationships with humans that God has established, "God has entered into relations with us in His revelations of Himself, and supremely in Jesus Christ; . . . through this Self-revelation we do know God to be the true God, and have real acquaintance with His character and will."[34]

The Nature of the Divine Attributes

What, however, is the nature of God's attributes in general? Can a simple knowledge of the attributes yield a concrete understanding of God? The answer is not as straightforward as we may like.

> The consensus of opinion in the early Church, during the Middle Ages, and at the time of the Reformation, was that God in His inmost Being is the Incomprehensible one. . . . Apart from the revelation of God in His attributes, we have no knowledge of the Being of God whatsoever. But in so far as God reveals Himself in His attributes, we also have some knowledge of His Divine Being, though even so our knowledge is subject to human limitations.[35]

Furthermore, there is no agreement among theologians on the precise list of attributes. Not only is our understanding of God subject to human limitations, but what an attribute is, exactly, is not clear. Thiessen referenced the thought of nineteenth-century theologian Henry B. Smith in this regard: "H. B. Smith recognizes the fact that perhaps some of the

---

33. Berkhof, *Systematic Theology*, 54.
34. Berkhof, *Systematic Theology*, 44.
35. Berkhof, *Systematic Theology*, 43.

so-called attributes are 'strictly speaking,' not attributes at all, but 'different aspects of the divine substance.' He includes among these spirituality, self-existence, immensity, and eternity."[36]

Be that as it may, what we *can* say is that God's *attributes* are not wholly distinct from his *essence*—which essence, as we have seen, is love as the moral element of God's character—but rather are a further delineation of what that essence is.[37] In Berkhof's thinking this reality was expressed as follows: "Because of the close relation in which the two stand to each other, it can be said that knowledge of the attributes carries with it knowledge of the Divine Essence. It would be a mistake to conceive of the essence of God as existing by itself and prior to the attributes, and of the attributes as additive and accidental characteristics of the Divine Being. They are essential qualities of God, which inhere in His very Being and are co-existent with it."[38] Thiessen put it more succinctly: "The terms 'essence' and 'substance' are practically synonymous when used of God . . . that in which the qualities or attributes inhere."[39] God's attributes, then, are intertwined with the divine essence, and vice versa. They are not identical with each other, but neither are they wholly distinct from one another. Yet the fact that the God-revealed attributes are the means by which humans know at least some of what God is like indicates that still more can be said to clarify the nature of the attributes.

One standard, classical statement concerning the attributes' nature was offered by Strong:

> The attributes of God are those distinguishing characteristics of the divine nature which are inseparable from the idea of God and which constitute the basis and ground for his various manifestations to his creatures.
>
> We call them attributes, because we are compelled to attribute them to God as fundamental qualities or powers of his being, in order to give rational account of certain constant facts in God's self-revelations.[40]

---

36. Thiessen, *Systematic Theology*, 119.

37. See, for example, that Strong claimed, "We cannot conceive of attributes except as belonging to an underlying essence which furnished their ground of unity." Strong, *Systematic Theology*, 245.

38. Berkhof, *Systematic Theology*, 45–46.

39. Thiessen, *Systematic Theology*, 119.

40. Strong, *Systematic Theology*, 244.

Strong's statement, unfortunately, carries the possibility of misinterpreting the nature of the attributes as something that humans assign to God. In particular, his assertion that the attributes are so called because humans *attribute* them to God is problematic. Strong's view is somewhat different from the doxological view of the attributes, which sees them as human expressions of how God can be in relationship with people. Nevertheless, the further explanation by Berkhof brings added clarity:

> The name "attributes" is not ideal, since it conveys the notion of adding or assigning something to one, and is therefore apt to create the impression that something is added to the divine Being. . . . it is preferable to speak of the "perfections" or "virtues" of God, with the distinct understanding, however, that in this case the term "virtues" is not used in a purely ethical sense. . . . His virtues are not added to His Being, but His Being is the *pleroma* of His virtues and reveals itself in them. They may be defined as *the perfections which are predicated of the Divine Being in Scripture, or are visibly exercised by Him in His works of creation, providence, and redemption.*[41]

Thiessen contributed his view of the nature of the attributes, which emphasized their objective character rather than human conceptions or constructs:[42]

> By the attributes of God in distinction from the substance of God we mean the qualities that inhere in the substance and constitute an analytical and closer description of it. They are to be thought of as objectively real and not merely as man's subjective mode of conceiving God, and as descriptions of the particular ways in which the divine essence exists and operates and not as denoting distinct parts of God.[43]

Strong wrote in the first decade of the twentieth century, Berkhof wrote in the 1930s, and Thiessen wrote ten years after Berkhof. The

---

41. Berkhof, *Systematic Theology*, 52; italics original.

42. Strong and Berkhof affirmed this same point. See, for example, that Strong wrote regarding the divine attributes that they "are not mere names for human conceptions of God—conceptions which have their only ground in the imperfection of the finite mind. They are qualities objectively distinguishable from the divine essence and from each other." Strong, *Systematic Theology*, 244. See also Berkhof: "The attributes are not mere names to which no reality corresponds, nor separate parts of a composite God, but essential qualities in which the Being of God is revealed and with which it can be identified." Berkhof, *Systematic Theology*, 41.

43. Thiessen, *Systematic Theology*, 123.

language they employed can at times be confusing to us simply due to the writing style of the respective times in which they wrote. In the last quarter of the twentieth century Hauerwas used updated language—even though he was referencing Aristotle—to express a similar notion of the divine attributes. Employing the term "virtue" instead of "attribute," he asserted, "A virtue involves both a set of objects or situations external to the self and a definite manner in which the subject composed himself with respect to them. A virtue as a characteristic of the self is to be defined 'by its activity and its object.'"[44] A divine attribute, then—or "virtue" as Hauerwas termed it—is part of who God is, but becomes known to us through God's actions toward us.

We now come to the matter of the importance of the divine attributes for growth in faithfulness. Recall that the point about the attributes is not whether they are noetic, objective statements about God's nature or doxological human expressions of praise to God (for they are both). The fact that we know them through God's revelation—his self-disclosure—is the crucial point about the attributes. Yet the doxological perspective in relation to our desire for faithfulness yields value, for fundamental to the doxological view is the fact of God in relation with creation.

God is ultimately ineffable in that we cannot completely know what God is like, for God in totality is beyond human comprehension. That does not mean, however, that nothing of God can be known. He is not completely ineffable, for through the divine self-disclosure via the general revelation of creation, the special revelation of the Scripture, and the incarnation of the second person of the Godhead we have received a partial divulgence of who God is. Berkhof wrote:

> We cannot comprehend God, cannot have an absolute and exhaustive knowledge of Him, but we can undoubtedly have a relative or partial knowledge of the Divine Being. It is perfectly true that this knowledge of God is possible only because He has placed Himself in certain relations to His moral creatures and has revealed Himself to them, and that even this knowledge is humanly conditioned; but it is nevertheless real and true knowledge, and is at least a partial knowledge of the absolute nature of God.[45]

---

44. Hauerwas, *Character*, 75.
45. Berkhof, *Systematic Theology*, 44.

Note that the knowledge is possible only because God has established a relationship with his created, moral creatures. This notion of God in relationship with us is key to our apprehension of the divine attributes as perfections by which each of us can help form our character in faithfulness.[46] Regarding a doxological understanding of the attributes Grenz commented, "Our descriptions of the God we know are attempts to describe God-in-relation. Through such statements we speak about the eternal relations of the triune God and the reality of God in relationship with creation, most importantly with us."[47] It is through God's relationship with us, experienced in part through perception of the divine attributes, that at least some of those attributes can be appropriated by us. That appropriation leads to greater faithfulness.

At this juncture it behooves us to become familiar with God's attributes as understood by faithful believers throughout history. Some are unique to God alone, and thus we—as God's creation—cannot participate in them, even though we are in relationship with God. Others we can share. It is these that will garner our greatest attention moving forward.

The doxological view espoused by Grenz holds that "the enumeration of the divine attributes is a proper result of our desire to describe God in relationship. The various terms extol the greatness of God in comparison with creation. These doxological descriptions speak either of God's eternality or his goodness."[48] This he contrasted with a more traditional view, which he ultimately rejected: "The classical description of the divine attributes as 'incommunicable' and 'communicable' presupposes a noetic understanding of attributive theological statements. It assumes that assertions concerning God assert propositional truths concerning the static divine essence apart from God's internal dynamic or his relationship to the world."[49] Yet the desire to view God's attributes within a context of divine/human relationships—one that clearly understands at least some of the attributes in the moral context of the goodness of

---

46. See, for example, Berkhof: "The Bible never operates with an abstract concept of God, but always describes Him as the Living God, who enters into various relations with His creatures, relations which are indicative of several different attributes." Berkhof, *Systematic Theology*, 43. See also that Grenz, who clearly takes the doxological view, expressed this reality when he wrote "the attributes are expressions arising out of our experience of the God who stands in relationship to humans and the world." Grenz, *Theology*, 90.

47. Grenz, *Theology*, 90.
48. Grenz, *Theology*, 91.
49. Grenz, *Theology*, 91.

God—does not necessitate rejection of the traditional incommunicable/communicable structure. Instead, within the divine relationship of the Trinity all of the attributes are shared, both incommunicable and communicable; in the relationship between God and God's creation (specifically humans) the created can participate in at least some of the divine attributes, the communicable ones.[50]

We hold, then, that proclamation and adoration of God through doxological expressions of the divine attributes, as well as objective affirmations of God's nature as expressed in the attributes, are both inherently relational, and thus are part of the moral realm of human experience. As such, the extent to which people are experientially like God is the extent to which they are faithful.

The attributes have been structured in several ways by various theologians. We have already indicated that eternality and goodness is one approach, and incommunicable and communicable is another. Others include metaphysical, relational, and moral;[51] non-attributes (that others mistakenly classify as attributes), non-moral, and moral;[52] and absolute/immanent and relative/transitive.[53] For our purpose of pursuing greater faithfulness we will look at just two approaches to classifying the attributes, for through these two we can ascertain the attributes that will help us become more Godlike.

The Incommunicable God and the Communicable God

The great benefit of classifying God's attributes into incommunicable and communicable is that we can clearly see in which parts of the divine nature we can participate versus those in which we cannot. Greater appropriation of the communicable attributes yields the fruit of increased faithfulness.

The most commonly affirmed incommunicable attributes are those that describe God as self-existent, self-contained, transcendent, incomprehensible, immanent, omnipotent, omniscient, omnipresent, immutable, infinite (perfect, eternal, and immense), and unified (free from

---

50. See Berkhof: "The most common distinction is that between *incommunicable* and *communicable* attributes. The former are those to which there is nothing analogous in the creature . . . the latter those to which the properties of the human spirit bears some analogy." Berkhof, *Systematic Theology*, 55; italics original.

51. See Pittenger, "God's Nature," 395.

52. See Thiessen, *Systematic Theology*, 119–33.

53. See Strong, *Systematic Theology*, 243–303.

division).[54] It is these attributes that distinguish God from the creation, and are possessed by God alone. Humans, as part of creation, cannot experience or appropriate any of these attributes as they exist in God.

Other attributes of God are the communicable ones. Humans can experience and express these attributes, not perfectly as God does, but nevertheless to an extent. They include God's righteousness, justice, goodness (benevolence, grace, mercy), knowledge, wisdom, holiness, veracity, kindness, and sovereignty (will, power, and freedom). Through appropriation and expression of these attributes humans enjoy the potential of reflecting God's nature at least somewhat, thus approaching faithfulness to God.

The Non-Moral God and the Moral God

It should be apparent that many of the attributes listed as communicable carry a moral sense. We engage them as part of our participation in the moral realm of human experience. Others of the attributes do not carry this moral sense. The distinction is not between what is commonly termed "moral and immoral," for both of those labels are part of the moral realm, commonly indicating either good or bad. Rather the distinction is between moral and non-moral. Some of the attributes do not lend themselves to ethical terminology or discussion; these are termed "non-moral attributes." The reason why this distinction is of value is that walking and growing in faithfulness are inherently moral concepts. It is helpful, then, to articulate God's moral attributes, and distinguish them from the non-moral.

Many of the attributes classified as incommunicable are also non-moral. For example, God as self-existent, self-contained, omnipotent, omniscient, omnipresent, and unified are non-moral; they do not entail subjects or content we associate with the moral realm. By contrast, the moral attributes—those in which we can participate by virtue of being human and part of creation—include righteousness, justice, goodness (benevolence, grace, mercy), knowledge, wisdom, holiness, veracity, kindness, and sovereignty (will, power, and freedom). It is through display

---

54. Our purpose is not to define or describe each of the attributes, but rather to identify those that are incommunicable and distinguish them from those that are communicable. For more detail on the attributes see standard systematic theology texts such as those by Berkhof, Strong, and Thiessen.

of the moral attributes that God shows us the ideals of the moral realm, and calls his followers to faithfulness through emulation.

At this point the natural tendency of many Western Christians is to try to translate or reduce the communicable, moral attributes of God into lists of principles, rules, or laws to be followed as a means to put the attributes into practice, thus being faithful. This approach is a mistake, for it both reduces God's nature to executable lists of conduct and ignores the fact that the attributes are not external to God, but rather essential elements of the divine nature. Jesus' use of the phrase "You have heard it said" followed by "But I tell you" in the Sermon on the Mount demonstrates the flaw in the approach employed by many today. What Jesus was doing was pointing out this very mistake. His followers were focusing on particular external rules or laws as a means to faithfulness. Jesus' corrective to them was to call them to true faithfulness, something much more internal, reflecting the character of God. We now turn to the kind of thinking Jesus was expressing when calling his followers to more than a simple following of principles or obeying of rules: something known as "character ethics."

8

Character Ethics

WHAT DO WE MEAN by character ethics, and where did it originate? What are its basic elements and how is it different from the dominant thinking about what it means to be morally upright? How can it help those who are seeking to be more faithful Christians?

ARISTOTLE'S MORAL THOUGHT

Aristotle, in the fourth century BC, is generally credited with formulating the kernels of what has become known as character ethics. Although it is not easy to describe his thought in current ethical terms,[1] for Aristotle character minimally appeared to mean that a person acts habitually via what he termed "virtues."[2] According to Hauerwas, "For Aristotle a habit is a characteristic (*hexis*) possessed inwardly by man, defined as 'the condition either good or bad, in which we are, in relation to our emotions.' These characteristics which form the virtues are dispositions to act

---

1. See Hauerwas: "Aristotle's ethical reflection cannot be easily summarized or captured by current ethical categories or alternatives. His ethics is at once teleological and deontological." Hauerwas, *Character*, 36.

2. See Hauerwas: "For Aristotle and Aquinas, therefore, to say that a man has character seems to mean at least that he has acquired certain kinds of habits called virtues." Hauerwas, *Character*, 69.

in particular ways."³ This language of dispositions is reminiscent of the attempts to define character that we reviewed earlier, and the virtuous condition, according to Aristotle, is "the state of character which makes a man⁴ good and which makes him do his own work well."⁵

Notice that the human situation—the character ethics—being described by Aristotle is depicted not in terms of conduct, but rather as the nature of an individual's being. Ethics fundamentally refers not to decisions or actions driven either by certain desirable ends or adherence to standards, rules, or laws. Terms such as "habit," "virtue," "inwardly," "emotions," and "disposition" describe that which composes character,⁶ rather than the *praxis* that results from character. This is the key quality of character ethics: it is formed by one's inwardness. Or, in Aristotelian thinking, this notion is expressed as "having a good moral character helps its possessor operate well and live up to her potential, thereby fulfilling her nature."⁷ It is the character that drives the conduct.

We may ask from where does the good, or desirable, character come? How is it constructed, or formed? A character habit—or virtue—according to Aristotle, is "a kind of 'readiness for action,' but a 'readiness for' that is not momentary but lasting. . . . Furthermore, the habits that make men good are formed through the agent's activity."⁸ It is habitual practicing of the virtues that inculcates them in the moral agent's being, solidifying them as part of the individual's character. Through such practice the individual can, in fact, actively form character.

Aristotle's conception of character virtues included a notion known as "the mean."⁹ Among other things, it entailed esteeming a moral stance

---

3. Hauerwas, *Character*, 70.

4. Again, we encounter a situation in which an author used exclusively male language to describe a human in a morally upright situation. The reader will have to understand that both genders, not just males, is the intention.

5. Albert et al., *Great Traditions in Ethics*, 50.

6. See that Hauerwas, in discussing both Aristotle and Aquinas, noted that "neither seemed to feel the need to make an explicit terminological distinction between the virtues, virtue, and character." Hauerwas, *Character*, 74. It is likely futile, then, for us to try to distinguish precise differences among the various terms used by Aristotle when describing the elements of what we now understand as character ethics.

7. Timpe, "Moral Character," para. 7.

8. Hauerwas, *Character*, 70.

9. See Albert et al.: "[A] master of any art avoids excess and defect but seeks the intermediate" and "Virtue, then, is a state of character concerned with choice, lying in a mean, i.e., the mean relative to us, this being determined by a rational principle, and by that principle by which the man of practical wisdom would determine it. Now it is

that could be endorsed by the prevailing social milieu, the majority, or the dominant society. As a result courage, as a character virtue, was to be embraced as the mediating stance between confidence and fear; temperance between pain and pleasure; liberality between meanness and prodigality; proper pride between undue humility and empty vanity.[10] The issue for current Christians seeking to be faithful—as were the earliest believers—is that the Christians in the first few centuries rejected such a mediating moral position when establishing themselves within society. Rather, not only were they extreme, but they exhibited character that was distinctly different from the prevailing social milieu. Furthermore, their social stance was modeled after that of Jesus, whom they sought to emulate as they lived in a society that was hostile to them. Aristotle's moral mean strikes us as eerily similar to the syncretistic thinking of many Western Christians today; adoption of it does not appear to be a defensible option for those seeking to enhance their faithfulness. Nevertheless, the fundamental elements of modern character ethics align well with our quest to rediscover and adopt the faithfulness stance endorsed by the early believers.

ESSENTIALS OF CHARACTER ETHICS

One way of understanding character ethics is to view it in contradistinction from the other two basic approaches to moral obligation.[11] The first, known as teleology or consequentialism, holds that what drives obligation in any moral situation requiring action is the ends or consequences that result from a particular decision. The proper decision is the one that achieves the desirable results as determined beforehand by a particular set of rules, conventions, or laws. In particularly difficult moral situations, or in cases when there is conflict between rules, the proper decision is the one that results in the greatest amount of good compared to bad. The second, known as deontology, obligates the moral agent to act so as to adhere best to a predetermined set of laws, rules, or standards.

---

a mean between two vices, that which depends on excess and that which depends on defect; and again it is a mean because the vices respectively fall short of or exceed what is right in both passions and actions, while virtue both finds and chooses that which is intermediate." Albert et al., *Great Traditions in Ethics*, 51.

10. Albert et al., *Great Traditions in Ethics*, 52–53.

11. For a more thorough discussion of teleology and deontology, see Frankena, *Ethics*, 14–17.

Adherence itself is deemed to be good, irrespective of the consequences. The notion of duty, as prescribed by the laws, rules, etc., is key to the deontological approach to ethics; the resultant consequences do not play a role in determining proper moral action.[12]

Character ethics stands in contrast to teleology and deontology in that it has in view not primarily the conduct of the moral agent, but rather the agent's character. That character is more fundamental to moral thought, and ultimately conduct, than an external driver such as rules or conventions. The individual's moral being is the primary focus of ethical deliberation, and thus forms the foundation for human experience in the moral realm. Hauerwas pointed out the significant benefit of the character ethics approach compared with others: "If the function of ethical discourse and argument is limited to judgment about specific action, it cannot help but pervert rather than enliven men's lives. Ethical argument concerned solely with discrete acts minimizes the moral life as it gives no direction or context of significance for why we should refrain from some things and do others."[13] The character approach to ethics is not just one option among other equals; it is the superior option, for it represents a more expansive and mature approach[14]—inclusive of the individual's moral self rather than simply the individual's moral acts—unlike the approaches of teleology and deontology. Brawley sought to explain the uniqueness of character ethics when he asserted, "Character ethics begins not with ethics as such but with what shapes human identity. . . . Before considering what ethical life looks like in actual existence, character ethics has to do with formation as the presupposition and source of that life."[15]

What is it that shapes human identity and forms a person's character? How does formation take place? Recall that whereas character is not fickle, it is malleable. That means that character is formed through habitual practice over a long period of time by which one learns what is morally good and what is morally bad.[16] Character thus formed is not

---

12. See Timpe: "At the heart of consequentialist theories is the idea that the moral action is the one that produces the best consequences. According to deontological theories, morality is primarily a function of duties or obligations, regardless of the consequences of acting in accordance with those duties. Both of these sets of theories are commonly described as ethics of rules." Timpe, "Moral Character," para. 12.

13. Hauerwas, *Character*, 232.

14. For a more thorough explanation of the progression and maturation of ethical obligation as found in the Bible, see Wozniak, *Living as the Living Jesus*, 171–95.

15. Brawley, *Character Ethics*, vii–ix.

16. The author of the Epistle to the Hebrews expressed this idea of repeated effort as

just a theoretical concept, nor is it for the faint of heart. Rather, it is what drives an individual's thinking, convictions, commitments, and conduct in the social milieu in which he or she is found, irrespective of how amenable or hostile the milieu is to the individual's religious/social stance. Old Testament scholar Walter Brueggemann expressed the very practical nature of character ethics as it engages the realities of the social situation of the faithful individual—the one who has sought to emulate the character of God: "The focus of character ethics . . . is always 'in history' of a concrete kind. . . . [T]he human agents who engage the character of God will inescapably enact their ethical character 'in history,' that is, in the arena of power and violence and ideology."[17] Such was the experience of the early Christians, whose character did not waiver and whose faithfulness remained steadfast, even in the face of abuse, torture, and death.

CHARACTER AND COMMUNITY

Thus far the focus of our character study has been on the nature of character, the character of God, and ethics as rooted in formation of the individual's character. There is, however, an essential driver of character we have only mentioned, but not yet explored: the role and influence of an individual's community on character formation.

In part 1 we noted that the Christians of the first few centuries did not live as isolated believers. Rather, they lived faithfully as participants in Christian communities. A new Christian not only *left* his or her old life in the Roman social milieu, but also *joined* a new community: a collective of Christian believers. In their defiance of Rome these Christians did so as community members, not as mere individuals. Recall that while he was being transported to Rome to face martyrdom Bishop Ignatius of Antioch was greeted by Polycarp of Smyrna; he then communicated with the church at Rome as well as several others, pleading with them not to interfere with his execution. Blandina was tortured and martyred in solidarity with a number of other Christians. She, being the last to die, looked forward to joining the others who had just been martyred, and was encouraged in facing death by the thought that soon she would be reunited with her fellow believers. Similarly, Perpetua was martyred in

---

the means to build character in 5:14: "But solid food is for the mature, who by constant use have trained themselves to distinguish good from evil."

17. Brueggemann, "Foreword," x.

solidarity with fellow believers, mutually encouraging the others and being encouraged by them as they faced death with joy. Remember that Le Chambon was a community that worked *as a united community* against the Nazi regime.

In all of these examples and many more, the influence of the community on its participants cannot be ignored. The formation of character is both driven and colored by the nature of the community.[18] For the early Christian communities—influenced, for example, by Mark's account of the life of Jesus—the communities' values were what distinguished them from the broader Roman society in which they found themselves. New Testament historian C. Drew Smith observed, "Within the political framework of the Roman Empire, the virtues of service, inclusion, humility, and economic simplicity become the norms that set Mark's community apart from the Roman culture, which places value on status, domination, power, and wealth."[19] That character, formed within the community members as they grew within the community and adopted its values, drove the early Christians' faithfulness, even unto death. Smith asserted that for the members of this community "crucifixion, not acquiescence to the political norms of the Roman Empire, becomes the norm of faithful existence and a form of internal cohesion and resistance against the politics of Rome."[20] Indeed, the early Christians were not acting in isolation as they continued in faithfulness to the point of suffering and even martyrdom. Rather, they were acting consistent with—and reflective of—the values, ethos, and character of the Christian communities in which they participated.

In reflecting on the thought of Hauerwas, his mentor—James Gustafson—characterized his mentee's thought: "The general shape of his work is this: we grow up in communities in which we share the narratives, the stories of the community. . . . The narratives and our participating in the community, in his case the 'Church' (very abstractly), give shape to our characters. Our characters are expressed in our deeds and actions."[21] Hauerwas himself reiterated the notion that the individual's

---

18. In this regard, see Brueggemann: "'Character ethics' refers to a way of thinking about and interpreting the moral life in terms of a particular vision of and a passion for life that is rooted in the nurture, formation, and socialization of a particular self-conscious community." Brueggemann, "Foreword," vii.

19. Smith, "Become My Followers," 217.
20. Smith, "Become My Followers," 213.
21. Gustafson, *Moral Discernment*, 147.

community heavily influences a participant's character by virtue of its beliefs and conduct: "The kind of character we have is therefore relative to the kind of community from which we inherit our primary symbols and practices. . . . However, an intentional community can provide a range of symbols that create boundaries for an ethics of character by suggesting the fundamental symbols that should give each man's character its primary orientation."[22] Gustafson explained the view that character is formed in community: "We are members of moral communities, and the outlooks, values and visions of these communities are shaped by their stories. As we participate in a community and its formative narratives our own moral outlooks and values are shaped by its narrative. . . . The critical issue, from a moral point of view, is what narratives ought to shape moral ethos and character."[23]

For the early Christian communities those symbols were the God of what came—in time—to be the Bible, his working in creation and history, and his incarnation in Jesus whose death provided salvation and life for the faithful members of the community. Fundamental to their understanding of God was God's self-disclosure via divulgence of the divine character. As part of their community participation and growth in faith, the individual learned of God and what it meant to be faithful to the God they knew. Meeks suggested how the community dynamic worked to influence those who had left the dominant social context in order to join the community, arguing that the community leaders "were able to use the virtues and . . . the character of God as warrants for their advice, because they could assume their audience knew who God was. They knew who God was because they had been taught . . . as part of the resocialization or 'conversion' process."[24]

The formation of the individual's character, then, occurs within the community in which she or he participates, and reflects the beliefs and convictions of that community. The early Christians, by virtue of embracing the Jesus message as conveyed through the gospel accounts and voluntarily aligning themselves in communities of other Jesus followers, intentionally formed (or perhaps reformed) their characters by embracing the God of the Christian communities and the associated divine character. It was this new-formed character, patterned after the character of God, that fundamentally drove their faithfulness.

22. Hauerwas, *Character*, 231.
23. Gustafson, *Moral Discernment*, 192.
24. Meeks, *Origins*, 161.

To an outside observer it may have appeared that the Christians were living according to certain laws or rules or principles; these, however, were not what motivated Christian moral conduct. Rather, it was the believers' desire and intention to be Godlike in character that empowered their conduct and drove their faithfulness to the one who called them to a different life: "You have heard it said . . . But I tell you."

If in all of this we look for a description of what character ethics looks like—as it was inculcated in the lives of the early, faithful believers and should be inculcated in the lives of believers today—we can do no better than the depiction offered by Brueggemann:

> Character ethics . . . resists the formulation of codes, rules, or commandments. . . . it works against a caricature of the Bible—and particularly the Old Testament—as a set of commandments that are too familiarly labeled as "legalism." The dynamic and generativity of character ethics is based on the conviction that a rightly appropriated social vision and a rightly disciplined habit of behavior will together provide sufficient guidelines and adequate resources for every moral issue, all the while assigning the human person great freedom alongside great responsibility as a moral agent who is embedded in a community and disciplined and informed by a particular text.[25]

Brueggemann's reference both to "the Bible and ethics" and a community informed by "a particular text" leads us to the question of character ethics and the Bible. The early believers learned both from the Old Testament and the written Gospel stories of Jesus' life. They also learned from the Epistles of the New Testament. If these texts, in the context of the Christian communities, drove character development of the early Christians, then should we not find character ethics in the Bible?

---

25. Brueggemann, "Foreword," vii.

9

Character Ethics in the Bible

WE KNOW THE MEANINGFUL narratives that drive the identity of the individuals who make up a community are fundamental and essential elements of character formation. Without them, the individual would be morally adrift, development of character would be without guidance, and community solidarity would not exist. To the faithful people of God, for thousands of years before the incarnation as well as the thousands of years since, those meaningful narratives are found in the Bible. In them is seen the character of God, and from them the faithful learn how the divine character can be appropriated by them both as individuals and as members of the broader faithful community. Brueggemann argued for the vitality of the sacred text when he wrote: "Character ethics is a practice of being (not doing) that is derived from and referred back to the character of God, the God of the script . . . It is impossible to overaccent the dynamic of this ethic as evidenced in the biblical text."[1]

Not all biblical passages display character ethics equally, or even display ethics at all. It is in certain passages, be they narrative, didactic, or poetic, where character ethics is most strongly seen. For Smith, Mark 8:27—10:52, in which Jesus taught and demonstrated what it means to walk in the Jesus way, is one such passage: "It is in these teachings

---

1. Brueggemann, "Foreword," ix.

that we find social identity formation and character formation to be the strongest."[2]

The power and essential nature of the text for character development cannot be understated. In a scathing denunciation of the failure of modern Western Christianity to embrace the character ethics approach, Brueggemann pointed out the stark contrast between a faithful community that adheres to its authoritative text—the Bible—and the corrupt, syncretistic nature of what is naively understood to be Christianity today: "In character ethics, social power is important and defining . . . Biblically grounded ethics characteristically acts with only 'the weapons of the weak.' . . . In current U.S. society, one can readily see the move toward 'the weapons of the strong' in religious communities, and one can, with equal readiness, see how that move is marked by idolatrous self-deception."[3]

Where, then, do we find character ethics in the Bible, and which passages are authoritative for formation of character and a life lived faithfully in the moral realm of human experience? An exhaustive review would constitute a very large book in itself, so thoroughness will not be attempted here. Several examples, however, will serve to show that character ethics is found throughout the Scripture.

CHARACTER ETHICS IN THE OLD TESTAMENT

The idea that the faithful in the Old Testament were required to obey God's commands is incontrovertible. Passages in the Decalogue such as Exod 34:10–11a,[4] Lev 18:4–5,[5] and Deut 28:1–2,[6] along with a host of

---

2. Smith, "Become My Followers," 213.

3. Brueggemann, "Foreword," x.

4. In Exod 34:10–11a God spoke to Moses: "Then the LORD said: 'I am making a covenant with you. Before all your people I will do wonders never before done in any nation in all the world. The people you live among will see how awesome is the work that I, the LORD, will do for you. Obey what I command you today.'"

5. In Lev 18 God gave extensive instructions to Moses, to be passed on to the Israelites, including verses 4–5: "You must obey my laws and be careful to follow my decrees. I am the LORD your God. Keep my decrees and laws, for the person who obeys them will live by them. I am the LORD."

6. In Deut 28:1–2 Moses made the following commitment to the Israelites just before they entered the promised land: "If you fully obey the LORD your God and carefully follow all his commands I give you today, the LORD your God will set you high above all the nations on earth. All these blessings will come on you and accompany you if you obey the LORD your God." Therein follows a list of blessings for obedience, and a much longer list of curses for disobedience.

others, make it absolutely clear that obedience was fundamental to the early biblical understanding of faithfulness. The requirement is reiterated outside of the Decalogue in, for example, Josh 23:6.[7] If such rote obedience was foundational to faithfulness for the people of God, then how can it be asserted that character ethics is found throughout the Old Testament?[8]

Fundamental to answering the question is the realization that the concept of moral faithfulness develops incrementally throughout the Bible. Initially, even prior to the fall, the moral sphere of human experience included obedience to God.[9] As God continued to disclose himself through the writings of additional Spirit-inspired authors,[10] more was revealed concerning the notion of faithfulness. Whereas disobedience was never condoned, what emerged through ongoing disclosure of the divine will was that rote obedience was insufficient and at times even rejected by God as evidence of faithfulness. The message of Amos in the eighth century BC, for example, was that whereas God's people diligently brought sacrifices, conducted religious festivals, and assembled according to the law, their concomitant disregard for truth and justice in the courts, over-taxation of the poor, oppression of the innocent, and embracing of bribery rendered their hypocritical adherence to required ritualistic religious customs morally perverse. Rather than their obedience (for which God indicated he had no regard), God wanted them to display the type of moral character that resulted in the establishment of justice and lives of righteousness.[11] This is evidence of moral velocity[12] through the Bible, as well as ongoing development and enhancement of the notion of faithfulness.

---

7. In his farewell to the leaders of Israel Joshua gave the following instruction in Josh 23:6: "Be very strong; be careful to obey all that is written in the Book of the Law of Moses, without turning aside to the right or to the left."

8. See, for example, Carroll, in which the editors assert that character ethics is concerned with "subtle ways in which Scripture molds believers and their communities. Character ethics is not as widely understood to be constitutive of Old Testament ethics as, say, the legal material in the Bible, but its less visible power to impact every dimension of human existence is nonetheless real and must not be underestimated." Carroll, *Character Ethics*, xviii.

9. See Gen 2:16–17b in which God's single command to Adam was that he not eat from the tree of the knowledge of good and evil.

10. See 2 Pet 1:20–21.

11. See Amos 5:11–24.

12. For more on the concept of moral velocity, see Wozniak, *Living as the Living Jesus*, 180–83.

The Character of David

In the context of faithfulness consider David, Israel's greatest king. If we simply look at his conduct we see someone who lived a life continuously characterized by violence, at times engaging in the wholesale slaughter of entire ethnic groups. Today we would refer to his actions as genocide. David did not leave a single man or woman alive for fear that they might report his conduct.[13] On one occasion, after defeating a particular ethnic group, he indiscriminately killed two-thirds of the defenseless prisoners of war.[14] It was because of his life of violence that David later was denied the honor of building God's temple.[15] Furthermore, David was a deceiver and liar, a murderer, an adulterer, and an intentional violator of God's ceremonial/religious law. He abandoned his first wife, then openly practiced polygamy and additionally maintained many lovers on the side. At one point he despised the word of God by knowingly doing evil,[16] and when a wealthy man snubbed his request for supplies David retaliated by attempting to kill him. He was a traitor to his country,[17] and at the end of his life passed on to his son a hit list consisting of two people the son was to kill: one who had been a loyal army commander for many years, the other an individual who at one point had insulted David but later repented and received from David a promise that he would not be killed. One expert's summary description of David's conduct is: "chock full of sexual and physical violence, passion, scandal, dysfunction, and outrageous moral excess."[18]

Can it be said that David was faithful to God? For many of us our automatic response, given his conduct, would be to say "no," or perhaps something stronger. This is because we have been conditioned to understand faithfulness to be external adherence to articulated lists, laws, or standards, or maybe an attitude that asserts faithfulness to be evidenced by such adherence. Yet both the Old and New Testaments credit God as testifying David to be "a man after his own heart"[19]—a moniker that he alone bears in all of Scripture. How can such a vile person—Israel's

---

13. See 1 Sam 27:9–11.
14. See 2 Sam 8:2.
15. See 1 Chr 22:8 and 28:2–3.
16. See 2 Sam 12:9.
17. See 1 Sam 27:1–2.
18. Kirsch, "Fourteen Things," para. 5.
19. See 1 Sam 13:14 and Acts 13:22.

greatest king, King David—be characterized as such (surpassed only by the example of Jesus, and perhaps Moses[20])? The key is to realize that faithfulness is not circumscribed by adherence to laws, standards, or rules, important as they may be. Rather, at its heart faithfulness entails formation and enhancement of character, patterned after the character of God, and *then* the essential ensuing attitude and conduct that reflect the divine character. In this element of conduct David failed often and severely. Faithfulness is something other than, and more fundamental than, external conduct. Notwithstanding the many moral failures associated with his actions, David—in his foundational moral being—set out on the path to form his character after the character of God. This is best seen in the Psalms of David, even with regard to his moral failures.

When the prophet Samuel was about to anoint young David as the future king of Israel, God told Samuel that it is the heart, not externals, that are morally vital.[21] Later David implored God to test the fidelity of his heart, for he had a continual focus on God's love and reliance on God's faithfulness.[22] In Ps 63 we see David's commitment to aligning his being with God's as he cried out "You God, are my God, earnestly I seek you: I thirst for you, my whole being longs for you" (v. 1); "On my bed I remember you; I think of you through the watches of the night" (v. 6); and "I cling to you; your right hand upholds me" (v. 8). This is David revealing the longing of his heart, a longing to pattern his being after the being of God. It is this longing that made David a man after God's own heart. This longing became reality in David's approach to his kingly duties, for he led God's people "with integrity of heart."[23]

What about the moral failures of David? If his heart truly was aligned with that of God, how can that fact be reconciled with his long-term, extreme, and repeated moral shortcomings? Do we see Godlike character even in the midst of David's failures? Whereas no answer ever may be completely satisfying, there are a few observations that help us see in David how faithfulness through character development should function, or perhaps rather how it fails to function when not developed consistently after the character of God. First, when anointed, David appears to have had a heart that was uncorrupted by either power or his social milieu. As

20. For more on the faithfulness of Jesus and Moses see Heb 3:1–6, as well as 11:23–28.
21. See 1 Sam 16:7.
22. See Ps 26:2–3.
23. See Ps 78:72.

his life continued, however, David grew in power, embraced that milieu, and even helped establish its moral standards, with the resultant conduct that is seen throughout his life. Instead of distinguishing and separating himself from the ways of his surroundings, he adopted them as his own. It is not surprising, then, to see him become a person of violence, revenge, lust, unfaithfulness, deception, lawlessness, and even murder—such conduct reflects both abuse of the power with which God had entrusted him and adoption of the values of his surrounding social milieu. This point cannot be overemphasized; aligning oneself with the prevailing moral environment inevitably results in one's attitudes, intentions, and conduct reflecting it. Recall that the early Christians, as a necessary exhibition of their faithfulness, intentionally distinguished themselves from the standards of their social milieu. David did not.

Second—in spite of his conduct—we see in David one who had not completely abandoned his sensitivity to and understanding of the ways of God. In Ps 51 David confessed his sin to God, acknowledging both his guilt and the just nature of God's judgment. He implored God to cleanse him, and submitted his broken spirit and contrite heart to the mercy of God. In verse 10 we observe David's desire that his character be realigned with that of God: "Create in me a pure heart, O God, and renew a steadfast spirit within me." David, then, was not only repentant and seeking God's forgiveness; he desired that his character, damaged because of his sin, be restored and renewed in yieldedness to the faithful character of God. For David, Ps 51 likely was not a one-time event, but a pattern of his life.

Third, David was not consistent and persistent in his effort to form his character after that of God. Character development, as we have seen, does not occur *at* a point of time, but rather *over* time as one continues to walk in the way of God by habitually training oneself to distinguish good from evil.[24] Thus we see in David one who lived cyclically: he repeatedly started on the path of character development, deviated from it due to his embracing of the values of the social milieu in which he lived, and subsequently repented of his actions and once again sought the heart of God.

The life of David, then, serves as a vivid example of the struggle associated with character development, for each person—like David—remains severely affected by the results of the fall. The story of his struggle is greatly informative for those individuals and communities that seek to walk the path of faithful character development.

---

24. See Heb 5:14.

Character Ethics in Israel

Character ethics also can be seen within the functioning community of Israel. Israel's historic narrative, repeated throughout the Old Testament, served to remind the people of Israel of who they were, and then to call them to what was obligatory—not because of the requirements of the law but *because of who they were as the people of God*. One example of how this worked is found in the sixth chapter of Micah. Verses 2 and 3 indicate that God had a case against Israel due to its lack of faithfulness. In the next few verses God rehearsed a nutshell version of his faithfulness to Israel throughout its history. What follows in verses 6 and 7 was a challenge to the notion that Israel's faithfulness should consist in adherence to requirements of the law, or ritual practices of the cult.[25] The clear implication is that for Israel to perform such rituals would not please God. Rather, as seen in verse 8, Israel's obligation was to reflect God's character of justice and mercy, and to do so in humility before God. Old Testament scholar M. Daniel Carroll R. captured this notion of community narrative and attendant obligation as follows: "Narratives not only can ground identity; they also clarify accountability. Narratives present the roles and mutual obligations that are consistent with the tradition. They offer examples of appropriate as well as negative behavior and attitudes . . . and thereby function as a historical framework for evaluating community life in the present."[26] He went on to indicate that "the prophet points to the ideal of important virtues for community life."[27] It is the appropriate attitudes—essential elements of character—that drive the associated appropriate behavior in reflection of virtues such as a propensity for both justice and mercy. In terms of the Israelite community/cult and its moral practices, "if the cult is interpreted within the framework of character ethics as a practice, then [Micah] 6:8 is not to be set over against the cult but instead is designated to reemphasize precisely what the cult is designed to do: promote the good and nurture the virtues. The cult is where the people are to be taught justice, mercy, and humility and learn about the God who seeks such qualities from the nation."[28] Char-

---

25. The use of the term "cult" refers to a number of characteristics, including Israel's understanding of itself as distinct from other people, communities, or nations; also the practice of making offerings to a deity, including Israel's sacrificial system.

26. Carroll, "He Has Told You," 111.

27. Carroll, "He Has Told You," 112.

28. Carroll, "He Has Told You," 112–13.

acter ethics, then, is at the heart of what Israel was to be: a functioning community that fundamentally and primarily reflected and enacted the character of God.

Much earlier in Israel's history—at the end of Moses' life—we see that God's chosen leader for the community was depicted in terms that initially appear to describe the strength of his conduct. Terms such as "signs and wonders," "mighty power," and "awesome deeds" point to external acts by which Moses' authority was established and his leadership position was confirmed. Old Testament professor Dennis T. Olson, however, gave us valuable insight into the actual message of Deut 34. Regarding verses 10 through 12 Olson observed:

> Moses' uniqueness stems from his unparalleled intimacy with God (knowing God "face to face"), on the one hand, and his uniquely powerful "signs and wonders," on the other hand. What is remarkable is that these words ("signs and wonders," "mighty deeds," "terrifying displays of power") are all technical terms applied consistently elsewhere in Deuteronomy to God alone (4:34; 6:22; 7:19; 11:3; 26:8; 29:3). Thus, paradoxically in a narrative that emphasizes his human mortality when he dies as Israel's leader outside the promised land, Moses is also remembered at the same time as a leader with godlike powers.[29]

It is not the display of power that is critical in this passage, but rather the divine character that Moses adopted and reflected as he worked within the community of Israel. It was to Moses that the law was given, but in the account of his death it is his Godlike character that was remembered.

If we look at the guidance Moses gave Israel for its future judges, we see again that character was to be foremost both in the choosing of judges and in their conduct when deciding cases. This is important, for the scope of the judges' work extended through the entire community of the people of God. It would be natural to think that a list of rules outlining proper conduct by judges would be primary among Moses' guidance. Such was not the case, however. Instead, judges were to avoid corruption and pursue justice.[30] No list of rules was found; rather, it was the individ-

---

29. Olson, "Between Humility and Authority," 55.

30. See Olson, in which he quoted biblical legal scholar Bernard Jackson's observations concerning the requirements for judges found in Deut 16:18–20. Jackson wrote, "The judges here are simply to act justly and avoid corruption. They are not asked to follow any particular rules." Olson's contention about this passage is that the verses specify "the character of the judges and the criteria for their judgments in arbitrating disputes." Olson, "Between Humility and Authority," 53.

ual judge's character that was paramount. That character, however, was to emulate the character of God. Olsen leaned on Rabbi Michael Goldberg's thought when he pointed out, "Michael Goldberg has argued that the ban on judges accepting bribes is grounded in Deuteronomy in the character of God. According to Deut. 10:17–18, God is one who 'is not partial and takes no bribe, who executes justice for the orphan and the widow, and who loves the strangers.' Human judicial practice is to be shaped by the character of the divine Judge."[31]

The examples from Amos, Micah, David, Moses, and Israel's judges are not exhaustive; rather, they are but a few of many instances where character ethics is not only found in the Old Testament, but serves as the foundation for faithfulness among the people of God. We will see that the same reality is found in the New Testament.

CHARACTER ETHICS IN THE NEW TESTAMENT

In the New Testament we find character ethics throughout, even in Revelation. Whereas an exhaustive review is beyond our scope—as it was with our look into the Old Testament—we can look at a few representative instances, starting with the character of God. Following that, the means of appropriating the divine character can be seen in the work of the Spirit; the practical outworking being that which we saw in the lives of the early Christians: commitment to God and rejection of the Roman social milieu, with faithfulness being expressed through a life of peace. Finally, the life of Jesus as an exemplar of the divine character and standard to be imitated will be introduced in anticipation of part 3.

The Character of God in the New Testament

Earlier we saw that fundamental to God's character is the element of relationship; it is an essential component of God's being. There is relationship among and within the three members of the Godhead, and there is relationship between God and the created order, including people. That relationship is expressed as divine love, both within the Godhead and from God to humans. Such love is experienced as God's goodness to all of humanity, in the form of mercy and grace, and constitutes the moral standard for all people.

31. Olson, "Between Humility and Authority," 53.

It is not surprising to learn of the comprehensive and foundational nature of love for God in the New Testament. Appropriation of the character of God by the faithful includes reciprocity: God in his moral essence loves created humanity, and humans are expected to emulate God's character by loving God in return. Brawley captured the importance of love of God, in relationship with God, as crucial for moral faithfulness by referencing the event from Jesus' life in which a Jewish legal teacher inquired of Jesus concerning the most important commandment. "The question of the first commandment expands the notion, expressed in Mark 7, that ethics derives from a heart that is in a proper relationship with God. A scribe inquires about ethics in the abstract: 'Which commandment is the first of all?' (12:28). Grounding himself in God's monotheistic character, Jesus repeats Deuteronomy 6:5 with some echoes of Joshua 22:5, enjoining love of God."[32] He continued by referencing the observation of theologian Dan Via that ethics so conceived means that proper moral conduct is not predetermined: "Via correctly discerns that ethics in Mark means giving up knowing in advance what one is to do. But Via makes the love command an exception."[33] What is obligatory is love patterned after the character of God's love, rather than rote adherence to the law or a list of rules. Indeed, ethics driven by character rather than laws or rules renders predetermination of upright conduct in all situations impossible, for no matter how extensive the list of obligations it cannot accommodate the range of ethical situations possible within the moral realm.

Ethics based in relationship is also found in the letters of Paul. For example, in his letter to the Ephesians Paul taught that the faithful must no longer live as do the gentiles, who are separated from the life of God. Rather, they were to put off the pre-Christian self, and replace it with the Christian self which was created to be Godlike.[34] It is the character of God they were to emulate, to the point that their entire beings were to take on Godlikeness. In the letter to the Colossians Paul repeated this theme when instructing the nascent Christians—who have shed the pre-Christian self and put on the Christian self—which has been formed in the image of God.[35]

---

32. Brawley, "God's Character in Mark," 67.

33. Brawley, "God's Character in Mark," 67. Brawley was quoting from Via's book, *Ethics of Mark's Gospel: In the Middle of Time* (Philadelphia: Fortress, 1985), 135.

34. See Eph 4:17–24.

35. See Col 3:10.

A similar theme is found in Paul's letter to the Galatians. This relational transition, from pre-Christian antagonism to God to Christian alignment with God, was expressed by Brawley: "In Galatians a metaethical relationship with God, which Paul calls being justified, is construed as the point of origin for social identity and understood to be a source for behavior."[36] As was the case in the Old Testament, the moral life is seen to be not rote adherence to the law or rules, but the expression of human character aligned with that of God.[37]

Living in the Spirit

Establishing a relationship with God, and aligning one's character with God's, is not a matter simply of human determination and effort. Rather, it is the Spirit of God who brings one into relationship with the divine. In the moral realm of the faithful, the Spirit "originates, maintains, develops, and guides *the new life* that is born from above, is nourished from above, and will be perfected above—a life that is heavenly in principle, though lived on earth."[38] In speaking to his disciples just prior to his arrest, Jesus described the work of the Spirit in the lives of the faithful as follows: "But the Advocate, the Holy Spirit, whom the Father will send in my name, will teach you all things and will remind you of everything I have said to you."[39] It is the work of the Spirit in the life of the faithful one that forms one's character after the character of the divine, and leads one to live life following the pattern of divine conduct. This is something not found in the Old Testament. Although the Spirit was active among God's chosen people, the Spirit did not guide the life of the individual as we find in the New Testament after the ascension. Jesus' departure triggered the release of the Spirit among and within the faithful in the new way of Jesus' example. The individual was enabled to live the new life born from above because of an active relationship with the Spirit. Brawley again

36. Brawley, "Identity and Metaethics," 118.

37. Brawley expressed this reality as follows: "Initially being justified is not a change in ethical quality or behavior, because it means a change in the relationship of a human being with God 'through faith in/of Jesus Christ.' But by no means does Paul neglect ethics. . . . Paul is compelled to spell out how ethical behavior is possible apart from law. In short, Paul believes in the power of God that acts dynamically through the relationship of being justified to produce life among those who are in Christ." Brawley, "Identity and Metaethics," 116.

38. Berkhof, *Systematic Theology*, 426; italics original.

39. John 14:26.

referenced Galatians to express the way the Spirit works in the moral life of the believer: "The fictive kinship of being children of God is confirmed by an experience that Paul refers to as receiving the Spirit, which is also contrasted with 'from works of the law' (3:2). Receiving the Spirit determines their identity, and they require no further determination of it by works of law."[40]

Notice that for Paul the work of the Spirit is contrasted with the law. The faithful one's being is molded by the Spirit to the extent that blind adherence to the many stipulations of the law not only is no longer necessary, it is found to be in conflict with the new life of the Spirit. It is not that the law is bad in and of itself, but it is the work of the Spirit, not the law, that is to guide the expression of one's character in the moral realm. "To live by the Spirit, though not antithetical to law (5:14), means that the present is open beyond the law. When Paul says that 'the whole law is summed up in a single saying, 'You shall love your neighbor as yourself,' there is no way for the Galatians to know what love will look like in a concrete situation before they encounter it. At that point Paul's exhortation is to live by the Spirit."[41]

The Early Christians

In part 1 we investigated the lives of the early Christians, including the values and traits that formed their character as well as their social stance of opposition to Rome. Even while enduring pressure, threats, persecution—and for some, martyrdom—the early Christians remained committed to a lifestyle characterized by peace—not just as a goal, but as their daily attitude characteristic of their faithfulness. Peace, however, was not chosen for its practical results—perhaps diminution of suffering under Rome—but as a means to emulate and even appropriate the character of God as taught and demonstrated by Jesus.[42]

How does a lifestyle of peace reflect the character of God, particularly given the dictates of God in the Old Testament that his faithful

---

40. Brawley, "Identity and Metaethics," 116.
41. Brawley, "Identity and Metaethics," 117.
42. See Swartley: "The gospel narrative as a whole presents Jesus as a paradigm for peacemaking. The manner of his birth, with the angelic proclamation, 'Peace on earth' (Luke 2:14), and Jesus' pattern of behavior before the authorities in his passion are the bookends of this peaceable Messiah." Swartley, "Peacemaking Pillars of Character Formation," 231.

people should engage in unbridled violence?[43] New Testament scholar Willard M. Swartley explained that peace as a depiction of God's character is only possible since the self-sacrificial peacemaking work of Jesus:

> The commands to make or pursue peace (2 Tim. 2:22; 1 Pet. 3:11; Heb. 12:14; Rom. 14:19) . . . draw upon the symbolic world that describes God's own character and action. Peaceful relationships are desirable and possible because of what God has done for us. God loved us even when we were enemies, and acted in Jesus Christ to make peace with us his enemies (Rom. 5:10). . . . This is the character of the new person described in many and diverse ways in the NT parenesis.[44]

It is in Jesus, then, and through the sacrifice of Jesus, that reflection of God's character has been made generally available to all who seek to be faithful. That character is worked out in the human moral realm—in the social milieu in which we find ourselves. No longer enemies of God to be destroyed by God's chosen few, through the work of Jesus we stand as God's privileged children who have the ability to pattern our character after that of God. This is the reality understood by the early Christians—the reality that drove their character, demonstrated consistently even in the dire social situations in which they found themselves.

It was during the threatening Roman situation faced by some of the early Christians that the apostle John wrote Revelation. In that book Jesus, the Lamb who was sacrificed, also makes war. Violence is associated with the Lamb in a number of places. Initially the Lamb is presented as the *victim* of violence (5:6), but then as the one filled with wrath from whom the kings of the earth flee—as do other high-ranking people, the rich, and all others—begging that the rocks and mountains fall on them so they may escape the Lamb's wrath (6:16). Later the Lamb, identified as Lord of lords and King of kings, engages in battle with ten kings aligned with the beast, defeating them because of who he is (17:12–14). A further description of the Lamb is given in 19:11–16. In this image the Lamb is clearly a warrior who engages in violence against the nations, meting out "the fury of the wrath of God Almighty."

How are we to understand the significance of the wrathful Lamb in light of the peacemaking character of God—a character that is to be pursued and enacted by God's faithful? Swartley's understanding of the

---

43. See, for example, 1 Sam 15:1–3.
44. Swartley, "Peacemaking Pillars of Character Formation," 236.

violent Lamb is insightful in this regard, for the Revelation context of the godlessness of Rome and its persecution of those seeking to be faithful is what yields the proper understanding. He appealed to the writing of Elisabeth Schüssler Fiorenza when he asserted, "What Revelation contributes to an understanding of peace is that when peace is taken away from the earth, the lives of Jesus' followers confess with heart, soul, and strength that God is sovereign . . . Revelation forces a choice between loyalty to the 'Herrschaft Gottes' or the 'Herrschaft Roms' and the only Christian possibility for the Revelator is a decision against the political-religious power of his time."[45]

We glean from this explanation that whereas peace is to be at the heart of the Christian's character—following the character of God—in a social context where the dominant governing entity has rejected God, the faithful are to reject the dominant entity. They are not to abandon peace, but are to abandon the social entity that has rejected the God of peace. This follows the pattern of Jesus' life, and is depicted in the first instance when the Lamb appears—as the peaceful one who was the victim of lethal violence. The believer is to maintain this element of the divine character in spite of the conduct of the evil power that dominates the believer's social context. The result may be what the Lamb experienced—execution—but that prospect is not to deter the faithful one.[46]

This image is precisely the stance we saw the early Christians take: staunchly against Rome without compromise irrespective of the potential consequences—even martyrdom—living a lifestyle of peace following the character of God. The influence of Revelation on their understanding of faithfulness in this life was consistent with what they learned from the written Gospel accounts of the life of Jesus. This example of faithfulness among the early Christians is distinctly distant from the view held by much of Western Christianity today—which I would argue to be a drastic departure from God's standard of faithfulness as found in the Scripture—in which alignment with the powers of secular government (believed to be consecrated by God), endorsement of the use of force, and employment of violence constitute the norm for many Christians

---

45. Swartley, "Peacemaking Pillars of Character Formation," 230–31.

46. See Swartley: "The Lamb is paradigmatic and normative for believers, a model in which one gives one's own life rather than taking another's. The power of the word, cross, and song of praise assures the fall of mighty Babylon, symbol for all deified political power." Swartley, "Peacemaking Pillars of Character Formation," 231.

and (in their minds) form essential elements of upright participation in the moral realm of human life.

Much of what we have seen in this section on character ethics in the New Testament can be capsulized in the notion of emulation of Jesus as the archetype of faithfulness to God. For the early Christians such emulation was the means by which they, as the believing and faithful community, appropriated and inculcated the divine character. This theme will be explored further in part 3, but as an introduction consider Swartley's thought on this subject: "A discipleship and imitation pattern lies at the heart of the NT. *Imitation* and *discipleship*, grounded in *imitatio Christi* and *Dei* (Eph. 5:2), are the means of forming moral character, which in turn shapes moral identity."[47]

CHARACTER ETHICS AND JESUS

The primary character of the Gospel narratives, of course, is Jesus. We have seen that when the early Christians encountered the written Gospels their moral stance within the social milieu in which they found themselves changed dramatically, fortifying their commitment to faithfulness. What was it about Jesus' life and character that caused such a huge change in the lives of the first Christians, and is there any element of their experience that we should recapture as God's faithful people today?

John wrote that love among Christians is completed in this way: "In this world we are like Jesus."[48] Even though Jesus is to be our standard, this does not appear to mean that Christians are simply to copy Jesus' conduct, for the phrase refers to Jesus' being: "as he is." It speaks to Jesus' character, and the need for the faithful to acquire, adopt, and inculcate it in order to be like him. Jesus provides us with a tangible model for character development, but the issue for us is how is it to be done?

A number of scholars—most of whom have been previously referenced—have suggested what it means for the character of Jesus to be paradigmatic for the faithful. Through their statements we may discern five aspects of divine character acquisition that signify the desired character development of the faithful. First, it is through the earthly person of Jesus that we find the paradigmatic divine character. The second person of the Trinity has existed eternally, yet it is only by means of the

---

47. Swartley, "Peacemaking Pillars of Character Formation," 228; italics original.
48. 1 John 4:17.

incarnation that the divine character has been modeled for acquisition by the faithful. Kenneth Kirk, Anglican bishop of Oxford in the early twentieth century, asserted that "the Christian ideal of character, as we have seen, is the person of Christ, as manifested in his earthly life. Nothing short of that suffices as a guide."[49] Being sure to reference the earthly Jesus and God's working through him, rather than citing the eternal divine Son, Hauerwas argued that "to be a Christian is to have one's character determined in accordance with God's action in Jesus. This determination gives one's life an orientation which otherwise it would not have."[50] We see, then, that the earthly, incarnate Jesus is where the character model for the faithful is to be found; the importance of maintaining focus on Jesus' earthly life for the development of the Christian's character cannot be underestimated.

Second, the character of Jesus is found by observing carefully the gospel depictions of his actions, not by seeking to ferret out a list of Jesus' character traits. Gustafson helps us understand this point. After agreeing that "the person of Jesus Christ is the paradigm for the life of the Christian community and of individual members of the community," he suggested that "the Gospels portray the paradigmatic person, not by stipulating a set of virtue-adjectives for his character, but by depicting the sorts of actions and relations that were thought to be characteristic of him," and concluded with "in him there was the embodiment of a way of life, a coherence between his teachings on the one hand, and his person and his actions on the other, that depicts what man is meant to be in his faithfulness and love to God and to others."[51] When reading the gospel accounts of Jesus' life we should not look for a description of Jesus' values, or even the traits of his character. Instead, by observing Jesus' actions we find the necessary outworking of the character of God. This is true irrespective of the literary genre depicting Jesus. Gustafson expanded his contention about Jesus' character being found in his conduct:

> The varieties of literature in the Gospels, the Beatitudes and the commands, the parables, the narrations of the actions of Jesus, line out the manner of life that is worthy of the gospel of Christ, the bearing toward one another that arises out of life in Christ Jesus. . . . there is also a normative or obligatory character to the way of life. Persons whose intentionality is reoriented by

---

49. Kirk, "Cardinal Virtues," 238.
50. Hauerwas, *Character*, 227.
51. Gustafson, *Moral Discernment*, 47.

the gospel ought to have its marks on their manner of life, their bearing toward one another.[52]

The character of Jesus, realized and inferred through observation of his conduct, is to mark Jesus' followers. Emulation of Jesus' actions, however, is insufficient to render faithfulness; rather, the divine character as seen when observing his conduct is what the faithful one is to pursue.

Third, Jesus' community of followers is the context in which individuals adopt and assimilate the character of Jesus. Earlier the subject of character and community was explored. It should come as no surprise, then, to learn that one of Jesus' foci was the formation of a community through which members increasingly would take on the divine character. C. Drew Smith observed that Jesus "is the paradigmatic human being who is bringing into existence a new community of individuals whose character is formed by his example."[53] Specifically concerning the believing community influenced by the Gospel of Mark, for instance, he asserted, "Mark's Jesus again serves as the paradigm of character formation as he claims to give his life for others (10:45). In doing so, he sets forth the norm of character formation in the Markan community."[54] Character indeed is formed within the Christian community, but it is formed through self-sacrifice for others.

Fourth, adoption of the character of Jesus occurs over time, as one increasingly adheres to Jesus. Inculcating Jesus' character is a transformative *process*, not an *event*. Through the process the faithful one's character is in continual change, from something void of the divine to growing conformity to God's character as found in Jesus. Hauerwas expressed this process as follows: "To have one's character formed in Christ is to always have one's life directed toward a fuller realization of that formation. Thus to have Christian character is to really be changed and directed by Christ, but not in a way that Christ becomes a possession in which I can feel secure, but rather it is to be subject to a restlessness that knows no end in this life."[55] It is of note that full adoption of the divine character is not achievable, just as in the theological realm full sanctification does not happen in this life. Further acquisition of the character of God is an ongoing challenge, no matter where the faithful one is in the process

---

52. Gustafson, *Moral Discernment*, 45.
53. Smith, "Become My Followers," 212.
54. Smith, "Become My Followers," 214.
55. Hauerwas, *Character*, 221.

of character transformation. The challenge, however, brings with it new experiences in the moral realm of human existence, and so character formation is anything but static for as long as one lives. Hauerwas captured this reality when he wrote, "Our character may indeed be formed by our adherence to Jesus Christ, but the significance of that must be constantly deepened and enriched through our experience. As our character becomes more and more formed in accordance with what God has done in Christ, such a formation directs us to and opens up aspects and possibilities in our existence that we had not before envisaged."[56]

Fifth, adoption of the character of Jesus will be accompanied by a growing distinction from the dominant character of the individual's social milieu. This should not surprise us, considering what we learned through our investigation of the early Christians. Swartley described the outward manifestation of the divine character as taught by Jesus to his disciples: "The focal images for character formation are taking up the cross, valorizing a child, and living as a servant, in contrast to seeking power, prestige, and position."[57] Adoption of Jesus' character does not come without a cost, however, for a character-driven life lived in contrast to the prevailing values of the social milieu inherently generates the wrath of the threatened milieu. Jesus fully paid the price of living according to God's character, and expects his faithful followers to do the same. "While Jesus does not explicitly state that each follower will incur the wrath of Rome, the political possibility and probability of such as an end is ever more increased when the disciples choose to model their lives after him, that is, when character is formed via the norms of Jesus."[58]

This last aspect should raise within us concern about current Western Christianity, for it generally does not reflect distinction from the surrounding culture, but rather full embracing of it. It comes not as an accommodation for the sake even of expediency, but as what Western Christianity believes to be a divinely ordained social stance of full syncretism without discretion or reflection. These Christians' social stance, devoid of the character of Jesus, drives us to question if they truly are faithful Christians in any sense.

It is highly beneficial to the quest for faithfulness that Jesus be the paradigm. His modeling of the character of God and its proper exemplification in his social milieu serve as the standard by which the believer

---

56. Hauerwas, *Character*, 222.

57. Swartley, "Peacemaking Pillars of Character Formation," 232.

58. Smith, "Become My Followers," 212.

is to build her or his character over a lifetime. Yet commitment alone to emulation of Jesus is insufficient for the faithful one to acquire, internalize, and inculcate the divine character. To overcome that insufficiency the Christian needs to—as Kierkegaard expressed it—become contemporary with Christ.

What does contemporaneousness with Christ entail? According to Kierkegaard, at its root it occurs in a context of suffering: "In the situation of contemporaneousness, to become a Christian (to be transformed into likeness with God) proved to be an even greater torment and misery and pain than the greatest of human torment."[59] If Kierkegaard was correct, then to be contemporary with Christ means to be transformed into God's likeness. Yet what is this but adoption of God's moral essence: the adoption of the divine character? It certainly is not—and cannot be—some sort of physical likeness to God. For Kierkegaard this transformation cannot happen if one focuses on the past, viewing Jesus as a historical figure whose story was recorded in the Gospels. "Only the contemporary is reality for me.... And thus every man[60] can be contemporary only with the age in which he lives—and then with one thing more: with Christ's life on earth; for Christ's life on earth, sacred history, stands for itself alone outside history."[61] Contemporaneity, then, means to live currently in fellowship with the living Jesus whose earthly life is contemporaneous with the faithful believer.[62] What of those who claim to be Jesus' followers, but will not join him in contemporaneity? In Kierkegaard's view contemporaneity was so vital that without it one was not a Christian.[63]

It is through ongoing, continual contemporaneity with the risen and exalted Jesus as depicted in the first chapter of Hebrews that the faithful

---

59. Kierkegaard, *Training in Christianity*, 58.

60. Like other authors we have encountered, Kierkegaard employed exclusively male language to refer to people in general—reflecting the convention of his time in the nineteenth century. The reader will have to try to enjoy the great benefits of Kierkegaard's writing, in spite of the unfortunate choice of male language.

61. Kierkegaard, *Training in Christianity*, 58–59.

62. See Kierkegaard: "What true Christians there are in each generation are contemporary with Christ, have nothing to do with Christians of former generations, but everything to do with the contemporary Christ. His earthly life accompanies the race, and accompanies every generation in particular, as the eternal history; His earthly life possesses the eternal contemporaneousness." Kierkegaard, *Training in Christianity*, 59.

63. See Kierkegaard: "If thou canst not prevail upon thyself to become a Christian in the situation of contemporaneousness with Him, or if He in the situation of contemporaneousness cannot move thee and draw thee to Himself—then thou wilt never become a Christian." Kierkegaard, *Training in Christianity*, 59.

one is enabled to acquire, inculcate, and align his or her character with that of Jesus. Yet how can this occur? Jesus was here among people during his earthly sojourn in the first century, but now no longer is here among us. Rather, he is ascended and glorified with the Father. So how is it that contemporaneity is possible? How does one experience being in the presence of Jesus? This is a question with which many scholars have struggled. Analytic theologian Joshua Cockayne provided a summary of the various major attempts to answer the question, then offered a solution of his own. Cockayne started by observing, "it seems pertinent to ask just what Kierkegaard means by this: How can a person enjoy contemporaneity with an individual who existed more than two thousand years ago? There are some competing interpretations of what Kierkegaard means by 'contemporaneity' in the secondary literature which can help us respond to this question."[64] One approach, he explained, holds that there is a type of "mystical experience" that allows for fellowship or communion with Christ. In this approach one is to practice Jesus' presence, and thereby become increasingly like the spirit of Jesus, aligning oneself to Jesus' life pattern.[65] The shortcoming of this approach, however, is that in the mystical experience and practice of Jesus' life pattern there is no actual contemporaneity with Jesus; it simply is something that is pictured and somehow presumed to be approached through copying Jesus' conduct, but the actual experience of the living Jesus by the faithful is nowhere to be found.

Another approach is a type of "epistemic contemporaneity" in which the actual experience of contemporaneity is not required. Instead, through a particular mindset that negates the historical/temporal element one can align with the historical Jesus, just as did his historical contemporaries.[66] Cockayne correctly pointed out the shortcoming of this approach: for Kierkegaard Jesus is not to be viewed by the faithful one as a figure from the historical past, and "imaginative co-presence will not capture what Kierkegaard has in mind by contemporaneity with Christ."[67]

Cockayne suggested that the proper way to understand Kierkegaard's contemporaneity is to see it in the practice of Communion. He asserted that Kierkegaard espoused the traditional Lutheran view of Communion: consubstantiation. In this view there is "a mysterious and miraculous real presence of the whole person of Christ, body and blood,

---

64. Cockayne, "Imitation and Contemporaneity," 8.
65. See Cockayne, "Imitation and Contemporaneity," 8.
66. See Cockayne, "Imitation and Contemporaneity," 8–9.
67. Cockayne, "Imitation and Contemporaneity," 9.

in, under, and along with, the elements."[68] Whereas Christ can also be elsewhere simultaneously, "the physical nature of Christ is locally present in the Lord's Supper."[69] As support for his assertion Cockayne argued that Kierkegaard took this view throughout his writing. He cited a passage in which Kierkegaard indicated that Jesus is present with the individual just as if he were close to earth and touching the earth, and also is at the altar when the faithful one is seeking him.[70]

Certainly this approach is superior to the previous two. However, it also falls short, for even if it is granted that contemporaneity can be achieved through the practice of Communion—understood as consubstantiation—engaging in Communion is not a continuous, unending practice throughout the individual's overall human experience. From the words of Jesus when instituting Communion, it is to be celebrated *periodically*, but not necessarily *continuously* without interruption.[71] The result—if contemporaneity were to occur only when the individual partook in Communion—would be that contemporaneousness with Christ would occur only during the current Communion event, then not occur again until the next Communion event. This on-again, off-again experience is not what Kierkegaard meant by contemporaneity, particularly since as a percentage of the individual's overall life experience Communion is a very small portion. Kierkegaard had in mind something that the Christian experienced not periodically or occasionally, but continually.

There is another approach which is more direct, allows for continuous, actual relationship between the faithful and Jesus, and aligns better than the others with Kierkegaard's notion of contemporaneity. Just prior to his arrest Jesus was speaking with his disciples about his departure. He promised to ask the Father to send them another advocate, not only to help them but to be with them forever.[72] They would know this Holy Spirit, who Jesus referred to as the Spirit of truth, because "he lives with you and will be in you."[73] He also promised, "I will not leave you as orphans; I will come to you,"[74] and assured the disciples, "you are in me and I am in

---

68. Berkhof, *Systematic Theology*, 652.
69. Berkhof, *Systematic Theology*, 652.
70. See Cockayne, "Imitation and Contemporaneity," 9–10.
71. See 1 Cor 11:25–26.
72. See John 14:16.
73. John 14:17.
74. John 14:18.

you."[75] So that nobody would misunderstand what Jesus was saying about his replacement by the Spirit, he clarified that the Spirit would not in any way be independent of Jesus, but convey only what Jesus directed: "He will not speak on his own; he will speak only what he hears . . . the Spirit will receive from me what he will make known to you."[76] Not only would Jesus be present continually with the faithful in the person of the Spirit, but the very message that the Spirit conveyed to them would come from the ascended Jesus himself. We reiterate the earlier question: How is it possible that the departed, ascended Jesus would be so intimately present with his disciples? The key is to understand that he would be so through the abiding presence and message of the Holy Spirit with Jesus' faithful.

Kierkegaard himself at one point suggested this same answer to the question of Jesus' actual presence—his contemporaneity—with his disciples after his ascension. There is only one place in the Kierkegaard corpus where he dealt with the Holy Spirit in any significant way. It is found in his 1851 book entitled *For Self-Examination*.[77] The impetus for the writing was the second chapter of Acts in which the Spirit descended upon the waiting disciples in a dramatic display of great power. In one section concerning the desperation of hopelessness we find this phrase: "entrust thyself to the Spirit, for with it thou canst talk."[78] Though only part of a sentence, it indicates clearly that for Kierkegaard communion with the divine is achieved through conversation with the Holy Spirit. This is the means by which contemporaneity takes place: the historical Jesus of the Gospel accounts sent another member of the one, triune godhead upon his departure from the earth. That Spirit of Jesus—the Holy Spirit—remains present with believers in order for believers to commune with the living Jesus. Earlier in the same section—entitled "It is the Spirit that Giveth Life"—Kierkegaard expanded on the notion of the Spirit's presence with the faithful. In the context of Rom 6:8[79] he reasoned, "With the coming of the life-giving Spirit it is as with the coming of the

---

75. John 14:20.

76. John 16:13, 15.

77. It would be natural to ask why the lack of specificity concerning the means by which contemporaneity could occur would be addressed by Kierkegaard in a different book. It is helpful to realize that both *Training in Christianity* and *For Self-Examination* were, according to Kierkegaard scholar and translator Walter Lowrie, published on the same date in 1851 and functioned as companion volumes. See the preface to *For Self-Examination and Judge for Yourselves! and Three Discourses 1851*, v.

78. Kierkegaard, *Self-Examination*, 102.

79. Rom 6:8: "Now if we died with Christ, we believe that we will also live with him."

'Comforter' which Christ promises the disciples. When comes the Comforter? He comes when all the dreadful things which Christ predicted of His own life have come first, and the like horrors which He predicted concerning the lives of the disciples—then comes the Comforter."[80] The clear point he made is that the Spirit, in the form of—and doing the work of—the Comforter, is present with the faithful in the most dire of times—as when the early Christians were living under the persecution of Rome and facing martyrdom. Being the Comforter, though, is only one function of the Spirit, among others, when present with people. The more fundamental learning from this passage is that the faithful can be in the presence of God by means of the Holy Spirit which Jesus sent—to be present with believers—after he left them via the ascension.

This fundamental learning was reiterated by Kierkegaard, perhaps to add emphasis to his assertion that the living Spirit truly is present with the faithful as an actual, super-reality outside of the physical realm. Speaking of the Spirit is not a poetic expression, or a fantasy, or a dream, or some other product of the imagination, but rather the actual living Jesus among his people. Kierkegaard wrote of the Spirit, "But it comes, it does not disappoint by failure to appear. Did it not come to the Apostles, did it disappoint them? Did it not come later to the true believers, did it disappoint them by failing to make an appearance? No, it comes, and it brings the gifts of the Spirit: life and spirit."[81] It is those gifts of life and spirit that are the means by which an individual connects with, and is contemporaneous with, the ascended and glorified divine Jesus, including his divine character.

There is one other place in Kierkegaard's treatment of the Holy Spirit where he described the Spirit's involvement with people. He chose to do so by telling the story of a wealthy man who bought a perfect pair of horses.[82] The man drove the horses himself, but after two years they were unrecognizable due to their breakdown, lack of stamina, and poor health. At that point the man called in the king's coachman to take charge of the horses. Within a month they had been restored to their prior glory. The conclusion was that the owner, not knowing how to be a coachman, caused the ruination of the horses, while the king's coachman, knowing

---

80. Kierkegaard, *Self-Examination*, 100.
81. Kierkegaard, *Self-Examination*, 100.
82. See Kierkegaard, *Self-Examination*, 104. In the ensuing pages Kierkegaard developed his understanding of the work of the Holy Spirit by presentation of the story of the horses.

exactly how to drive horses for their greatest benefit, caused the horses to thrive.

Kierkegaard used this story as an analogy of the working of the Holy Spirit in the lives of people. We have potential, but devoid of a vital linkage to the authoritative and knowledgeable One who knows how best to cause our thriving we have only ourselves to drive our lives, developing our character within the limits of our humanity to our ruination. For Kierkegaard it was not always so. "Once there was a time when it pleased the Deity (if I may venture to say so) to be Himself the coachman; and He drove the horses in accordance with the coachman's understanding of what it is to drive. Oh, what was a man not capable of at that time!"[83] He then referenced the apostles, convinced that their Lord and Master Jesus was God yet devoid of him after his ascension, waiting for the Spirit's arrival. Only subsequently—after the Spirit's arrival and alighting on them—were they well-driven to spread Christianity throughout a hostile Roman Empire.

This, for Kierkegaard, is what it meant to be contemporaneous with Jesus. The Holy Spirit sent by Jesus to be with the faithful, guiding them in the way of Jesus, is how the early Christians were formed to be like Jesus—not only in conduct, but more importantly in character.

---

83. Kierkegaard, *Self-Examination*, 105.

10

Character and the Image of God

Throughout part 2 the focus has been on character as the foundational expression of faithfulness, with particular emphasis on the relationship between the character of the faithful believer and that of God. We have learned that God's character forms the pattern for the one who seeks to be faithful, and that the heart of faithfulness is continuous character enhancement formed after God's character itself. The extent to which believers are experientially like God in character is the extent to which they are faithful. They understand that having been commanded to be holy as God is holy, pursuing moral Godlikeness is the fundamental notion of what it means to be faithful.

This reality places the responsibility for character development—as the path to increasing faithfulness—squarely on the individual, for he or she plays a major role in forming character. Yet aligning one's character with that of God is more complex than exercising simple human commitment and effort alone, for it entails the active work of the Holy Spirit to guide formation of the faithful individual's character after the divine pattern. Nevertheless, character development certainly requires the active, intentional involvement of the individual. Character development, however—and thus faithfulness—is not automatic once one becomes a follower of Jesus. Rather, the *directed* volition of the moral agent—not the moral intentions to which one leans naturally—is essential to becoming more Godlike in character. Such directed volition forms one's malleable character in the direction constrained and guided by one's predetermined beliefs.

A primary challenge faced by the one seeking to be faithful is to understand accurately the nature of God's character. We learned that fundamentally both God's character and essence are love, and that God's expectation of his faithful followers is that they emulate his love character in their relationships with their fellow human beings. Such emulation involves enacting the divine attributes that depict—in tangible form—God's love character. Those attributes have been conveyed to people by God's intentional self-disclosure, quintessentially seen in the earthly life of Jesus as well as his glorified and exalted life subsequent to the ascension. The tangible model for human character development however—one that most clearly reveals the divine character as it can be appropriated by the individual seeking to be faithful—is the life of the incarnate second person of the Trinity as captured in the four Gospels found in the Bible.

This may be helpful as far as it goes, but for the one who aspires to realize *de facto* the character of God in her or his own character, how is the necessary appropriation to be done? We know that such character appropriation occurs over time as a transformative process rather than in a momentary event, and that it involves some sort of habitual imitation or reflection of Jesus' character in some way. We also know that the Holy Spirit is continually with the faithful believer as a means to commune with the living Jesus. In addition, the believing community in which the individual participates has a role to play in character development through proclamation of the biblical narratives that color the community's nature. Such narratives function both as rails that align the individual along the path of character formation and as inspiration for the individual along the transformative way.

The key to understanding how to "put on the new self, created to be like God"[1]—as the apostle Paul put it in his letter to the Ephesian Christians—is to realize that inherent in the creation of human beings was conveyance of the divine image, and that it is the image of God that is to be nurtured and grown as the means to forming one's character after the character of God. Paul captured this concept by repeating to the Colossian Christians what he had pressed upon the faithful at Ephesus: "put on the new self, which is being renewed in knowledge in the *image*

---

1. Eph 4:24.

of its Creator."[2] In this regard, recall the thought of Kierkegaard, who understood character to be something engraved on the individual; the challenge we face is both to identify the engraver and to determine how the engraving takes place. Understanding the image of God is the starting point to do so.

THE PROBLEM OF THE IMAGE OF GOD

The term "image of God," or the oft-used Latin form, "*imago Dei*," is a commonly used one in theological circles. Its source is verse 26 of the first chapter of Genesis, which in part reads, "Then God said, 'Let us make mankind in our image, in our likeness.'" The next verse affirms that God indeed followed through: "So God created mankind in his own image, in the image of God he created them; male and female he created them." Given these verses, the fact that humans—both male and female—were created in God's image is rarely debated. However, the agreement ceases at that point. Beyond the *fact* of creation in the *imago Dei*, there is little concordance regarding the *meaning* of the fact.

In developing views regarding the meaning of the image of God, theologians have few specific scripture references to consult. "The Bible contains only five texts that directly connect humankind to the image of God. Although the idea is not absent from the New Testament, being mentioned in 1 Cor. 11:7 and James 3:9, the exegetically significant references are in the Old Testament, more particularly in the early chapters of Genesis (Gen. 1:26–27; Gen. 5:1–3; Gen. 9:5–6)."[3] Anthony Hoekema, twentieth-century systematic theology professor, added, "One could also think of Psalm 8 as describing what man's creation in God's image means, but the phrase 'image of God' is not found there."[4] He went on to assert, "Clearly, according to the Scriptures man[5] was created in the image of God. It is also clear that, in distinction from other creatures, only man

---

2. Col 3:10; italics added.

3. Grenz, *Social God*, 184. There are, however, other verses that contribute to our understanding of the image of God, including Rom 8:29, 1 Cor 15:49, 2 Cor 3:18, 2 Cor 4:4, Eph 4:24, Col 1:15, Col 3:9–10, and Heb 1:3a.

4. Hoekema, *Created in God's Image*, 11.

5. Hoekema explained, "I use the word *man* here and frequently in what follows as meaning 'human being.'" Hoekema, *Created in God's Image*, 1, note 1. Although he went on to acknowledge that "it is a pity that the English language has no word corresponding to the German word *Mensch*, which means human being as such, regardless of gender," he nevertheless persisted in using this outdated and unfortunate convention.

has been made in God's image. What is not so clear, however, is the answer to the question 'In what does the image of God consist?'"[6]

That the issue still has not been resolved is evidenced by the fact that in 2022 systematic theologian Lucy Peppiatt reiterated the difficulty: "The Scriptures do not tell us precisely the nature of this connection between God and humanity . . . so this raises a multitude of questions."[7] Is it no wonder, then, that Grenz concluded, "With the possible exception of human sin, perhaps the single most debated topic of Christian anthropology is the meaning of the designation 'image of God,'"[8] and later added, "historians do not even agree as to how many distinctive understandings of the divine image have come to be proposed in the Christian tradition."[9] He then wisely cautioned, "The lack of unanimity among Old Testament scholars regarding the meaning of the biblical concept of the *imago Dei* as set forth in Gen. 1:26–28 suggests that the divine image ought not be viewed from too narrow a perspective."[10]

THE OLD TESTAMENT ON THE IMAGE OF GOD

Although the meaning and nature of the image of God may not be clearly depicted in the Bible, it behooves us nevertheless to review the few passages that form the basis for the range of notions about the *imago Dei*. If we focus the review only on those passages that give content about the image itself, we are limited to just four. The first three appear in Genesis, and the fourth in Ps 8.

The most fundamental biblical passage on the image of God is found in Gen 1:26–28. It indicates that after completing the rest of creation, the Creator as the pluralistic God announced that the next part of the divine creation process would be to make humankind in God's image and likeness. There is a stated purpose for creating human beings in this way: so that they may exercise dominion over the rest of the earthly creatures. Humankind as both male and female was then created in God's image. Subsequently God commissioned them to be fruitful and fill the earth, as well as to exercise the dominion over the other creatures just mentioned.

---

6. Hoekema, *Created in God's Image*, 33.
7. Peppiatt, *Imago Dei*, 3.
8. Grenz, *Theology*, 168.
9. Grenz, *Social God*, 141–42.
10. Grenz, *Social God*, 200.

There are several items of note about this passage. First, it is only human beings, both male and female, that were created in God's image. The *imago Dei* is something specific and unique to people, not shared with any other part of the created order. Second, the creation occurred in both God's image and God's likeness. The difference between the two has been argued for centuries, but the preponderance of thought regards the two as one and the same, emphasizing a common reality.[11] Third, the declaration "Let us make mankind in our image" references a divine plurality, rather than various divine attributes.[12] Since it is the Creator who is speaking, perhaps it references interaction between the Father and the Son as Creator (see Heb 1:1–2). Fourth, the commission to be fruitful and to exercise dominion occurs after creation of male and female in the image of God, not simultaneous with it. The commission, then, is not part of the image, for the completed creation of the people occurred prior to the commission.

The next passage is Gen 5:1–3. Sequentially it occurs after the fall and the murder of Abel by Cain. The broader passage is concerned with the generations subsequent to Adam. The first two verses, however, reiterate some of what was stated in the Gen 1 passage, namely that humankind—both male and female—was created by God in the divine likeness. They go on to add that God blessed the people, and gave them the name "humankind."[13] In the third and subsequent verses there is a sudden switch in subject matter, with a focus on events that occurred 130 years after the creation referenced in the first two verses and beyond. Verse 3

---

11. See, for example, Keil and Delitzsch: "On the words, '*in our image, after our likeness*' modern commentators have correctly observed, that there is no foundation for the distinction drawn by the Greek, and after them by many of the Latin Fathers, between . . . (*imago*) and . . . (*similitudo*), the former of which they supposed to represent the physical aspect of the likeness to God, the later the ethical; but that, on the contrary, the older Lutheran theologians were correct in stating that the two words are synonymous, and are merely combined to add intensity to the thought." Keil and Delitzsch, *Commentary*, 1:63. See also Eastvold: "In Gen 1:26a . . . the two phrases function synonymously . . . The translation of one term thus determines the interpretation of the other." Eastvold, "Image in the Old Testament," 243.

12. Keil and Delitzsch, *Commentary*, 1:62. See also, "The potencies concentrated in the absolute Divine Being are something more than powers and attributes of God; that they are *hypostases*, which in the further course of the revelation of God in His kingdom appears with more and more distinctness as persons of the Divine Being." Keil and Delitzsch, *Commentary*, 1:62–63.

13. The Hebrew word is *adam*. It is translated "humankind" in RSV (2001), "mankind" in NIV (2011), and "human beings" in Today's New International Version (2006).

indicates that after the 130 years Adam had a third son "in his own likeness, in his own image"—one who was named Seth.

Several things can be observed from this passage. First, it occurs subsequent to the fall, so whatever it indicates regarding the image of God is in the context of both humanity and much of the rest of creation cursed due to the sin of Adam and Eve.[14] It also occurs subsequent to the banishment from the Garden of Eden, so does not take place in an environment of moral innocence but rather the sin-tainted moral milieu which continues to today.[15] Second, there is an equality between male and female in that both are said to have been created in the same moral fashion, in the likeness of God and sharing the same name: "mankind." Third, when Adam's son Seth appears, it is said that he was in Adam's likeness and image. Since Adam's likeness and image was that of God, so was Seth's.[16] By strong implication the rest of post-fall humankind has been created in the same fashion, in the *imago Dei*; however, the possible effects of sin on the divine image are not indicated in the passage.

The final Genesis passage is 9:5–6. It occurs immediately after the great flood and is part of the Noahic or Universal[17] covenant. Verse 5 indicates that God will require an accounting when a human life is taken, be it by another human being or by an animal. In verse 6 God declares that the one who sheds the blood of another person will have their blood shed at the hands of other people. The reason given for this one-for-one human life sacrifice is that God made humankind in the image of God.

We observe in this passage the high value God placed on human life, and that ironically occurring immediately subsequent to God's destruction of all living creatures on earth with the exception of Noah and the other inhabitants of the ark.[18] Another observation, given the context of the passage, is that the universalism of God's pronouncement indicates that all people are created in the *imago Dei*, irrespective of time, location, ethnicity, or any other factor. In particular, it includes all those born

---

14. See Gen 3:14–19.

15. See Gen 3:23.

16. See Leitch, "The likeness of man to God and the image of Adam in Seth are brought together in the same treatment (5:1–3)." Leitch, "Image of God," 256. See also Keil and Delitzsch, "As Adam was created in the image of God, so did he beget '*in his own likeness, after his image*;' that is to say, he transmitted the image of God in which he was created." Keil and Delitzsch, *Commentary*, 1:125.

17. See Gen 9:8–9, in which God declared that the covenant was being established with "every living creature on earth."

18. See Gen 7:21–23.

subsequent to both the fall and the flood. Third, the fact that creation of humankind was in the image of God endows people with a level of dignity and value that is incalculable—beyond that of life itself.

The last Old Testament passage dealing with the image of God is Ps 8, even though the term does not occur in the text. The key verses are 5 and 6, the first of which indicates that humankind has been made a little lower than God and has been crowned with glory and honor. Verse 6 adds that humankind has been given the assignment to rule over the rest of God's creation, reflecting the thought of Gen 1:26 and 28b.

The early verses of Ps 8 set the stage for understanding verses 5 and 6, for they establish the wide gap between God's glory and majesty and the present state of humanity: privileged that God would even be mindful of people. Nineteenth-century German theologian Franz Delitzsch characterized the state of humankind in verse 4: "It describes man from the side of his impotence, frailty and mortality . . . this weak and dependent being is, nevertheless, not forgotten by God."[19] Yet, despite the incomprehensible gap between God and the people he created, humankind has been granted a position just slightly lower than God; in addition glory and honor—in some way patterned after that of God—have also been granted to them. Delitzsch summarized the point of Ps 8 when he stated, "The primary thought of the Psalm is this, that the God, whose glory the heavens reflect, has also glorified Himself in the earth and in man."[20] Very recently theology and culture professor Ron Ruthruff—in writing on Ps 8—reminded us of the thought of Karl Barth: "Karl Barth said we are like God not in substance but relationally. This means we bear the image of God in communities of shalom, justice, and love. We bear the image of God caring for the more-than-human world in the same way the Divine has cared for humankind."[21]

There are other biblical passages that reference or suggest the image of God, but the four just reviewed are generally considered the ones on which an understanding of the *imago Dei* should be formed. Others will be mentioned later in the chapter when dealing with either the life of Jesus or believers' growth in faithfulness. Next, let us review the major views regarding the nature of the image of God, all predicated upon the four passages just considered.

19. Keil and Delitzsch, *Commentary*, 5:153.
20. Keil and Delitzsch, *Commentary*, 5:149–50.
21. Ruthruff, "Creation in Context (Psalm 8)," 2.

NOTIONS OF THE IMAGE OF GOD

Notwithstanding the enduring ambiguity concerning the image of God, a number of general notions about its meaning have been proposed, all of which claim fidelity to the relevant Old Testament material. There are many permutations of the basic ones, which we will not explore; the basic ideas themselves will serve to help us understand the general range of thought throughout history concerning the *imago Dei*. It should be noted that the notions are not mutually exclusive, and that the lines separating one notion from another can be fuzzy. Overlap among them is possible. However, upon knowing the various basic notions we may ask how they—if any of them—help us understand how to appropriate the character of God.

Image as Structure

Of the various views about what characterizes the image of God, the most common, and the one that has endured the longest, is the notion that when human beings were created they were endowed with traits that mimic those of God. It is known as the structural or substantialist view since it affirms that something in the human structure or substance is somehow Godlike. This view dominated Christian thought until at least the time of the Reformers,[22] and remains the common understanding among many Western Christians today.

In this view there is no agreement on what the Godlike traits actually are, but they could include moral virtues, essential attributes, capabilities, or characteristics inherent in the nature of humanity.[23] The most common assertion is that humans are created in the image of God in that they are rational, including being both willful and free. Grenz explained, "Since the patristic era, the Christian concept of reason as comprising the divine image has routinely been linked to the faculty of will or volition. In fact,

---

22. See Peppiatt: "For many centuries, the substantialist account of the *imago Dei* dominated the church's teaching, with theologians largely defining the image in terms of an attribute that human beings possessed that was believed to mirror an attribute of God." Peppiatt, *Imago Dei*, 10.

23. See that A. H. Leitch asserted the image of God meant "likeness in the inner man as it is embodied in a physical manifestation—powers of thought, of communication, of transcendence, creativity, a sense of humor (which is a kind of transcendence), powers of abstraction, and what are generally put together in personality, i.e., self-consciousness, and self-determination." Leitch, "Image of God," 256–57.

most early Christian theologians did not bifurcate reason and will but viewed them as two aspects of the single rationality with which God had endowed humans."[24] Peppiatt added that the image of God in humans so understood includes "intelligence and will; their rationality, freedom from necessity, and capacity for self-determination."[25]

Irrespective of what specifically constitutes the divine attributes that humans share with God, the structural understanding of the *imago Dei* maintains that there is something specific within the substance of human beings—unique in all of creation—that mimics or mirrors God in some way. That something distinguishes people from other created beings in that they are Godlike in a way shared by no others.

If growth in faithfulness is equated with increasing formation of one's character in the likeness of God's, then according to the structural view of the *imago Dei* the faithful follower would increasingly reflect God's definable and communicable attributes, particularly the moral ones.

Image as Function

Another notion of the image of God maintains that it primarily designates a *function* that human beings are to play. In being like God they have been commissioned to represent God while remaining under divine authority.[26] Grounding this understanding of the *imago Dei* in creation, theologian Ryan Peterson explained, "every human person's identity is determined by the reality described in Genesis 1:26–28: a human knows who she is and how she is oriented within creation when she recognizes that she is made in God's image. . . . everyone's 'fundamental orientation' is established in the fact that they are made by God to represent God in the world."[27]

Peppiatt used the representational notion of the image of God to argue that the functional view is not just different from the structural one, but that it is superior. In the context of seeing humanity as God's coworkers for good on the earth—including the establishment of peace—she stressed that "once it is established that the imago Dei in humanity lies in the calling to represent God among God's creatures, the theology

---

24. Grenz, *Social God*, 144.
25. Peppiatt, *Imago Dei*, 10.
26. See Peppiatt: "Humanity has a God-given role in creation that carries with it both an authority and a responsibility to mediate the rule, reign, and presence of God on the earth while under God's rule themselves." Peppiatt, *Imago Dei*, 27.
27. Peterson, *Imago Dei*, 3.

of the imago Dei may be utilized to argue or demonstrate that the calling upon human beings is not simply to *be* God's image on the earth, but to enact an ethical and missional imperative, as God's image-*bearers*—to carry the presence of God to the world."[28]

In what specific way, we may ask, are people to represent God and to bear the divine image? Specifically, what are humans to do in fulfillment of the commission to represent God? The most prevalent idea is to see human representation of God as exercising dominion over the rest of creation. Hoekema endorsed this view as at least part of what the *imago Dei* means, appealing to the first chapter of Genesis for substantiation: "from Genesis 1:26 we may infer that dominion over the animals and over all the earth is one aspect of the image of God. In exercising this dominion man is like God, since God has supreme and ultimate dominion over the earth."[29] Yet dominion for dominion's sake—and God desiring a partner to manage his creation—is too simplistic an understanding of the purpose of humans bearing the divine image. It is erroneous to think that being in God's image connotes license for humans to be domineering, as is asserted by some. Instead, the purpose God had for creating people in his image is so that they might ultimately reflect God himself. Grenz expressed this purpose well when explaining the basis for the functional view of the *imago Dei*: "There is but one God, and the entire world is the creation of that God. The Creator has given this creation to humankind to manage. But our management has as its goal that we show to creation what God is like. Consequently, we do not manage creation for our own purposes, but for the sake of that higher goal, namely, in order that we might serve as the mirror of the divine character."[30]

Interestingly Grenz linked the image of God to the motivation for our quest to form our character after God's: so that by doing so faithfully we might fulfill our ultimate purpose in creation, namely, reflecting the moral character of God. The image of God, then—not only as a fact of our creation as humans, but as a reality we are to cultivate as typifying our daily experience—is the means by which we live faithful lives that convey to others the goodness of God.

According to the functional view of the image of God, faithfulness entails acting within the rest of creation as God's character demands, not

---

28. Peppiatt, *Imago Dei*, 29; italics original.
29. Hoekema, *Created in God's Image*, 14.
30. Grenz, *Theology*, 177–78.

for the purpose of controlling creation but as the means to reflect to creation the divine character.

Image as Relationship

A third view of the *imago Dei*—one promulgated by the Reformers—is that it consists not in something inherent in the essence of the human being, or a function for which people were created, but rather in the relationship between humans as the creation and God as the Creator. This view is based upon the nature of the Godhead itself: three persons who exist in relationship. The image of God is the mimicking of that relational reality of God.[31] Theologian Richard Lints explained, "The *imago Dei* is fundamentally a relational term but one with a peculiar relationship in view. It draws attention to the way in which the image reflects the original as its primary relation. The image is conceptually like a shadow, ontologically dependent upon the object it reflects. It is the imaging relationship rather than the image itself that is the primary vantage point throughout Scripture."[32]

Why was it that the Reformers sensed the need[33] to formulate a relational view of the *imago Dei*? It has to do ultimately with the work of Christ to address the result of the fall after Adam and Eve sinned. Grenz explained that the relational view "does not perceive the image of God primarily as a formal structure of the human essential nature, but as a standing before God. The divine image is essentially a special relation with the Creator which Adam lost, but Christ restores."[34] It is the salvific work of Christ, central to the theology of the Reformers, that drove their understanding of what humans are: people who were in ideal relationship with God prior to the fall, now with the hope of relational restoration only through Christ's self-sacrifice on their behalf.

---

31. See for example, Peppiatt: "This social view . . . claims that the oneness of God consists primarily of the three persons in relation rather than in their shared essence. This view of the Trinity is then mapped on to human relations, which are deemed to reflect something of the essence of existence both in God himself and in human being." Peppiatt, *Imago Dei*, 62.

32. Lints, *Identity and Idolatry*, 153.

33. See Grenz: "The Reformers were compelled to replace the structural understanding of the image of God that had grown to dominance over the first fifteen centuries of Christian theology. In its stead, they offered a relational understanding." Grenz, *Theology*, 171.

34. Grenz, *Theology*, 171.

Picking up on this idea of one's worthiness—however attained, but in the Christian context attained only via the work of Christ—Peppiatt focused on the heart of the image of God as relational: "The image of God is realized or fulfilled through participating in a reconciled relationship with God and possibly also with one another."[35] That notion of "one another," as well as the relational nature of the triune God, strongly suggests a communal element of the *imago Dei*. Formation of our character by enhancing in our daily experience—or "realizing," as Peppiatt expressed it—the image of God with which we were endowed *de jure* via creation is accomplished not in individual isolation, but within the faithful community of God. Such is a reflection of the community within the Godhead itself.[36] Grenz captured this essential nature of the community for realization of the image of God in one's life when he concluded:

> Because God is a social reality, it is only in relationship—in community—that we are able to reflect the divine nature. Hence, we can only exemplify the divine image within the context of community, specifically, the community of the people who together acknowledge the lordship of Jesus the Christ. For this reason, we are dependent on the community of Christ in the task of reflecting the image of God. . . .
>
> In so far as we take part in the life of the community of Christ's followers, we are the image of God.[37]

Earlier in part 2 the necessity of developing character, and thus faithfulness, within the context of the Christian community was emphasized. It is the community that forms the social milieu that incubates character, and it is the community's fundamental narratives—in the case of the Christian community, the narratives of the earthly life of Jesus as found in the Gospels and the post-ascension life of Jesus as found in New Testament letters such as the Epistle to the Hebrews—that both direct character development and provide its content. Formation of the image of God *de facto* in the life of the one aspiring to faithfulness is the tangible expression of character development after the character of God. Thus

---

35. Peppiatt, *Imago Dei*, 47.

36. See, for example, Grenz, in which he argued that "ultimately the image of God should focus on community. As the doctrine of the Trinity asserts, throughout all eternity God is community, namely, the fellowship of Father, Son, and Holy Spirit who comprise the triune God. The creation of humankind in the divine image, therefore, can mean nothing less than that humans express the relational dynamic of the God whose representation we are called to be." Grenz, *Theology*, 179.

37. Grenz, *Theology*, 501.

character and the *imago Dei* are parallel, the former consisting of the communicable part of God's essence fully realized within a human being, and the latter being the actualization of that essence in that person's daily life lived in the moral sphere of the Christian community.

Image as Identity

A more recent view of the image of God holds that it has to do with human identity, a term that focuses on the uniqueness of human beings in contrast to the rest of creation.[38] The view is inherently ontological, concentrating on who or what people are in distinction from the rest of the created order. Lints held that the image of God understood as identity also included notions of human meaning: "Affirming that the language of *imago Dei* is a claim about human identity is to say that the *imago Dei* is part of the wider theological framework in which human meaning is embedded."[39]

If the nature of who human beings are—their identity—is determined by the fact of their creation in the divine image, then the *imago Dei* is not something that they merely *bear*, nor is it an *element* of who they are. Rather, it is the *essence* of who they are in their totality. Lints held that in addition to distinguishing humankind from the rest of the created order, the image of God appropriately embraced and exhibited by people demonstrates the identity of God as distinct from that of idols (or anything not God). He wrote, "The notion of a light shining or reflecting the identity of God into and against the idols is the function of the *imago Dei* rightly considered. The identity of God illuminates the identity of the *imago Dei*."[40] If such is the case, then the image of God as found in humankind is their identity, which is somehow *linked* to God; it is not something with which God imbued people as unique creatures clearly distanced from the divine, but rather it is the means by which God keeps people close to himself as no other creatures are. In this reality is found both human meaning and the nature of human dependence upon God.[41]

---

38. See Peterson, *Imago Dei*, 3.
39. Lints, *Identity and Idolatry*, 23.
40. Lints, *Identity and Idolatry*, 42.
41. See Lints: "'Image' or 'likeness' language argues for a dependence upon an original. Whatever else may be said of an image, it must be clear that the image depends upon whatever it is an image of for its meaning. . . . Humans may possess many diverse qualities, but the emphasis of Genesis 1 is that whatever else may be true of them, they

The *imago Dei* understood as the identity of both individual humans and humankind strongly suggests that growth in faithfulness means increasing Godlikeness at the core of one's self-understanding.

A reality we must not ignore in our pursuit of faithfulness is the fact that the fall somehow affected the image of God in people. Whether the change was in the essence of the image *de jure* or entailed a *de facto* change expressed in everyday human moral experience—or both—is a matter we will investigate next.

THE IMAGE OF GOD AFTER THE FALL

Irrespective of which view or combination of views of the *imago Dei* is accurate, if humans subsequent to the fall experienced the image just as it was before the fall, their life in the moral realm pursuing the character of God would be considerably different from what it actually is. The pursuit would not be nearly the struggle that it is, and the gap between human reality and the goal of faithfully exhibiting the character of God would not be as broad as we experience it to be. Since this is the case, it behooves us to learn how the fall affected the pristine image of God in people as originally created. Knowing that, we may be better positioned to understand the individual's moral and ontological starting point when seeking to be faithful to God.

The first question we face is whether the image of God survived at all subsequent to the fall. We saw references in both Gen 5 and Gen 9 to humans in the image of God after Adam and Eve's first sin, which would appear to indicate that the image carried on from generation to generation. Martin Luther, however, believed that the image was completely lost, and a young John Calvin believed the same but later softened his position.[42] Yet, he held that the entire image was negatively affected by the fall, and that in the extreme.

---

fundamentally image Elohim, their Creator. . . . The *imago Dei* does not appear as a place marker for an otherwise long list of human traits and qualities. . . . The *imago Dei* is the reminder that humans image God. It also suggests this is an important and probably the most important, dimension of human existence, which the author of Genesis 1 desired to communicate." Lints, *Identity and Idolatry*, 59–60.

42. See Van Vliet, who wrote, "Calvin's position in 1559 is more nuanced than it was in 1536. He still teaches total depravity. And yet, in some way something of that original image of God lingers after the fall. It is 'almost'—not utterly—blotted out." Van Vliet, "Calvin's Teaching on the Image of God," para. 6. See also Brandon, "John Calvin on the Image of God."

More recent views of the effect of the fall outline a wide range of consequences. Among them are broken fellowship with God, a guilty conscience, shame, the corruption of human nature, expulsion from the pristine environment of the Garden of Eden, and overall cursing of the creation.[43] In addition, both physical and spiritual death resulted from the fall. Also, three other consequences were depravity, or moral corruption and the inability to rectify that situation; guilt, or accountability before God for violation of God's moral law; and penalty, or the resultant loss inflicted by a just God as vindication for such violation.[44]

A number of the consequences can be viewed as negatively affecting specifically the image of God, particularly the morally laden ones such as broken fellowship between humankind and God, a sense of guilt and shame, loss of harmony with the rest of creation, and corruption of the human self and moral sense. Grenz pointed out the general effect of the fall on the *imago Dei*: "In that it destroyed the primordial experience of community, the sin of Adam and Eve marked the immediate marring of the divine image."[45] He went on to describe the longer-term effects of sin on humanity: "Persons placed in creation to reflect the character of God no longer show forth the image of the Creator."[46] Not to be missed is the essential linkage Grenz drew between God's character and the image of God; they are, in fact, integral to one another and are two facets of the same jewel.

It is important to point out that even though sin severely affected the image of God in humans, it nevertheless was not lost; rather, the image of God remains the key understanding of what it means to be human as distinct from the rest of creation, and gives humankind its core identity. In their basic essence people are the *imago Dei*. This is the image of God *de jure*, even though the individual still bears all of the effects of the fall.[47] Hoekema pointed out the biblical basis for affirming that the *imago Dei* has not been destroyed, and still exists irrespective of the level to which people have fallen into sin. Regarding Jas 3:9 he wrote, "One passage clearly teaches that fallen man still bears the image of God and

---

43. See Thiessen, *Systematic Theology*, 255–72.
44. See Strong, *Systematic Theology*, 590–93 and 637–64.
45. Grenz, *Theology*, 192.
46. Grenz, *Theology*, 207.
47. See Grenz: "The divine image, although marred, remains present to each person.... The residue of the divine image within us is a dimension of general revelation." Grenz, *Theology*, 137.

is, therefore, a New Testament echo of the Old Testament material... In James 3:9 we read: 'With the tongue we praise our Lord and Father, and with it we curse men, who have been made in God's likeness.'"[48] His conclusion was that "what the passage does say with the utmost clarity is that, whatever the Fall has done to the image of God in man, it has not totally obliterated that image."[49]

Given that humans still are the image of God despite the effects of sin, how is one whom God created to reflect God's character through pristine demonstration of the *imago Dei*—but no longer does so—to become faithful to God's original intent? The need for renewal of the image of God is foundational to the quest for faithfulness. Yet renewal entails a process by which one moves from the current state to the ideal one—or at least makes very significant progress during the process. The ideal to which the faithful aspire needs to be known in order to discern the path along which the process should progress. Gaining that knowledge is our next task.

JESUS AS THE IMAGE OF GOD

God's character and essence are love, and emulation of such is what God expects of the faithful. Yet how is the divine character to be known? If the image of God fundamentally is the reflection of God's character and essence—the moral element of the divine being as somehow imbued in people by virtue of creation—then what does that image look like in its ideal form? How, in short, can we *view* the image of God?

There are a few New Testament passages that yield at least a hint of an answer. Just prior to his arrest, while Jesus was speaking words of comfort to his disciples, Philip—apparently speaking for the group—said to Jesus, "Lord show us the Father and that will be enough for us."[50] Jesus replied, "Don't you know me, Philip, even after I have been with you such a long time? Anyone who has seen me has seen the Father. How can you say, 'Show us the Father'?"[51] Jesus was explaining to Philip that in seeing Jesus Philip was seeing the *imago Dei*. Among other things, Jesus is the image of God *on display*, in visible form. As such, the character of God is

---

48. Hoekema, *Created in God's Image*, 19.
49. Hoekema, *Created in God's Image*, 20.
50. John 14:8.
51. John 14:9.

made available for observation via the life of Jesus. Recall the earlier discussion on image as relationship and image as identity; in Jesus' response to Philip he is conveying both of these views of the *imago Dei*. In the earthly life of Jesus the nature of Jesus' relationship with the Father was on display, as was the divine essence.

Second Corinthians 4:4 and Col 1:15 use identical language to state that Christ or the Son, respectively, "is the image of God." The Colossians verse then adds "the invisible." The word for "image" is *eikón*, a word that—in the respective contexts of the verses—places all the emphasis on Jesus' equality with God.[52] The adjective "invisible" adds a curious bit of meaning, in that we naturally think of an image as something visible to the eye. However, the meaning of *eikón* is not confined to the visible. Rather:

> The peculiarity of the expression is related to that of the ancient concept, which does not limit image to a functional representation present to human sense but also thinks of it in terms of an emanation, of a revelation of the being with a substantial participation (μετοχή) in the object. Image is not to be understood as a magnitude which is alien to the reality and present only in the consciousness. It has a share in the reality. Indeed, it is the reality.[53]

The intent of *eikón*, then is not a diminished version of the original. Rather, it illuminates the original's essence.[54] In 2 Cor 4:6 we find this reality expressed in slightly different language when it speaks of "God's glory displayed in the face of Christ."

At the beginning of the letter to the Hebrews there is further explanation of the nature of the *imago Dei* as found in the Son, although the term was not used. Rather, the author used two New Testament *hapax legomena*,[55] both in verse 1:3,[56] to describe the image of God. The first, *apaúgasma*, is the word translated "radiance." In context it means that when one sees the Son, she or he is seeing God. There is no diminution of the divine glory when looking at the Son. Instead, "the Son is the one

---

52. See Kittel and Friedrich, *TDNT*, 2:395.
53. Kittel and Friedrich, *TDNT*, 2:389.
54. See Kittel and Friedrich, *TDNT*, 2:389.
55. The term *hapax legomenon* means "being said once," and refers to a word that occurs but a single time in a body of literature (in this case, the New Testament).
56. Hebrews 1:3 reads, in part, "The Son is the radiance of God's glory and the exact representation of his being."

who presents the invisible God in a way humans can perceive."⁵⁷ In the Son, then, God can be discerned by human beings.

Later in the verse we find the second word, *charaktēr*. It is translated "exact representation," and was applied secularly to refer to the result of a die being used to produce a coin. In the verse, however, there is a qualifier: the exact representation is of God's being. When viewing the Son one is viewing the image or counterpart of God's being, the divine essence. Thus the character of God is on display in the Son for the purpose of human perception. In this, the Son is God's image made available to humanity.

How has the New Testament material concerning the image of God as found in Jesus generally been understood? In reviewing a range of conceptions several fundamental notions emerge. First, Jesus is seen as the *ideal* instance of the image of God. The pre-incarnate Son, being a member of the Godhead, was not an approximation of God, and in his human state, as Jesus, remained fully divine. Upon the incarnation the divine essence was not lost, neither was it truncated. Rather, it continued unabridged throughout the earthly life of Jesus, and as such was the pristine exemplification of the *imago Dei*. Comparing the image of God as seen in fallen humanity with that seen in Jesus, Peppiatt asserted, "Whereas the image of God in humanity is once either totally obscured or completely lost, it is imparted once again through the first image-bearer, Christ. Jesus Christ is seen to be both the archetype and the prototype of the image."⁵⁸ Hoekema simply stated, "Since Christ was totally without sin (Heb. 4:15), in Christ we see the image of God in its perfection."⁵⁹ Grenz employed different language to emphasize that the image of God in Jesus not only was perfect, it was unique. Citing Col 2:9⁶⁰ as substantiation, he argued, "The attribution of 'fullness of deity' to Christ in the Colossian hymn serves as a contextual defining motif for the understanding of the *imago dei* as an accolade for Christ, and it indicates why this commendation must ultimately be reserved solely for him. As the one who manifests fully the deity of his Father, Jesus alone is the image of God."⁶¹ We have seen that the image of God has not been lost in humanity, but Grenz's description of the uniqueness of the image

---

57. Wozniak, *Living as the Living Jesus*, 144. For a more thorough explanation of the Son as the essence of God, see Wozniak, *Living as the Living Jesus*, 144–46.

58. Peppiatt, *Imago Dei*, 53.

59. Hoekema, *Created in God's Image*, 22.

60. Col 2:9 reads, "For in Christ all the fullness of the Deity lives in bodily form."

61. Grenz, *Social God*, 217.

as seen in Jesus calls our attention to the observable difference between the image in people and the image displayed in Jesus. In Jesus it was ideal; in humans it falls far short, even in the best instances.

Second, the image of God has been made *visible* in Jesus. God expects the faithful not only to bear the image of God, but also to reflect that image to the rest of creation. Yet how is creation to know when it has seen the *imago Dei*? In Jesus the question is answered, for when the Son became incarnate God became revealed in visible form for all of creation to see. Lints connected this revelation to the New Testament understanding of Jesus as the image of God: "In the New Testament the *imago Dei* is most directly connected to Christ (2 Cor. 4:4; Col. 1:15). In the case of Christ he is the 'exact representation' and that by which the invisible God has become visible."[62] He referenced John 1:18 to bolster his argument that not only is the divine Son in close relationship with the Father, but is the one who has made the unseen God known to humans. Hoekema went beyond the notion that in Jesus the image of God is made visible, to assert that God is visibly *reproduced* in Jesus: "One can tell by looking at the Son exactly what the Father is like. It is hard to imagine a stronger figure to convey the thought that Christ is a perfect reproduction of the Father. Every trait, every characteristic, every quality found in the Father is also found in the Son, who is the Father's *exact representation*."[63] Not only, then, is Jesus the *imago Dei* in the ideal, he also is the heretofore unseen divine image exposed and made completely visible.

The third notion many have proposed concerning Jesus as the image of God is that as the *imago Dei* he revealed God's *identity* as well as the divine *character*.[64] It is through the observable image of God in Jesus that God's nature is made known, both ontologically and morally. The revelation to humankind of who God is, however, was not simply to increase human knowledge. Rather, Jesus on earth as the divine image had a more communal purpose, one intended to restore the damaged image of God in humankind to that which it was prior to the fall: the means for perfect harmony with God. It was to that end that Jesus was incarnated. Grenz captured the reason behind Jesus disclosing God's nature: "Ultimately, the divine image is Christ, for he reflects perfectly the perfect character of God. . . . The image of God which Jesus Christ reveals to us, however,

---

62. Lints, *Identity and Idolatry*, 103.
63. Hoekema, *Created in God's Image*, 21; italics original.
64. See Peterson, *Imago Dei*, 1.

is the destiny to which God calls us. His purpose is that we show forth the character of God as the Triune One, the community of love."[65]

Jesus as the ideal image of God made visible in order to disclose who God is, both in being and in character, was God's bidding to people to live in faithfulness. To do so, the human character must be reformed in the likeness of God's character. That involves reappropriation of the *imago Dei* as it was prior to sin and as revealed in Jesus, so that the individual is not only the divine image *de jure* by virtue of creation, but also lives continually in the moral realm of human experience as the image of God *de facto*.

FAITHFULNESS AS REAPPROPRIATION OF THE IMAGE OF GOD

The divine essence was made known—in fact, was put on display for all to see—in the earthly life of Jesus. Only in Jesus can God be discerned by humans. The incarnate Son is the perfect image of God exposed within the created order. He also is nothing less than divine disclosure of the heart of God: the divine being, will, and character manifested in a form that people can comprehend. When God revealed his heart in Jesus he laid out his ultimate desire and end for those created in his image: to be like—to reflect—God. Infinitely more personal, intimate, and relational than any list of laws, rules, principles, or directives, the ethic of God's heart is not comportment with a code but rather conformity with the divine image in a relationship characterized by "he who has seen me has seen the Father." Embracing the quest to achieve such harmony with the divine is the ethic after God's own heart. It also is the essential core of faithfulness.

The goal of living in such faithfulness is not to *become* God; such was not the intent of creating woman and man in God's image. Instead, just like the image on a coin is not the master die by which the coin was fashioned, faithfulness in the image of God is perfect *reflection* of God's heart to the rest of creation. The way to achieve that reflection is the path laid out for the one who aspires to be faithful; the journey requires reappropriation of the *imago Dei*. What, however, does that mean? Several verses in the New Testament point the faithful one in the right direction.

---

65. Grenz, *Theology*, 189.

The New Testament and the Image of God

In his letter to the Roman Christians Paul reassured them that God had predestined them for a particular end: "to be conformed to the image of his Son."[66] God's intention and ensured destination for the redeemed in Christ is that they will perfectly bear and reflect the divine image just as does the Son. This concept was reiterated by Paul in his first letter to the Corinthian Christians, using the language of bearing "the image of the heavenly man," who in the context of the letter is the Son.[67] Such is the ultimate destination for God's faithful at the eschaton, which should serve as a motivating reassurance as they pursue growth in faithfulness. What, however, happens in the meantime?

Two verses, also from Paul's letters to nascent Christian communities in the Roman Empire, hint at the nature of the *imago Dei* prior to the eschaton. In his second letter to the Corinthian Christians, written about a year after the first letter, Paul indicated that he and they "are being transformed into his image."[68] The language indicates a change that is taking place, perhaps one that is outwardly visible. The notable point is that in their present situation the Corinthians are experiencing change from what they currently are to increasing conformity to the divine image. In writing to the Colossian Christians Paul reiterated this concept, indicating that they had "put on the new self, which is being renewed in knowledge in the image of its Creator."[69] This progressive change into greater conformity with God's image that characterized the Corinthians also characterized the Colossians, but was accompanied by increasing knowledge of some sort. The surrounding verses appear to indicate that the increasing knowledge referred to understanding the moral implication of living increasingly like the image of God: severe lifestyle change from conducting themselves according to the standards of their prevailing social milieu to conducting themselves after the pattern set by Jesus.

In his letter to the Ephesian Christians the "putting on" language found in Colossians occurs in the form of putting on the "new self, created

---

66. See Rom 8:29: "For those God foreknew he also predestined to be conformed to the image of his Son, that he might be the firstborn among many brothers and sisters."
67. First Corinthians 15:49 reads, "And just as we have borne the image of the earthly man, so shall we bear the image of the heavenly man."
68. See 2 Cor 3:18.
69. See Col 3:10.

to be like God in true righteousness and holiness."[70] Here the image is referred to as Godlikeness, and is something that is "put on," indicating that traversing the path leading to perfect reflection of the image of God involves the active will and participation of the faithful one. More will be said about that later in the chapter. At this point, however, it is clear that conformity with the image of God as seen in Jesus is the guaranteed ultimate destiny of the faithful. It is also clear that in the ensuing time faithfulness involves making progress toward that ultimate reality through active engagement of the will on the part of the one aspiring to be faithful.

Character and the Image of God

We have learned that to be faithful one needs to develop character after the character of God, and also pursue being the image of God as was Jesus. Yet what is the relationship between the divine character and the divine image?

King David, whose character had been severely corrupted by his own sin, earnestly desired that his character be restored, renewed, and realigned with that of God. Centuries later members of the early Christian communities formed their identities, and hence their characters, by embracing the character of God. Their faithfulness was driven by that ongoing embrace as they looked to Jesus as the archetypical example of the divine character on display. Yet the story of the earthly Jesus was not sufficient for them to grow their character as the divine character borne by the incarnate Son. Rather, they were driven to live in relationship—or covenant—with the resurrected, ascended, glorified Son, and in that relationship to grow into the divine character. Indeed, they desired to live in contemporaneity with the living Lord of All.

In that ongoing relationship the early Christians lived with the reality that they were still on earth, and so looked to the accounts of the earthly Jesus for guidance concerning living out the divine character they were acquiring. Recall that the gospel depictions of Jesus' earthly life take the form of actions, teachings, and relationships that characterized his ministry. In them is found the character of God displayed and enacted; they reflect God's character for all to see. That reflection, however is the image of God. It is God's character—his essence, being, and attributes—made apparent and visible. As such the reflection is the means by which

---

70. See Eph 4:24.

the divine character is expressed on earth in the lives of people. Indeed, this is the purpose for which they originally were created in the image of God. Grenz summed up this reality when he wrote, "as Christ's people we are to show forth the divine reality—to be the image of God. To be the people in covenant with God who serve as the sign of the kingdom means to reflect the very character of God."[71]

There is an inescapable implication of the notion that the image of God is our fundamental identity to the extent that we are closely linked to and reflective of God: humankind—in order both to understand themselves and to realize in themselves the full expression of the *imago Dei*—must understand and pursue the divine character.[72] Growth in the image of God is the means by which that is done. Not only is the faithful individual to *learn* of God, she or he must also pursue being *like* God—reflecting God—in the moral realm of human experience, and that within the specific social milieu in which she or he lives. If God's intent in creating people was that in their fundamental identity they were to be Godlike—ontologically distinct in that they are the *imago Dei*—then to be faithful to that divine intent people must understand, become, and display the character of God. In short, the faithful one must move from being only the image of God *de jure* to being also the image of God *de facto*.

God's Self-Disclosure

Learning, acquiring, and reflecting the character of God seems to be an impossible task, since our natural tendency is to assume we need to do so by leveraging our own resources. Such is not the case; were it so, nobody—no matter how committed and devout—could achieve the goal of faithfulness, or even come close. Somewhere near the beginning of the path of faithfulness is the realization that God is neither abstract nor ineffable. Rather, he has disclosed himself to humans, and thus we are not left to our own devices to understand the divine character.

Most serious believers understand and affirm that God has disclosed himself through the Scripture. Learning the Bible is a means to

---

71. Grenz, *Theology*, 483.

72. This was expressed well by Peterson: "The *imago Dei* is humanity's identity, and this identity is basic to all human existence. God created humanity to establish an earthly image of God in the world. . . . Understanding the meaning of the *imago Dei*, therefore, demands that we have knowledge of God's identity and character. We must know who God is and what God is like." Peterson, *Imago Dei*, 1.

learning about God—his nature, being, identity, character, and attributes. We have already discovered that the bedrock of the divine essence is love, and that God's love character has been disclosed via divine attributes—the observable heart of God as found in the Bible. Through learning the divine attributes God spurs the one seeking to be faithful as a stimulus to creating one's character after that of the divine. This is a start toward faithfulness, primarily involving the intellect.

There is a more fundamental way—ontologically, logically, and chronologically—that God disclosed himself to humans: creation of both man and woman in the divine image. It is not that God created people as divine; Adam and Eve were not, and neither are we. Rather the first people were created as the perfect *reflection* of the divine—the divine image imposed upon humans (at a minimum), but also God's image within and throughout them as the unique *definition* of humanity at its core. People themselves were God's self-disclosure in tangible form for all of the rest of creation. Sin, however, obliterated that perfection, and left all subsequent humans as the *imago Dei* severely distorted, damaged, and obscured.

God's third means of disclosing himself was through the incarnation. In the second person of the Godhead made flesh, God again put on display for all of creation the *imago Dei* in all its perfection. Recall Jesus' response to Philip's inquiry about seeing the Father: "Anyone who has seen me has seen the Father." Perfect relationship with the Father was made observable in the earthly life of Jesus, and serves as the exemplary standard by which faithful relationship with God is to be judged. It also is the call—to those in their fallen state as the sin-damaged image of God—to begin their quest to reappropriate the *imago Dei* as disclosed in perfection both in the original creation of humanity and the subsequent incarnation of the Son. That quest is the path of faithfulness.

The Place of Active Engagement

Once the individual is on the path to faithfulness, what is she or he to do? Earlier we saw that the divine character is something that has to be seized, and that character development requires the active involvement of the individual. The one desiring to form his or her character after the character of God through pursuit of the full-orbed *imago Dei* must assume the role and responsibility of an active moral agent in order to drive and determine character development. This conduct, guided by one's beliefs, is sanctification expressed in moral terms.[73]

Such activity must be done in the context of the Christian community, for it is the community's foundational narratives—primarily those involving the earthly and post-ascension life of Jesus—that give content to the faithful one's beliefs. Remember that the early Christians' faithfulness was fostered within the community context of the first believers. As they grew within the community, increasingly adopting its values and affirmations, they also grew in character—a character that steeled them in their faithfulness even in the face of death. Growth in faithfulness is most successfully accomplished not in isolation, but within the believing community.

Simply learning of Jesus within the Christian community is not sufficient to realize in oneself the image of God as found originally in Adam and Eve and later in the incarnate Son. Faithfulness involves more than intellectual assent; it entails commitment to a lifestyle of volitional conduct patterned after the conduct of Jesus. However, simple emulation of Jesus' actions is not what it means to be faithful; instead emulation is driven by the desire to acquire the divine character *as displayed* in Jesus' teachings and behavior. Hoekema cited the thought of Dutch theologian G. C. Berkouwer to argue that learning what the image of God is like and inculcating the image as the essence of our daily experience requires learning from the life of Jesus. Hoekema wrote, "Berkouwer further observes that we can learn about the meaning of the image by looking at Jesus Christ, who is the perfect image of God (see 2 Cor. 4:4; Col. 1:15). . . . This also implies that to be renewed in the image of God means to become more and more like Christ (Rom. 8:29; 2 Cor. 3:18)."[74]

The one on the path of faithfulness, seeking to form her or his character after that of God's by becoming increasingly like the *imago Dei* revealed supremely in Jesus, is not left alone in that endeavor. In the Holy Spirit one is present with Jesus, living in contemporaneity with Jesus, for contemporaneity means to live in fellowship with the living Jesus. While doing so, "the activity of the Holy Spirit makes evident in our lives the qualities or character which Jesus vividly revealed to us as constituting the character of God. In this sense, Christ—the revealer of God—must be 'formed' in us (Gal. 4:19). As this transpires, we truly become the image

---

73. See Hoekema: "Sanctification, therefore, ought to be understood as the progressive renewal of man in the image of God." Hoekema, *Created in God's Image*, 56.

74. Hoekema, *Created in God's Image*, 63.

of God."[75] That transpiring, however, does not occur in a single event, or periodically through a sequence of discrete events; rather, it occurs continuously throughout the lifetime of the one desiring to be faithful, as he or she continues to walk in the way of Jesus. Consistency in that walk results in character formed, and the image of God increasingly seen *de facto* in the individual. In this regard Hauerwas reflected upon Calvin, arguing that:

> Calvin is insistent that the Christian life is no settled state, but a dynamic growth in righteousness. . . . Thus he says that he would "interpret repentance as regeneration, whose sole end is to restore in us the image of God that has been disfigured and all but obliterated through Adam's transgression . . . this restoration does not take place in one moment or one day or one year; but through continual and sometimes even slow advances God wipes out in his elect the corruptions of the flesh . . . the closer any man comes to the likeness of God, the more the image of God shines in him."[76]

What, however, is the role of the Holy Spirit in the renewal process of the faithful one, who increasingly demonstrates the image of God? How does the Spirit of God, working within the individual, enable progress?

The Role of the Holy Spirit

The story told by Kierkegaard of the rich man who bought a pair of faultless, high-bred horses yields a great picture of the role of the Holy Spirit in the journey of the faithful to reappropriation of the *imago Dei*. The man certainly was active in the situation, and even diligent in his engagement. Yet the result was ruination due not to lack of activity on the part of the man, but rather lack of ability to know how he was to be active. It was not until the king's coachman became involved that the horses thrived. In like manner, the Holy Spirit's involvement in directing the believer along the path of faithfulness is essential; indeed the Spirit activates the individual's potential for growth in character, giving guidance along the most beneficial path for moving from being the image of God *de jure* to *de facto*. Hoekema captured this notion of both the faithful individual and the Holy Spirit partnering in the quest to become in daily life the

---

75. Grenz, *Theology*, 265.
76. Hauerwas, *Character*, 216–17.

image of God: "Since human beings are creatures, God in the person of the Holy Spirit must sanctify them; since they are also persons, they must themselves be responsibly involved in their sanctification."[77] He went on to describe the Spirit's work as continual, not intermittent or a solitary event: "As we continually reflect the glory of the Lord, we are continually being transformed into the image of the one whose glory we are reflecting. This transformation . . . comes from the Lord, who is the Spirit."[78] Such transformation is the engraving of the divine character to which Kierkegaard referred.

Even through the work of the Holy Spirit, the faithful believer will not become the image of God in perfection as was Jesus. That is reserved for the eschatological future, when God will make all things new. Yet the faithful need not despair. Within the relational context of the Christian community great progress can be made toward realizing the reappropriation of the *imago Dei*. In fact, progressing toward the perfect image of God is an element and responsibility of faithfulness. Grenz expressed this obligation when describing the relationship between the image of God achievable here and now with its ultimate expression in the eschaton. "Those who are destined to be the new humanity and as such to reflect the divine image, and therefore are already in the process of being transformed into that image, carry the ethical responsibility to live out that reality in the present."[79] Thus there is great hope for believers who engage continually, habitually, actively, and in partnership with the Holy Spirit forming the divine character. In so doing they are reappropriating the *imago Dei*, for that is what it means to be faithful.

Faithfulness and Social Stance

The vast majority of those who make up the dominant social milieu *have not* pursued faithfulness by intentionally building their character after

---

77. Hoekema, *Created in God's Image*, 8. See also Hoekema's reference to Calvin's thought: "For Calvin the renewal of the image of God is both the work of God's grace and the responsibility of man. The Holy Spirit must renew us through the Word, but we, enabled by the Spirit, must respond to that Word by faith." Hoekema, *Created in God's Image*, 47.

78. Hoekema, *Created in God's Image*, 24.

79. Grenz, *Social God*, 251–52. Grenz expanded this thought: "The Spirit engages in the work of transformation . . . so that as a people imbued with the character of Christ, who is the image of God, they might together reflect God's own character and thus shine as the *imago dei*." Grenz, *Social God*, 334.

the character of God, nor have they sought to become the *imago Dei*—the observable reflection of the divine nature—in their daily experience in the moral realm. That being the case, we would expect that those who *have* pursued such faithfulness would establish themselves within the society in a manner vastly different from those who have not. The values, virtues, attributes, commitments, intentions, judgments, and conduct of the faithful have been driven by the character they—responding to the directing of the Holy Spirit—have built, and thus they have been driven in a manner wholly different and distinct from the nominal character of the dominant populace. Aristotle's notion of "the mean" reflects the moral stance of the prevailing social milieu—a stance distinctly rejected by the early Christians when establishing themselves in society. Their character of faithfulness would allow for nothing less, requiring them to take an extreme social stance when viewed from the perspective of those who embraced "the mean." In contrast, the bulk of Western Christianity today has chosen the way of the dominant social milieu, living in social syncretism and adopting "the mean" approach to its moral stance. As such, it has rejected the path of faithfulness.

The early Christians sought to follow the Jesus way, pursuing his perfect depiction of the image of God. Their outlook and orientation was that of Jesus, rather than the surrounding society, and as such rendered them in conflict with the world's norms, patterns, and values. Not only did their social stance expose the failure of those of the surrounding society to live out God's intent for them as created beings in his image, it also was viewed as a threat to the norm (as was Jesus within his social environment). The resultant wrath on the part of the dominant ones against the faithful ones should not come as a surprise, for that too was part of the pattern set by Jesus. Yet the faithful persevered in their faithfulness, continuing the habitual practice that had become the standard by which they walked in the Jesus way. Today's Western Christianity would benefit greatly from adopting the way of the early Christians, reappropriating the image of God and thereby setting out on the path of faithfulness.

PART THREE

Faithfulness and the Christian Life

ACQUIRING THE CHARACTER OF God through reappropriation of the *imago Dei* naturally leads to the observable expression of the image. Recall that the notion of image inherently entails reflection, just as when producing a coin by means of a die inherently results in the coin's face reflecting the die's image. When used skillfully the die replicates an image that reflects *without flaw*—or as the writer of the Epistle to the Hebrews expressed it when speaking of how Jesus reflects the divine character, he is "the exact representation of his being."[1]

In living out the image of God *de facto* the character of God influences—perhaps even directs—our functioning in the moral realm. The degree to which it does so is a depiction of our level of faithfulness. The reappropriated *imago Dei* affects moral conduct somewhat in a passive way since the individual's character to a great degree is now the character of God. However, it further generates in the individual something of the divine will. Thus, the individual also actively pursues expression of Godlikeness.

Jesus, being the perfect example of the *imago Dei*, perfectly reflected the divine character and the divine will throughout the earthly life he lived in his society—in the moral realm of human experience. In Jesus' life God's image and character were put on display for all to observe. It was this display that the early Christians held as the archetypical example of what faithfulness meant in daily living, and thus they sought to follow

1. See Heb 1:3.

Jesus in the manner in which he exhibited God's character. Unfortunately, vital elements of Jesus' living out the divine character have been forgotten or lost by much of Western Christianity in the twenty-first century. This problem, however, is not something new; in the mid–twentieth century Yoder expressed concern over the loss when he wrote, "Seldom has the exemplary quality of Jesus' social humanity been perceived as a model for our social ethics."[2] He went on to lament the selective nature of orthodox Christianity's endorsement of Jesus' social involvement, labeling it "the tradition that has been able to appropriate much of the New Testament idiom without catching its central historical thrust."[3] Yet what is Jesus' social humanity, his social involvement? Is it not his living out and reflecting the *imago Dei* within the social milieu in which he lived? It is incumbent upon Christianity today—both individual Christians and the Christian collective, the church—to correct the problem of today's Christianity by re-embracing the lost vital elements of Jesus' exemplification of God's character, and thus to live faithfully before God as did the early Christians.

Before launching into a life of faithful conduct it is important for the faithful one to understand the broad-brush constituent elements that exhibit the divine character as displayed by Jesus, for to follow Jesus as he lived is to reflect the *imago Dei*. Doing so constitutes faithfulness. Giving definition to those elements is the purpose of the chapters that make up this part. The hope is that the one seeking to live faithfully will be substantially equipped for the task.

Much of what Jesus did in displaying God's character is captured in his teachings, particularly the Sermon on the Mount. In reflecting on the Sermon's purpose, Bonhoeffer captured Jesus' intent, asserting: "The only proper response to this word which Jesus brings with him from eternity is simply to do it."[4] To do the Sermon as Jesus did it is to live a life of faithfulness; to recapture for ourselves in this century what the early Christians embraced in theirs.

---

2. Yoder, *Politics of Jesus*, 131.
3. Yoder, *Politics of Jesus*, 131n32.
4. Bonhoeffer, *Cost of Discipleship*, 219.

11

Faithfulness: Attitude and Intention

NOT ALL ELEMENTS OF the divine character as displayed by Jesus are of the same ilk. They vary in certain regards, such as the degree to which they are overt and obvious, the subtlety—or lack thereof—with which they are expressed, or the frequency in which they occurred in Jesus' life. In general, however, they may be grouped into two categories: those which pertain more to attitude and intention, and those associated with commitment and conduct.

Those of the first category were summarized in capsule form by the apostle Paul in his epistle to the Philippian Christians. The overall umbrella under which they were grouped is that of a mindset. In the second chapter of the letter Paul wrote, "have the same mindset as Christ Jesus."[1] Conceptually the notion Paul was seeking to impart was attitudinal rather than purely intellectual.[2] From ancient times the word Paul used for "mindset" carried the sense of "inner attitude,"[3] and within the Pauline corpus conveyed the sense of "disposition."[4] In the mid-twentieth century

---

1. Phil 2:5b.
2. See Bauer: *"have thoughts or (an) attitude(s), be minded or disposed . . . have the same thoughts among yourselves as you have in your communion with Christ Jesus."* Bauer, *Greek-English Lexicon*, 874; italics original.
3. Kittel and Friedrich, *TDNT*, 9:221.
4. Kittel and Friedrich, *TDNT*, 9:233.

Dr. Paul Rees—an early visionary in the movement to awaken Western orthodox Christianity to the essential nature of social milieu involvement on the part of those claiming to be faithful—asserted that Paul was directing the Philippians, "Be having this disposition or spirit in yourselves which was in Christ."[5]

It is clear that Paul was referencing the moral realm, specifically the attitude that should guide Christians' involvement in the social sphere. The earthly life of Jesus was to be the example they followed, beginning with his disposition. That disposition, however, was primarily demonstrated by Jesus through three attitudinal characteristics that he intentionally adopted as he lived a life reflecting the character of God. Paul captured them in the three subsequent verses: self-emptying, obedience, and suffering.

SELF-EMPTYING

If Jesus' depiction of the divine character involved self-emptying, then self-emptying must somehow be included in the character of God. Yet where do we see this divine element displayed? Many potential answers to this question could be explored, but the one that is obvious and undeniable is that God the Father emptied himself when he "did not spare his own Son, but gave him up for us all."[6] The Father could have retained and maintained the nominal relational reality among and within the Godhead, but instead gave up and gave over the Son for the benefit of humanity. The Son was not spared by the Father; rather, the Father emptied himself of the intimacy he had shared eternally with the Son, in order that created humanity might be reconciled to God. The ultimate expression of that voluntary, intentional divesting of intimacy occurred when Jesus cried out at his crucifixion, "My God, My God, why have you forsaken me?"[7] Whereas the Trinity was not dissolved as a result of the Father's giving over the Son, neither was it unaffected by the incarnation. This is how the Father displayed self-emptying.

The apostle John expressed this notion when he wrote, "For God so loved the world that he gave his one and only Son, that whoever believes

---

5. Rees, *Philippians, Colossians, Philemon*, 38.
6. Rom 8:32.
7. Mark 15:34.

in him shall not perish but have eternal life."[8] The emphasized parts of that verse often are God's love, the Son, believing, and eternal life. Yet the giving on the part of the Father was essential for the beneficial results to occur. Without the Father's self-emptying humanity would have no hope of reconciliation to God.

The Son's Self-Emptying

The first attitudinal characteristic of Jesus' life as explained by Paul was similar to what the Father displayed in giving the Son. It is captured in two specific Greek words: *harpagmòn* (in "something to be used to his own advantage"[9]) and *ekenōsen* (in "he made himself nothing"[10]). The fundamental root for *harpagmòn* connotes stealing, snatching, raping, seizing, or taking as plunder or booty,[11] although twentieth-century New Testament scholar C. F. D. Moule argued that there is no secular evidence that the rare form of the word found in Phil 2:6 carried the sense of plunder or booty; rather, it simply meant to snatch or take.[12] Even though there has been considerable debate over phrases in the text associated with *harpagmòn*, such as "being in very nature God" or "equality with God," as well as the timing of the events referenced in the passage (e.g., before, during, or after the incarnation), our focus is on the fact that the Son *did not* snatch or take. This was the first element of his self-emptying.

What was it, however, that the Son did not grab? From eternity he shared the divine nature, as well as the divine glory and prerogatives. Since he already enjoyed them, there was no need for him to take or grab them. The divine nature, however, is not the focus in this passage, for the Son continually bears that nature from eternity to eternity; rather the passage deals with the divine glory and prerogatives. It is the *benefits* associated with and derivative from God's glory and prerogatives that the Son chose not to take. Nineteenth-century theologian J. B. Lightfoot—whose

---

8. John 3:16.
9. See Phil 2:6.
10. See Phil 2:7.
11. Kittel and Friedrich, *TDNT*, 1:472–73.
12. Moule, "Further Reflections," 268, 272. See also Meyer: "It is accordingly to be explained: *Not as a robbing did He consider the being equal with God*, i.e. He did not place it under the point of view of making booty, as if it was, with respect to his exertion of activity, to consist *in His seizing what did not belong to Him*." Meyer, *Philippians*, 69; italics original.

thought is widely regarded as foundational to a proper understanding of this passage—paraphrased verse 6 as follows, "*Though* He pre-existed in the form of God, *yet* He did not look upon equality with God as a prize which must not slip from His grasp."[13] Seizing with a strong grip the prize that was already his was what the Son determined not to do. In Lightfoot's words, what the Son chose to empty himself of was "the insignia of majesty."[14]

Why was it that the Son chose not to take the benefits of the divine glory and prerogatives? The heart of the answer appears to lie in the fact that to do so was inconsistent with the divine nature, for inherent in that nature is self-giving, not retaining. If we recall that the divine character, when experienced by God's creatures, takes the form of love, then the self-giving of God is the natural—even essential—expression of God's character. New Testament scholar Jennings Reid expressed the relationship between God's nature and his self-giving when he wrote, "His self-giving was the natural result of who he was as divine Love, a love that naturally and inevitably expressed itself in outgoing concern for others, even for the most depraved and despicable specimens of mankind."[15] It is consistent within the nature of the Godhead, then, that the Son should express his divinity by giving of himself, even to the point of complete self-emptying.

Moule suggested that the opposite of *harpagmòn*—which is what characterized the Son—is giving away rather than taking.[16] He asserted that the point of the passage is, "instead of imagining that equality with God meant *getting*, Jesus, on the contrary, *gave*—gave until he was 'empty.'"[17] Just as we saw that the character of God entailed giving, so with the Son. For him to be divine meant that instead of taking, he gave.[18] So Moule concluded that to understand properly how the Son displayed his equality with God one must see that "the self-emptying was evidence of how Christ understood that equality with God which he possessed inalienably."[19]

---

13. Lightfoot, *Philippians*, 111; italics original.
14. Lightfoot, *Philippians*, 112.
15. Reid, *Jesus*, 81.
16. See Moule, "Further Reflections," 272.
17. Moule, "Further Reflections," 272; italics original.
18. See Moule, in which he summarized this thought by asserting that Paul used "the gospel story of God's self-giving in Christ as a way of saying 'Be generous and self-sacrificing towards one another, for this is the most God-like thing you can do; it is precisely here that we can recognise Christ's divinity.'" Moule, "Further Reflections," 270.
19. Moule, "Further Reflection," 275.

The Son gave of himself, but to what extent did he do so? The second word that conveys the self-emptying of the second person of the Trinity—*ekenōsen*—suggests the answer. There is little sophistication or complexity associated with the word; it simply means to empty,[20] hollowness,[21] to evacuate,[22] void of content as well as ineffectiveness.[23] It was used to describe secular realities such as an animal that had lost its offspring or a mother who had lost all of her children.[24] The emptying of the pre-incarnate Son referenced in verse 7 connotes a choice not to exploit the divine form—such as the glory and prerogatives discussed previously—but rather laying that form aside completely so that the Son could instead give.[25] This willful action constituted the sacrifice associated with the Son's self-emptying at the moment of incarnation.

Our understanding of the nature of the emptiness the Son took upon himself is enhanced if we observe what he chose to take on instead of seizing equality with God. We see it explained in verse 7: he took on himself human form, with all of its limitations and frailties, and he assumed a servant's role. In verse 8 we see that subsequent to such self-emptying he also lived a life of humility and obedience to the point of enduring torture to death on a Roman cross. Jesus' obedience and suffering are treated later in the chapter, so at this point the focus will be on his assuming human form and the servant's role that typified his earthly life.

The creation of humanity is generally regarded as the crown of creation, for not only were people created at the culmination of God's creative work, but only humans were created in the *imago Dei*. When the Father, through the Son,[26] created Adam and Eve, the pinnacle of the created order appeared, and as such was given the task of ruling over all other created beings.[27] This lofty view of humanity, however, is not what Paul had in mind when in verses 7 and 8 he indicated that Jesus was made in human likeness. Rather, his point was that the eternal Son assumed the *frailties* and *limitations* of humanity. Nineteenth-century German Lutheran theologian Heinrich August Wilhelm Meyer saw an essential

20. Bauer, *Greek-English Lexicon*, 429.
21. Trench, *Synonyms of the New Testament*, 180.
22. *Analytical Greek Lexicon*, 228.
23. Kittel and Friedrich, *TDNT*, 3:659, 60.
24. Kittel and Friedrich, *TDNT*, 3:661.
25. Kittel and Friedrich, *TDNT*, 3:661.
26. See Heb 1:2.
27. See Gen 1:28.

connection between the Son's self-emptying and his assumption of human form, asserting "the empirical appearance . . . was an integral part of the manner in which the act of self-emptying was completed."[28] Not only did the Son exchange the divine immensity for the realities of human flesh, such as hunger, thirst, pain, and weariness; he also did so for the realities of the human spirit, such as temptation, grief, and frustration. Yet more than these, Jesus becoming human entailed the humanly inconceivable exchange in which the Creator assumed the position of the created.

It is important to note that Paul used a plural form of the word for human in describing what Jesus did when taking the form of a created being. His purpose was to show that Jesus was not just one man, but that he took upon himself the nature of the human race. As such, he became the race's representative in his servanthood, obedience, and suffering.[29] He also became the race's ultimate example of the self-giving of God, and thus the archetype for the rest of humanity to emulate in its quest for faithfulness.

Paul indicated that as human Jesus took a particular form upon himself. In contrast with the form of God—which he abrogated—he assumed the form of a servant. The word for servant (*doûlos*) actually refers to one who is enslaved. It is to be viewed in contrast with the master or a free person,[30] not as someone hired to perform tasks for another. Given the history of slavery in the West it is natural to assume that a slave is primarily an owned and severely abused one—a person who, among other things, is compelled under threat of violence to perform economically beneficial labor for an owner, and that without compensation. Moule, however, offered a different concept of the fundamental nature of slavery as found in the Roman Empire during the first century, and specifically why *doûlos* is used in verse 7 as a descriptor of Jesus: "Slavery would deny a person the right to anything—even to his own life and person . . . more than any actual maltreatment that a slave might or might not receive . . . Jesus so completely stripped himself of all rights and securities as to be comparable to a slave, constitutes a poignant description of his absolute and extreme self-emptying—even of basic human rights.[31]"

It appears that the concept Paul is seeking to convey regarding the slavery Jesus took on himself entailed primarily not violent abuse and

28. Meyer, *Philippians*, 74.
29. Lightfoot, *Philippians*, 112.
30. Bauer, *Greek-English Lexicon*, 204.
31. Moule, "Further Reflection," 268.

even torture—although we will see later that it indeed involved those as well—but throughout his life meant deprivation of his fundamental humanity. He appeared as a human, but functioned as something much less—as one who gave up even basic human rights.

We may ask, "If Jesus was a slave, whose slave was he?" Meyer accurately answered the question, asserting that "Paul, in the word [*doúlou*], thought not of the relation of *one serving in general* . . . But of a slave of *God* (comp. Acts iii. 13; Isa. lii.)."[32] For Jesus, being God's slave was a divine commission to serve others, and thus he characterized his earthly ministry as "I am among you as one who serves,"[33] and "the Son of Man did not come to be served, but to serve, and to give his life as a ransom for many."[34] The latter statement additionally includes the extreme giving which is fundamental to the divine character.

From the point of view of faithfulness this perspective is reasonable and consistent: the faithful one must simply adopt the stance of God's slave. In this Jesus was the example for others seeking to be faithful, including the early Christians who sought to live as God's slaves within their social milieu, just as Jesus had in his. That notion of being God's slave has essentially been lost by today's Western Christianity; the degree of that loss is the extent to which twenty-first-century Christians fall short in faithfulness.

Self-Emptying throughout Jesus' Life

If Jesus' self-emptying was displayed in his taking on the form of humanity—understood as extreme limitations compared with the privileges of his divinity that he enjoyed prior to the incarnation—we should be able to see how that human frailty influenced his earthly ministry. Furthermore, his stance as the slave of God would have had significant effect on his life on earth. Having no rights of independence, but rather thinking and acting in submission to the Father, would have colored—and restricted—the events of his life. To explore all of the biblical examples of the empty Jesus is not our goal; rather, thinking about a few examples will suffice to see the giving character of God—and thus the *imago Dei*—in the life of Jesus.

---

32. Meyer, *Philippians*, 75; italics original.
33. Luke 22:27.
34. Matt 20:28.

Prior to looking at examples from Jesus' life, however, it will be helpful to see their precursors in the lives of several Old Testament characters.

Old Testament Precursors of Jesus' Self-Emptying

One of the defining events of God's approach to his faithful people is the event in the life of Abraham in which God directed him to sacrifice his beloved son Isaac.[35] Abraham obeyed God, who provided an alternative sacrifice just as Abraham was about to kill his son. Yet Abraham was obedient to God, and in his obedience he was reenacting the giving element of the divine character. For his self-giving faithfulness to God's command Abraham heard these words from the angel of the Lord: "I swear by myself, declares the Lord, that because you have done this and have not withheld your son, your only son. I will surely bless you."[36] The parallel to the self-giving of the Father is striking: the Father did not withhold his only begotten Son, and in faithfulness Abraham—though earlier in time than the incarnation—mimicked the character of the Father.

In addition to giving after the pattern of the Father, Abraham was preenacting the self-emptying of the Son. In not withholding Isaac—by not grabbing for himself the benefits of the son he already had—Abraham was prefiguring the Son's refusal to snatch (*harpagmòn*) the benefits of the glory he already shared with the other members of the Godhead. His obedience to God was proof that he "feared God"—the textual rendering of the faithfulness concept we have been exploring.

The life of Moses serves as another picture of the self-emptying of the Son. Moses had escaped from Egypt and had settled into a routine life as a shepherd. At one point God appeared to Moses in the form of a burning, yet unconsumed, bush. Shortly thereafter—in Exod 3:10—God's selection and sending of Moses occurred: "So now, go. I am sending you to Pharaoh to bring my people the Israelites out of Egypt." Moses immediately replied to God with what appears to be either a challenge or a protest: "But Moses said to God, 'Who am I that I should go to Pharaoh and bring the Israelites out of Egypt?'"[37] What follows is a dialogue between Moses and God in which Moses tried in a number of ways to escape God's selection of him. For example, he asked God how he should

---

35. See Gen 22:1–19.
36. Gen 22:16–17.
37. Exod 3:11.

respond if the Israelites asked what God's name was.[38] Later he asked God, "What if they don't believe me or listen to me and say, 'The Lord did not appear to you'?"[39] That was followed by a protest in which Moses complained that he was not eloquent, and was slow of speech.[40] Each time God reassured Moses in various ways. Finally Moses simply asked, "Please send someone else,"[41] to which God responded with anger.

Moses was God's chosen servant to carry out the divine will. He had no choice in the matter, and eventually yielded to God's commission. It turns out that Moses—as the one God had chosen to carry out his plan—yielded to God. Yet to do so Moses had to empty himself of his former life situation; he could not continue as a shepherd who also enjoyed the relationships within his family, and at the same time be God's servant.

The life of Moses was a precursor to the life of Jesus. Jesus emptied himself of the familial situation he enjoyed within the Godhead so that he could take upon himself the position of God's slave. Both Moses and Jesus protested,[42] but in the end served God in yielded faithfulness.

The lives of certain prophets serve as one final precursor of the self-emptying of Jesus. If we look into God's commission of Ezekiel, for example, we see that he had no independent choice about being the servant of God in the way that God wanted him to serve. Ezekiel was a priest living in Babylon during the time of the exile in the sixth century BC. At one point Ezekiel heard the voice of God order him to stand up, then tell him, "Son of man, I am sending you to the Israelites, to a rebellious nation that has rebelled against me."[43] The commission continued with such divine orders as "You must speak my words to them, whether they listen or fail to listen, for they are rebellious. But you, son of man, listen to what I say to you. Do not rebel like that rebellious people";[44] "Son of man, go now to the people of Israel and speak my words to them";[45] and "Son of man, listen carefully and take to heart all the words I speak to you. Go now to your people in exile and speak to them. Say to them, 'This is what

---

38. See Exod 3:13.
39. Exod 4:1.
40. See Exod 4:10.
41. Exod 4:13.
42. In the case of Moses, the protests were the ones found in Exod 3 and 4; in the case of Jesus the protest was found in his Gethsemane prayer.
43. Ezek 2:3.
44. Ezek 2:7–8.
45. Ezek 3:4.

the Sovereign Lord says,' whether they listen or fail to listen."[46] Ezekiel had no choice to accept or refuse God's selection of him, and no latitude regarding what he could say to the Israelites. His situation is reminiscent of Jesus' statement, "For I did not speak on my own, but the Father who sent me commanded me to say all that I have spoken."[47]

Ezekiel's response to God' selection, commission, and restriction of him is noteworthy: "The Spirit then lifted me up and took me away, and I went in bitterness and in the anger of my spirit, with the strong hand of the Lord upon me. I came to the exiles who lived at Tel Aviv near the Kebar River. And there, where they were living, I sat among them for seven days—deeply distressed."[48] At his selection by God Ezekiel became God's slave, void of any independence to live as he chose. That situation was not a one-time occurrence, but continued throughout Ezekiel's life. Similarly Jesus was God's slave, doing only what God directed him to do, throughout his life, including his crucifixion. Such is the model of faithfulness that Jesus established as the standard for all his followers who aspire to be faithful to him.

Jesus' Humanity on Display

In the second chapter of the Epistle to the Hebrews the writer presented the most complete picture in the New Testament of the humanity of Jesus. With statements such as "we do see Jesus, who was made lower than the angels for a little while"; "he suffered death"; "he suffered"; "Jesus is not ashamed to call them brothers and sisters"; "Since the children have flesh and blood, he too shared in their humanity"; "he had to be made like them, fully human in every way"; and "he himself suffered when he was tempted";[49] the writer made it clear that Jesus was completely human. In the Gospels we see Jesus' humanity on display through, for example, a range of emotions. At the tomb of Lazarus Jesus was deeply moved—even to the point of weeping—over the death of his beloved friend.[50] He also wept over Jerusalem for rejecting him.[51] At times he was frustrated over

---

46. Ezek 3:10–11.
47. John 12:49.
48. Ezek 3:14–15.
49. See Heb 2:9–18.
50. See John 11:33–38.
51. See Luke 19:41.

the disciples' inability to comprehend the truth he was trying to convey about himself.[52] When predicting his death he was troubled in his soul.[53]

At other times the physical limitations of Jesus' humanity were exposed. Just prior to his temptation he had not eaten for forty days, and thus was hungry.[54] His strength left him when, after a severe beating, he was unable to carry his cross and Simon of Cyrene was compelled to carry it for him.[55] While on the cross—the time when he experienced the most extreme physical torture—he expressed that he was thirsty.[56]

Jesus' taking on human form, including its limitations, did not—in and of itself—display the character of God. The *imago Dei* did not consist of the physical elements of humankind. We may ask, then, to what end did the Creator taking the form of the creation serve to display the character of God?

It is crucial to realize that for Jesus to serve as a true model of the divine character—enacted through the life of the faithful one—he had to assume *fully* the nature of the creation. Were he not fully human, he could not serve as the paradigm of faithfulness for other humans. Thus he had to show that he indeed was human flesh just like other human flesh, had human emotions just like other human emotions, and had human mind just like other human minds. This he did, as our brief overview of his humanity has demonstrated.

The Character of God Displayed in Jesus' Giving

We have seen that fundamental to the divine character is the self-giving of God. Not only was this shown in the process of creation, but it is seen supremely in God's giving of his only begotten Son—the second member of the Trinity—for the salvation of needy humankind. We would expect to see Jesus, as the perfect example of the divine character, give—as a tangible depiction of the character of God—for the benefit of others at their time of need. Jesus indeed lived a life of continuous giving for others,

---

52. See, for the example, the incident where the disciples failed to comprehend the meaning of the feedings of the 5,000 and 4,000 (Mark 8:17-21), as well as Philip's failure to recognize that in seeing Jesus he was seeing the Father (John 14:6-9).

53. See John 12:23-28.

54. See Luke 4:1-2. See also Mark 11:12 for a time later in Jesus' ministry when he was hungry.

55. See Matt 27:32.

56. See John 19:28-29.

but one experience from his life serves as a clear and simple picture of what Godlike giving looked like. This incident would form a picture that could be recalled later by various followers of Jesus attempting to be faithful while living life within their respective social milieus. In the second chapter of John's Gospel we learn of a time when Jesus was at a wedding, and there was insufficient wine for the wedding guests. To us in the West it may seem like a problem perhaps easily resolved and not terribly significant, but in the local shame culture of the first century it was a huge problem fraught with the potential for serious consequences. Jesus was somewhat coerced into the situation by his mother; yet once he was presented with an issue he could resolve, he gave for the benefit of others in their time of need. Notice that in verse 10 we learn that Jesus not only produced the required quantity, but that his gift was of the highest quality. His approach showed the character of God on display in a tangible situation of people in need.

It may be objected that Jesus did a miracle in order to rectify the troubling situation, and that his followers seeking to be faithful cannot simply turn water into wine as did Jesus. Whereas that may be true, the point of the story *from the perspective of faithfulness* is that reflecting the character of God fundamentally entails self-giving: the emptying of self for the benefit of others in their time of need. The story does not concern the deepest of human need, such as what to do about sin, but it is a direct and clear picture of how the faithful one is to respond to the *reality* of need in a way that reflects the divine character—the character resident in the individual who has focused on character development to the point of living the image of God *de facto*.

There is no indication that in the wedding incident Jesus himself was in any sort of need. How to live out the character of God when one is not at one's best is the next step in learning what faithfulness means. In the incident in which Jesus encountered a Samaritan woman at a well,[57] the narrative opens by stating that Jesus was both tired from his journey and in need of a drink of water. He asked the woman for a drink, to which she responded with something of a cultural barrier to her doing so, citing the cultural norm that Jews did not associate with Samaritans. Jesus, then, was in need himself, and his need was not being met. Yet instead of continuing to focus on his need, he turned the conversation to the giving of God, telling the woman that had she known who he was and asked him

---

57. See John 4:5–42.

for a drink, he would have given her living water. As was the case with the wedding, Jesus demonstrated the character of God in a practical situation within his specific social setting. That demonstration—irrespective of the fact that he himself was in need—was to give as God gives, with the result being eternal life.

Jesus as the Slave of God

We learned that the next element of Jesus' self-emptying was his adopting the stance of God's slave, void of his own independence. Later in the story of Jesus' encounter with the Samaritan woman Jesus stated that his food "is to do the will of him who sent me and to finish his work."[58] Was he indicating by such a statement that he could not continue his life on earth without doing God's will? It appears to be so. By making such a claim Jesus set a very high faithfulness standard for his followers: they either were to do God's will or experience some form of starvation of their relationship with God. Throughout John's Gospel we see this rather extreme theme repeated in various forms. For example, in chapter 6 Jesus described himself as the bread of life, and asserted that just as he lives due to the Father, so "the one who feeds on me will live because of me."[59] A few verses earlier he had taught, "unless you eat the flesh of the Son of Man and drink his blood, you have no life in you. Whoever eats my flesh and drinks my blood has eternal life, and I will raise them up at the last day."[60]

Jesus knew clearly that he was not independent, his self-understanding coming from his background in the Scripture, particularly Isaiah. Several places in Isaiah the image of God's servant is portrayed. It was these passages, known as "servant songs," that influenced Paul as he described Jesus as the slave of God in Phil 2.[61] Reid asserted that "the servant songs . . . made a profound impression on the mind of Jesus. More than any other portions of scripture, they were to define the role

---

58. John 4:34.
59. John 6:57. See also verses 32–35 and 51.
60. John 6:53–54.
61. See Reid, in which he pointed out that "there is a close relationship between the hymn in Philippians 2:5–11 and the servant portrayed in Deutero-Isaiah. In other words, the writer of the hymn presents Jesus Christ as the embodiment of the servant in Deutero-Isaiah. There are a number of servant passages referred to as 'servant songs.'" Reid, *Jesus*, 58. He then listed the passages as Isa 41:8–10; 42:1–9, 18–20; 49:1–13; 50:4–11; 52:13—53:12; and 61:1–3.

he was to fulfill. He saw himself as a true servant of the Lord, wholly obedient to God and wholly compassionate and empathetic to the needs of others. This called for a life of outgoing service in their behalf."[62] The Isaiah picture of the Servant of God was the prototype for how Jesus lived out his role as God's slave, including the seeking of justice, opening of the eyes of the blind, calling Israel back to faithfulness, being a light to the gentiles, bringing good news to the poor and comfort to those who mourn, and taking on himself the iniquity of humankind—including the associated punishment, even to the point of death on a Roman cross.[63]

In his account of Jesus' life Matthew also made the connection between Jesus' earthly ministry and the servant of God foretold in Isaiah.[64] In the passage he quoted, God described the future Jesus as "my servant whom I have chosen." The clear indication is that Jesus did not act independently; rather, he was serving his master, the Father.

Shortly before his death Jesus washed his disciples' feet.[65] Upon finishing the washing, immediately he told them that he had just left them an example of how they should treat each other, then characterized his conduct as a depiction of his relationship with the one who had sent him: "no servant [*doũlos*] is greater than his master, nor is a messenger greater than the one who sent him."[66] Yet immediately prior to the foot washing, Jesus clarified his position vis-à-vis the Father: "I did not speak on my own, but the Father who sent me commanded me to say all that I have spoken. . . . So whatever I say is just what the Father has told me to say."[67] These examples show that Jesus did not act on his own accord. Rather, he was sent by the Father as the Father's slave to do the will of the Father.

One incident from the life of Jesus prior to the crucifixion reveals the extent to which he was compelled by the Father and did not act on his own. The crucifixion, of course, was the ultimate depiction of Jesus yielded to the Father's will. Some of the faithful in subsequent centuries would be called to follow Jesus on his path to death. For most, however, Jesus' struggle with the Father in the Garden of Gethsemane is the ultimate picture of living as the slave of God. The incident is found in all three of the

---

62. Reid, *Jesus*, 62.

63. See Isa 52:13—53:12. In this regard see Stassen and Gushee's treatment of "Seven Marks of God's Reign" in Stassen and Gushee, *Kingdom Ethics*, 25–28.

64. See Matt 12:16–21.

65. See John 13:1–11.

66. John 13:16.

67. John 12:49–50.

Synoptic Gospels,[68] but Matthew's account yields some detail that aids in seeing not only Jesus' struggle but also his ultimate submission as the slave of God. In his first prayer Jesus expressed his will that his upcoming crucifixion be taken from him, then submitted his will to the will of the Father. When he prayed the second time, however, he acknowledged that it was not likely that his crucifixion was avoidable, then asked that the Father's will be done. Herein we see that although self-emptied, faithfulness in submission to the will of God entailed a severe struggle even for Jesus. It brought him to agony as he struggled with what the Father expected of him. Yet, being God's slave, faithful demonstration of the self-giving character of God required no less of him.

Self-Emptying and Jesus' Followers

Jesus' self-giving to the point of emptiness, as well as his taking the position of a slave, not only were the means by which he identified with humanity and displayed the character of God; they were at least a portion of the standard by which faithfulness on the part of his followers was to be measured. To make that point clear to his potential followers—as well as to those in subsequent generations who aspired to faithfulness—Jesus showed that his follower was to do simply that: follow him in self-giving and assume the position of a slave to others.

In his interactions with others and his associated teaching, Jesus called his followers to his standard of faithfulness in three distinct ways. First, he instructed them concerning the level of self-giving that he required. Second, he gave them examples of the self-giving of those who were faithful. Third, he showed them what faithful servanthood looked like. Let us look at samples of each from the life of Jesus.

At one point in his life Jesus was approached enthusiastically by a man seeking to know what he had to do to gain eternal life.[69] After confirming with Jesus that he had kept the commandments, Jesus looked at him and loved him. The encounter was not an intellectual one; it was not about what the man knew or how he had adhered to the religious requirements of his day. Rather, it concerned relationship with Jesus, the one who loved him. To that end, Jesus told the man that he still lacked one thing, which Jesus did not identify specifically. Instead, he told the

---

68. See Matt 26:36–46, Mark 14:32–42, and Luke 22:39–46.
69. See Mark 10:17–22.

man to sell everything, give it all to the poor, and follow Jesus. The man was unwilling to meet Jesus' demand of his followers and, being saddened by what faithfulness required of him, left Jesus. Here we see that Jesus required his followers to give up that which they held dearly, and instead to give in the extreme; in Jesus' words, "sell everything you have." The requirement is reminiscent of Jesus not grasping the benefits he enjoyed as the Son, but rather self-giving to the point of being completely empty. Meyer commented that Jesus' requirement of the man "*completes the weighty demand of that which he still lacks.*"[70]

The requirement to give up everything he had, while very much like Jesus' self-emptying, strikes us as at least somewhat extreme. Yet New Testament scholar David Garland gave some perspective on this requirement for twenty-first-century believers: "The command to sell all sounds quite unreasonable to us, but most in the ancient world would have heard it as radical but sound advice for those who were seriously devout."[71] This is helpful, for Jesus was conveying just that—that his followers had to be seriously devout, in order to be associated with him. Garland went on to explain the lesson Jesus was teaching his disciples through this incident, "The disciples are to learn from this encounter that God required something more than reverence for Jesus as a good teacher and earnest attempts to obey God's commands."[72] Indeed, Jesus' requirement for those who would be faithful is that they self-give to the point of selling "everything you have."

On another occasion Jesus was teaching the large crowd that was following him.[73] He spoke hyperbolically, indicating that anyone who wished to be his disciple must hate both one's life and one's family members. He followed that by stating a disciple must carry his or her cross and follow Jesus. These statements appear extreme, but at the turn of the twentieth century British theologian Alfred Plummer pointed out that making such shocking comments was typical of Jesus' style: "Jesus, as often, states a principle in a startling way, and leaves His hearers to find out the qualifications."[74] Nevertheless, such a radical requirement would have stunned many of the crowd at what it would cost them to become Jesus' followers.

70. Meyer, *Mark and Luke*, 133; italics original.
71. Garland, *Mark*, 396.
72. Garland, *Mark*, 400.
73. See Luke 14:25–33.
74. Plummer, *Luke*, 364.

Subsequently Jesus gave two examples demonstrating that it is prudent to count the cost of an activity prior to engaging in it. These two, along with Jesus' prior statements, served as the thought pattern in which potential disciples must engage prior to deciding to follow Jesus. His conclusion was that "those of you who do not give up everything you have cannot be my disciples."

Once again we see Jesus' requirement that the faithful at least be willing to give quite significantly, and actually do so in order to follow him. That self-sacrifice includes family relationships, one's own life, and all one's possessions. His point was that faithfulness is not something one elects for a period of time (or to a limited degree), followed by a season of waning, and perhaps subsequent faithfulness once again. Mid-twentieth-century British theologian A. R. C. Leaney summarized Jesus' teaching by suggesting that the passage is "intended to point one moral only: a disciple must be sure that he can see his discipleship through to the end."[75] Plummer had a similar comment about the passage, asserting that it teaches "that to become Christ's disciple involves something which ought to be well weighed beforehand. This something was explained before, and is shown in another form here, viz. complete self-renunciation."[76]

There are other examples from Jesus' life in which he taught that faithfulness entails extreme self-giving, parallel to the complete emptying he assumed at the incarnation.[77] These two, however, should serve to demonstrate that in his teaching Jesus required followers to emulate his example of not grasping what they had, but giving it up.

The second way in which Jesus called his followers to his standard of faithfulness was to give examples of those who did. The incident in which Jesus encountered Zacchaeus[78] stands out for one particular reason: it concerns a person who had only just begun his journey of faithfulness. Zacchaeus, a hated tax collector generally regarded as a sinner, merely wanted to see Jesus as he passed by. However, Jesus invited himself to stay with Zacchaeus at his house. As Jesus later described it, this was an act of "the Son of Man came to seek and to save the lost." At the end of the encounter Jesus declared that salvation had come to Zacchaeus's house. Yet Zacchaeus had responded tangibly to Jesus, paying back fourfold anyone he had cheated and giving half of his possessions to the poor.

75. Leaney, *Luke*, 215.
76. Plummer, *Luke*, 365.
77. For example, see Mark 8:34b–35 and Luke 9:59–62.
78. See Luke 19:1–10.

Whereas Zacchaeus had not given everything he had, as Jesus required in the teachings we just reviewed, he had given quite significantly *as a first act of following Jesus*.

At one point in his ministry Jesus was teaching in the temple. He observed that many rich people gave large sums, but that a widow had given a very small amount. His judgment of the matter, however, was that the widow had given more than all the others, since she—although in poverty—had given everything she had, even what she had to live on.[79] This striking example of faithfulness—and the cost of it—is a vivid parallel to the extent to which Jesus gave up what he had: he gave to the point of becoming empty, hollow, and void. The impoverished widow served as an example to those who would follow Jesus of his initial expectation of them.

The third way in which Jesus conveyed his standard of faithfulness was to show what servanthood looked like. As we have seen, he himself took the form of a slave—bereft of rights and self-determination, yielded completely to God—but what did he require of those who would be his faithful followers? Well into Jesus' earthly ministry two of his disciples, James and John, asked Jesus to "let one of us sit at your right and the other at your left in your glory."[80] After a brief discussion Jesus told the two that it was not up to him to grant their request. The rest of the disciples became indignant with James and John, at which point Jesus told them that aspiring to executive position and authority was something they were not to pursue. Rather, "whoever wants to become great among you must be your servant, and whoever wants to be first must be slave of all. For even the Son of Man did not come to be served, but to serve, and to give his life as a ransom for many."[81] The root word describing the servant that Jesus' followers were to be is *diákonos*. A form of the same word was used by Jesus to characterize his own role as one who served. The fundamental meaning in the context in which Jesus used it refers to a master's servant.[82] German church historian Hermann W. Beyer wrote in the mid-twentieth-century that in the context in which Jesus used the word it was composed of "many different activities such as giving food and drink, extending shelter, providing clothes and visiting the sick and prisoners. The term thus comes to have

---

79. See Mark 12:41–44.
80. Mark 10:37.
81. Mark 10:43–45.
82. Kittel and Friedrich, *TDNT*, 2:88.

the full sense of active Christian love for the neighbour and as such it is a mark of true discipleship of Jesus."[83]

This understanding captures the "servant" nature of what Jesus was demanding, but wherein do we find the sense in which Jesus was the slave of God, devoid of independence and acting only as the Father directed? Beyer went on to explain a further element of *diákonos*, arguing that it "is one of those words which presuppose a Thou, and not a Thou towards whom I may order my relationship as I please, but a Thou under whom I have placed myself."[84] Now it is clear that Jesus' call to the faithful to serve paralleled his stance as the *doūlos* of God, the slave of the Father. In the same passage Jesus used *doūlos* to refer to any who want to be first. They must assume not only the position of a slave, but that of the slave *of all*. We see, then, that in addition to requiring his followers to empty themselves as did Jesus he also required them to follow him in assuming the stance of a slave, void of independence and self-determination.[85]

OBEDIENCE

After emptying himself, adopting the stance of a slave, and taking the form of humanity, Jesus became obedient to death, according to the Phil 2 passage. The author of the Epistle to the Hebrews wrote that the Son "learned obedience through what he suffered"[86] and as a consequence "became the source of eternal salvation for all who obey him."[87] What is this obedience, and how does it function as a model for the faithful?

In modern Western culture it is common to view obedience as an action: comportment with the directive of some sort of authority, be it a person's executive orders, an institution's laws or rules, or a subculture's unwritten but clear expectations. There is no doubt that someone who does not comport is subject to a charge of disobedience. Yet obedience is more than simple action. More fundamentally, it is an attitude. In an article published in *Europe's Journal of Psychology* concerning obedience in US young adults, the authors concluded:

---

83. Kittel and Friedrich, *TDNT*, 2:85.
84. Kittel and Friedrich, *TDNT*, 2:85.
85. Other instances in which Jesus described the servant role required of his followers are found in passages such as Matt 10:19–20 and Luke 17:7–10.
86. Heb 5:8.
87. Heb 5:9.

> Obedience and disobedience are not just behaviors, as clearly identified by multiple scholars across time . . . Instead, obedience and disobedience are composed and can be considered as attitudes. Thus, this study allowed us to refer to the construct (dis)obedience, not only from a behavioral standpoint, but, instead, also evoking concepts related to affects and cognitions, which enabled us to defined it as an attitude.[88]

Whereas overt *acts* of obedience are vital, they are not the core of the obedience God requires of his faithful followers. One can obey outwardly, yet rebel inwardly; that is not faithfulness. Rather, faithfulness starts with a heart attitude that reflects the heart of Jesus when he humbled himself to the point of obedience. It is this view of obedience that we are about to probe.

It is important to understand what obedience meant both in the culture in which Jesus lived and in the Old Testament religious background that formed his spiritual milieu. To that end, the words translated "obedience" in both the Old and New Testaments are key. In both instances they are derivative from words translated "to hear,"[89] and carried the fundamental notion of harkening or giving ear to something.[90] In Greek mystery religions as well as Gnosticism revelation came primarily through seeing rather than hearing, and "monuments which have come down to us with pictures of religious acts also make it clear that the sacred moment of the mystery or cult is one of vision."[91] The religion of the Old Testament, however, is quite different, in that "the Word, which is either heard or to be heard"[92] is primary. Thus "the hearing of man[93] represents correspondence to the revelation of the Word, and in biblical religion it is thus the essential form in which this divine revelation is appropriated."[94] Recall that the consistent message of the prophets was to hear God's word. "This prevalence of hearing points to an essential feature of biblical

---

88. Pozzi et al., "(Dis)Obedience in U.S. American Young Adults," para. 43.

89. See Thompson: "The words most often used for 'obedience,' 'obey,' are derivatives of the words 'to hear' in Hebrew, Greek, and Latin." Thompson, "Obedience," 465.

90. *Analytical Greek Lexicon*, 414.

91. Kittel and Friedrich, *TDNT*, 1:217.

92. Kittel and Friedrich, *TDNT*, 1:217.

93. This is yet another instance in which a distinctly male word was used to represent both genders. This unfortunate convention of the time in which the author was writing is no longer acceptable use; it is hoped that the reader will be able to look past this convention and see the broader message the author intended to convey.

94. Kittel and Friedrich, *TDNT*, 1:216.

religion. It is a religion of the Word, because it is a religion of action, of obedience to the Word. The prophet is the bearer of the Word of Yahweh which demands obedience and fulfillment."[95]

It is this revealed-word nature of Old Testament religion that exposes the link between hearing and obedience. Not only do the respective words belong to the same word group, but the concepts are joined: there is no true obedience without first hearing the word of God, and the word of God has not truly been heard if obedience does not follow. It should come as no surprise that this concept carried over into the New Testament, given the Old Testament foundation for the New. Even in the visually observable elements of the New Testament, their meaning is in the message the events conveyed.[96]

What is it, then, that composes the word to be heard? Most fundamentally it is the salvific message and the corresponding demand for response. "Hearing, then, is always the reception both of grace and of the call to repentance.... There thus arises, as the crowning concept of the obedience which consists in faith and the faith which consists in obedience."[97] Herein we see the essential link between obedience and faithfulness.

The obedience of Jesus followed this pattern of hearing the word of God and responding with both an attitude and actions of obedience; together they pointed to the salvific reality to be generated ultimately by the emptied, obedient Jesus. The attitude was first seen in his determination to adopt the position of a slave, deprived of rights—even the right to his fundamental humanity—and void of any independence. Instead, he thought and acted in submission to the Father. Philosopher Thomas Gregory expressed Jesus' obedient attitude when he wrote, "Not only Christ's work, but also His person can be understood in terms of His obedience. For John, Jesus is the Son of God because of His perfect unity with the Father. Such unity is established upon the basis of the perfect obedience of Jesus, whose meat and drink it is to obey the will of God (John 4:34) and to do the things that are pleasing to Him (8:29)."[98]

---

95. Kittel and Friedrich, *TDNT*, 1:218.

96. See *TDNT*: "The NT often tells of things seen, but these usually acquire their true significance in what is heard, as in the case of the message of the nativity, the voice at the baptism, the voice at the transfiguration ... the visions of Paul ... and the visions of the Apocalypse." Kittel and Friedrich, *TDNT*, 1:219.

97. Kittel and Friedrich, *TDNT*, 1:220.

98. Gregory, "Obedience," 484.

The notion of obedience to God as the fundamental expression of faithfulness was first introduced during God's interaction with Adam, in which God commanded Adam not to eat of the fruit of the tree of the knowledge of good and evil.[99] It continued in the dramatic incident in which God commanded Abraham to kill his son, Isaac.[100] At the time of the exodus obedience to God was the central notion that defined Israel's faithfulness. In the seventh century BC Jeremiah captured this notion when he wrote the message God gave him to convey to the people of Judah: "For when I brought your ancestors out of Egypt and spoke to them, I did not just give them commands about burnt offerings and sacrifices, but I gave them this command: Obey me, and I will be your God and you will be my people. Walk in obedience to all I command you, that it may go well with you."[101] At the time Israel's kingship was established the requirement for obedience included not only the Mosaic law, but additionally everything else God had commanded. Throughout its history fidelity to the covenant God had made with Israel was the single determinant of the level of Israel's faithfulness.[102] As a means to ongoing fidelity subsequent generations rehearsed Israel's history, but that rehearsal necessarily entailed not only reiterating the facts of God's dealing with Israel, but also the associated obedience always expected of God's faithful. Ethicist Allen Verhey captured this idea of remembering as a spur to obedience when he wrote, "The art of remembering always involved storytelling—and it always had the shape of obedience. To remember the Lord, to own the stories of God's glory, of God's works of power and grace, always meant in Israel to discern God's will and to do it."[103]

The social context of expected obedience to the law was the environment in which Jesus lived. Faithfulness and moral uprightness were defined by adherence to the covenant law. This Jesus did without fail, but he also lived and conveyed his message in a reality more extensive than simple outward obedience. Since he lived within the context of the old covenant's *requirement* of obedience, we should not be surprised to see that he couched his message within the *language* of obedience. Yet, for Jesus, mere outward obedience was not sufficient to define faithfulness. The notion that obedience is fundamentally an attitude drove Jesus

---

99. Gen 2:17.
100. See Gen 22.
101. Jer 7:22–23.
102. See Jer 11:1–8.
103. Verhey, *Remembering Jesus*, 24.

to expand and change the foundational meaning of obedience, and thus faithfulness. For Jesus there was no obedience if not obedience of the heart, irrespective of outward conduct. Thus he redefined murder to include anger against a sister or brother; adultery he redefined to include the heart's attitudes and intentions; and the faithful one's righteousness had to surpass that of the religious leaders.[104]

There was another instance in which Jesus demonstrated that the common understanding of obedience—and thus faithfulness—was insufficient. At one point a religious leader asked Jesus which of the commandments was the most important.[105] Initially Jesus gave the answer to be expected in his religious context: he quoted Deut 6:4-5.[106] At that point he could have stopped, for his answer was sufficient and complete in the legal milieu in which he lived. Jesus, however, knew that the answer was insufficient to convey his expectations of obedience by his followers, and thus he added a second commandment to his answer. In doing so he challenged the adequacy of the teacher's question as well as the appropriateness of the legal religious requirements for demonstrating faithfulness. Once again he expanded the notion of obedience by quoting part of Lev 19:18: "The second is this: 'Love your neighbor as yourself.' There is no commandment greater than these." There was no need for Jesus to add the second commandment to his answer, except to convey a new understanding of what obedience meant for God's faithful, and his expectation of those who said they were his followers.

Jesus not only changed and expanded the meaning of obedience, he also learned obedience. We saw in Heb 5:8 that it was through his suffering that obedience was learned. What does this mean? In what sense can obedience be learned by someone who never was disobedient? Typically the wisdom of obedience is learned through the consequences of disobedience. Yet for sinless Jesus obedience was something he had to learn, and it was through his suffering that the learning occurred. Thus it is in this experience of Jesus' learning obedience that we observe the close connection between obedience and suffering. The learning was not intellectual; it was experiential. It was only by enduring both physical and emotional suffering that Jesus acquired an experiential understanding

---

104. See Matt 5.
105. See Mark 12:28-34.
106. Jesus' quote of Deut 6:4-5 reads, "Hear, O Israel: the Lord our God, the Lord is one. Love the Lord your God with all your heart and with all your soul and with all your mind and with all your strength."

of obedience—or more accurately, the consequences of obedience. This experiential understanding completed Jesus' humanity. As twentieth-century theologian F. F. Bruce expressed it, "He set out from the start on the path of obedience to God, and learned by the sufferings which came His way in consequence just what obedience to God involved in practice in the conditions of human life on earth."[107]

The author of the Epistle to the Hebrews expressed the joining of Jesus' obedience to his suffering by quoting from Ps 40, but attributing the words to Christ.[108] His conclusion was that mere obedience to the law is not what God desired, but rather obedience to the Father's will: "Here I am, I have come to do your will. He sets aside the first to establish the second. And by that will, we have been made holy, through the sacrifice of the body of Jesus Christ once for all."[109] This change in the understanding of what obedience to God entailed ushered in a new order and a new understanding of faithfulness.[110]

We have seen that Jesus lived in a social and religious milieu that required external obedience to the law of Moses as well as to the other commands of God that had occurred throughout the history of Israel. To this requirement he was obedient, but at the same time he pointed out his contemporaries' lack of obedience to the underlying required attitude that formed the basis for the external law-based covenant.[111] This dissonance between the society's understanding of obedience and the teaching of Jesus on God's expectation of obedience resulted in fierce opposition on the part of the leaders of his religious context, to the point of their plotting Jesus' death.[112] Yet presenting the corrective to the common understanding was the task to which Jesus was called by the Father: doing it constituted obedience, but that obedience resulted in Jesus' suffering. Ultimately his lifelong pattern of steadfast obedience to the Father led

---

107. Bruce, *Epistle to the Hebrews*, 103.

108. See Heb 10:5–7: "Therefore, when Christ came into the world, he said: 'Sacrifice and offering you did not desire, but a body you prepared for me; with burnt offerings and sin offerings you were not pleased. Then I said, "Here I am—it is written about me in the scroll—I have come to do your will, my God."'"

109. Heb 10:9–10.

110. See Bruce: "The sacrifices in which God is said to take no pleasure are the sacrifices prescribed by the ancient cultic law of Israel; now that cultic law is to be superseded by a new order, inaugurated by Christ's perfect obedience to the will of God." Bruce, *Epistle to the Hebrews*, 235.

111. In this regard see, for example, Luke 11:37–54.

112. In this regard see, for example, Matt 12:1–14.

to the ultimate act of both obedience and suffering, his death. Grenz observed, "Above all, however, Jesus sensed that his dying marked the highest obedience to the will of his Father. He sensed the confirmation of the obedient nature of this act repeatedly throughout his sojourn and again near the end of his life, as our Savior struggled for the final time in the Garden of Gethsemane on the night of his arrest."[113]

After his resurrection Jesus again conveyed the urgency and necessity of obedience for the one who would be Jesus' faithful one. Just prior to his ascension he commissioned his followers to make disciples of all nations.[114] The first part of that instruction was to baptize new believers in the name of the triune God. The second part, however, was the ongoing and long-term task subsequent to baptizing them: "teaching them to obey everything I have commanded you." In his final words on earth Jesus focused on obedience to what he had commanded. This constituted not belief in a system or a body of content, but rather a moral obligation of all those who were to claim "Jesus is Lord." It was not optional, and adherence had to be complete. This is what faithfulness meant for Jesus' followers, built upon the example of Jesus' complete obedience to the Father.

That Jesus was perfectly obedient to the Father and also required obedience of his followers is clear, but how does Jesus' experience and example of obedience function in the life of the one who aspires to faithfulness? The idea that Jesus changed and expanded the meaning of obedience comes into play at this point. At the end of the first century the apostle John captured Jesus' augmented understanding of obedience, recalling Jesus' teaching the day before his crucifixion: "We know that we have come to know him if we keep his commands," and later "this is love for God: to keep his commands."[115] Six decades earlier Jesus had not only linked his followers' love for God with keeping Jesus' commands, he had drawn a direct parallel between that and his love for the Father through obeying the Father's commands.[116] Jesus' obedience, then, serves as a direct *paradigm* for the believer seeking to be faithful, and entails the enmeshing of love and obedience.

The notion of obedience to what Jesus—as one's Lord—commanded is key to understanding Jesus' contrasting imagery of houses built on

---

113. Grenz, *Theology*, 336.
114. See Matt 28:19.
115. 1 John 2:3 and 5:3, respectively.
116. John 15:10.

either a foundation attached to solid rock or without any foundation at all.[117] Such obedience is fundamental to the faithful one's ability to endure and withstand the challenges of his or her social setting, just as it had been for Jesus. For the early Christians this reality of obedience to Jesus being the means by which they endured—even to the end of life—was what it meant to be faithful, at least in part. Equating Jesus' commands with the word of God, Gregory captured this concept when he asserted, "Speaking in parables and in direct discourse, Jesus portrays the believers as those who hear the Word of God and do it (Matt 7:24; Mark 4:20; 7:32–37; Luke 8:21). Obedience is the hallmark of the personal decision, trust, and commitment which are involved in faith."[118] For the early Christians, obedience to Jesus was normative; it was inconceivable that one could be Jesus' follower and not be obedient to him as Lord.

SUFFERING

We have already seen the close connection between Jesus' obedience and his suffering. In the Phil 2 passage the progression from self-emptying, to adopting the position of a slave, to taking human form, to ultimate obedience to the Father, ends with Jesus "becoming obedient to death—even death on a cross!"[119] His ultimate obedience led to his ultimate suffering.

Jesus' suffering followed the pattern that God had for his faithful throughout history. We have seen how Abraham suffered for being faithful to God. Similarly Moses suffered many times in fulfilling his appointment by God to lead the Israelites from bondage in Egypt to the promised land. Jesus himself affirmed the history of suffering that followed the prophetic call: "in the same way they persecuted the prophets who were before you."[120] During his speech before the Sanhedrin just prior to his martyrdom Stephen asked the Jewish leaders, "Was there ever a prophet your ancestors did not persecute?"[121] Indeed, it was part of the prophet's lot both to speak out against the religious leadership and to suffer for doing so. British Baptist pastor Edmund Huddle summarized the suffering burden of the Old Testament prophets when he wrote: "they

---

117. See Luke 6:46–49.
118. Gregory, "Obedience," 483.
119. Phil 2:8b.
120. Matt 5:12b.
121. Acts 7:52.

were placed in the stocks (Jer 20:2); they were kept in chains (Jer 40:1); they were slapped in the face (1 Kings 22:24); they were imprisoned in cells, dungeons and cisterns (Jer 37:15–16 and 38:6) in some cases just on bread and water (1 Kings 22:27); they were threatened with death (1 Kings 19:1) while others were actually put to death (2 Chron 24:21, Jer 26:20–23)."[122] He went on to give many examples of prophets who were persecuted, perhaps the most striking of which was his depiction of Zechariah: "the son of Jehoiada the priest, was stoned to death for rebuking the people who turned aside to Ashera poles and idols, and for forsaking the Temple."[123]

Prophets suffered in ways other than only physically. At times their messages were rejected; they were threatened, falsely accused, and ridiculed; some were hauled into captivity; and at times they were used by God as suffering examples to the ones to whom God had sent them. Ezekiel is a stunning instance of this last type. At one point God caused Ezekiel's wife to die, whom God himself described as "the delight of your eyes."[124] Furthermore, God did not permit Ezekiel to mourn, weep, or act in any other way like one who was grieving. Ezekiel's response to this news from God was, "So I spoke to the people in the morning, and in the evening my wife died. The next morning I did as I had been commanded." What was the purpose of this extreme personal suffering on the part of Ezekiel? One pastor described it in this way: "God had Ezekiel suffer this affliction so he could show the Jewish captives in Babylon just how evil the nation of Judah had been and God's punishment that was required because of their wicked ways."[125] Ezekiel suffered grievously not for his own sin, but due to the evil of Judah.

There is a long history, then, of prophetic suffering prior to the incarnation. Jesus was the inheritor of that history, and as such was to become the next participant in it. Systematic theologian Gordon R. Lewis captured the necessity of Jesus' suffering when he explained, "To accomplish His purpose, Jesus had 'to suffer many things, and be rejected by the elders and chief priests and scribes, and be killed, and on the third day be raised' (Luke 9:22; cf. 17:25; 24:26; Matt 16:21; Mark 8:31).... The risen Lord explained, 'Thus it is written, that the Christ should suffer and on the third day rise from the dead' (Luke 24:46). Peter declared that

---

122. Heddle, "Persecuted Prophets," para. 7.
123. Heddle, "Persecuted Prophets," para. 12.
124. See Ezek 24:15–24.
125. Boyd, "Prophets," 1.

God had foretold by the mouth of all the prophets that His Christ should suffer."[126] Faithfulness to the Father demanded that Jesus suffer; indeed, he was ordained to it.

It is clear, then, that Jesus was aware that the path of suffering was the path laid out for him. The inevitability of his suffering was pointed out by Grenz as being not only an indispensable part of Jesus' experience, but likely the heart of his purpose: "he saw suffering and death as the probable end of his ministry, perhaps even as an essential part of his mission. . . . Yet Jesus' attitude toward his death went beyond mere cognition of its imminence. More than passively acquiescing to the inevitable, Jesus saw this event as the focal point and climax of his mission."[127]

It is important to notice, as Paul explicitly made clear in the Phil 2 passage, that Jesus' obedience not only led to extreme suffering and death, it led to a particular type of death: death on a cross. The author of the Epistle to the Hebrews pointed out that Jesus "suffered death, so that he might taste death for everyone."[128] After asserting that "His full humanity and exposure to death was the condition for the achievement of redemption,"[129] theologian William Lane elucidated a critical truth about the term "tasted death," commenting that it "is a Semitic expression which captures vividly the reality of the violent death on the cross which Jesus endured for others."[130] And so, as I argued elsewhere, "He died a violent death involving intense suffering for a long period of time, and the entire social context surrounding Jesus' death included extreme humiliation, extensive injustice, gross misunderstanding, and many other elements of human experience that rendered his particular experience leading up to death a negative one in the extreme."[131]

The suffering Jesus experienced via crucifixion was not only physical, extreme as that was. As was the case with other faithful prophets, he also suffered social rejection, disgrace, and humiliation. Concerning

---

126. Lewis, "Suffering and Anguish," 531.

127. Grenz, *Theology*, 336. Grenz emphasized the essential nature of Jesus' suffering when, referring to Mark 8:27–30, he wrote, "The Evangelist points out that, beginning with the incident at Caesarea Philippi, Jesus emphasized how the Son of Man must first suffer before entering into his glory." Grenz, *Theology*, 338.

128. Heb 2:9.

129. Lane, *Hebrews*, 45.

130. Lane, *Hebrews*, 45.

131. Wozniak, *Living as the Living Jesus*, 119–20.

society's view of crucifixion at the time of Jesus' death, Bruce described it as follows:

> To die by crucifixion was to plumb the lowest depths of disgrace; it was a punishment reserved for those who were deemed of all men most unfit to live, a punishment for sub-men. From so degrading a death Roman citizens were exempt by ancient statute; the dignity of the Roman name would be besmirched by being brought into association with anything so vile as the cross. For slaves, and criminals of low degree, it was regarded as a suitable means of execution, and a grim deterrent to others. But this disgrace Jesus disregarded, as something not worthy to be taken into account when it was a question of His obedience to the will of God.[132]

Here we see the extent of Jesus' suffering *in the context in which he lived*. He not only endured to the end, he also showed by his example how to approach suffering within one's social milieu. His followers were given the model of how they were to understand the suffering that would accompany their fidelity, and how to view the ones in their respective societies that were imposing it.[133] Even after his resurrection Jesus—the victor over his agonizing and humiliating death—spent time with his followers convincing them that the kingdom of God entailed suffering, just as he had suffered. As his followers—those who identified with Jesus—they should expect to experience the same thing he had: suffering of all kinds at the hands of those who opposed them. It appears that the message was successfully conveyed to at least some of his faithful, for according to theologian Leo Lefebure, "When threatened with martyrdom, early Christians looked to the example of Jesus Christ for their primary model for understanding how to accept unjust suffering. Many tried to find something positive amid suffering."[134]

There is another way in which Jesus understood himself and the suffering to which he was called. Later, his followers came to see him in

---

132. Bruce, *Epistle to the Hebrews*, 352–53. To add emphasis to his point concerning the general revulsion at execution by crucifixion, Bruce quoted from Cicero, Roman philosopher and statesman of the first century BC: "Let the very mention of the cross be far removed not only from a Roman citizen's body, but from his mind, his eyes, his ears." Bruce, *Epistle to the Hebrews*, 352–53n42.

133. In this regard Grenz wrote concerning Jesus' example to his future followers, "Through his own example he models the pathway to life—the manner of living that his disciples are to follow (John 13:12–15)." Grenz, *Theology*, 337.

134. Lefebure, "Suffering in the Early Christian Church," 33.

the same light. We have seen that in Isaiah is found the figure of the Suffering Servant of the Lord. The poems, or servant songs, that depict the Suffering Servant[135] in general paint the picture of the one who was the gentle, faithful, bringer of justice (42:1-4). He was the one who endured beatings, mocking, and spitting (50:6); was disfigured beyond recognition (52:14), and was despised and rejected (53:3). He was a man of suffering and pain (53:3), who took up the pain and suffering of others (53:4). In doing so he was pierced crushed, punished, wounded (53:5), and became the one who bore the iniquity of all others (53:6). He was oppressed, afflicted, slaughtered (53:7), and numbered with transgressors while bearing the sin of many (53:12).

The thought of Grenz regarding the Suffering Servant yields clarity concerning Jesus' self-understanding in this regard, as well as the view later believers had of Jesus as the Suffering Servant. Grenz explained, "At the heart of Jesus' conception of his task lay his unparalleled employment of Isaiah's motif of Suffering Servant . . . In his earthly ministry servanthood predominated. Jesus understood his task as that of suffering in obedience to his Father and on behalf of the people. He must experience rejection, even death in fulfillment of his vocation."[136] He went on to tie Jesus as the Suffering Servant to Jesus' character, thereby linking Jesus' suffering to his faithfulness to the Father. According to Grenz, Jesus' character expressed as the Suffering Servant serves as the model for the faithful to emulate. "In his vocation as the Suffering Servant we discover the character of Jesus, which is our standard. In his life and death, Jesus reveals that God's design for us is that we live as obedient servants of our heavenly Father and minister—even suffer—for the sake of others."[137] In understanding Jesus as the Suffering Servant of the Lord, those who aspire to faithfulness see a tangible image of faithfulness in action. It was not much of a leap for the early Christians to view Jesus—the one they sought to follow—in light of the Suffering Servant pictured in Isaiah.[138]

---

135. See Grenz: "The background of this designation lies in the servant poems of Isaiah (Isa. 42:1-4; 49:1-6; 50:4-11; 52:13—53:12). We no longer can discern who the author saw as the Suffering Servant. This figure may refer to the nation of Israel as a whole, to the prophetic community in general who suffer in their mission, or to one specific prophet, perhaps even Isaiah himself. Nor did Jesus ever explicitly use the title for himself. Nevertheless these poems provide a fruitful context in which to understand the vocation of Jesus." Grenz, *Theology*, 336-37.

136. Grenz, *Theology*, 338.

137. Grenz, *Theology*, 339.

138. See Grenz: "The early community made explicit the servant-Christology

The Epistle to the Hebrews emphasized that one purpose for Jesus' suffering was to identify with, live as, and be in solidarity with humanity.[139] In doing so, he became experientially qualified to function as humanity's high priest. Bruce commented:

> Any priest must be one with those whom he represents before God, and this is equally so with Christ as His people's high priest. In order to serve them in this capacity, He was obliged to become completely like His brethren—apart from sin, of course... He suffered with them and for them, and through His sufferings was made perfect—qualified in every way to be their high priest. He is merciful, because through His own sufferings and trials He can sympathize with theirs; He is faithful, because He endured to the end without faltering.[140]

Bruce tied Jesus' suffering to his faithfulness when he observed, "It is difficult to decide whether His faithfulness here is His steadfast loyalty to God . . . or His utter trustworthiness so far as His people are concerned. . . . it may not be necessary to decide too narrowly between them."[141] Jesus' suffering not only was an existential alignment with those for whom he emptied himself in order to die, but also was a demonstration of faithfulness on multiple levels.

Suffering as temptation is particularly in view as one means by which Jesus showed solidarity with humanity.[142] The tempted one suffers continually, as long as temptation is endured. The suffering ends, however, when one succumbs. Such is the common lot of humanity. However, Jesus uniquely never succumbed to temptation, and so his suffering continued—more than that of any other person. His suffering in temptation, however, uniquely qualified him in a way that no other experience could: it enabled him to help others when they suffer.[143]

The early Christians viewed the suffering Jesus as the model they were to emulate. He had suffered and had promised that all who would be faithful to him would likewise suffer. They sought to walk the path

---

implicit in Jesus' self-understanding. They interpreted Jesus' actions (Matt. 8:16–17) and above all his death (Acts 8:32–35) by appeal to Isaiah's Suffering Servant." Grenz, *Theology*, 337.

139. See Heb 2:9–18.
140. Bruce, *Epistle to the Hebrews*, 52.
141. Bruce, *Epistle to the Hebrews*, 52.
142. See Heb 4:15.
143. See Heb 2:18.

he had trod, and to follow after him; that included his suffering. Lefebure described their thinking, noting particularly the moral aspect of their outlook. He asserted, "Many Christians would see the acceptance of suffering as a way of sharing in the sufferings of Jesus Christ and of becoming more closely united to him ... for early Christians, suffering offered a path to align one's life with the values of Jesus Christ."[144] As an example, Lefebure focused on the thinking of Ignatius and his desire to imitate Jesus, specifically in his suffering.[145] Ignatius "saw his suffering as the culmination of his becoming a disciple of Jesus Christ: 'If I suffer, I shall become a freedman of Jesus Christ, and I shall arise free in him.'"[146] He concluded, "Ignatius was acutely aware that he was being led to likely martyrdom, and he interpreted his upcoming suffering as a way of sharing in the passion and death of Jesus Christ and of perfecting his identity as a Christian disciple."[147]

Not all early Christians were as resolute in their commitment as Ignatius, but many aligned with his thinking because it reflected what faithfulness to Jesus entailed. Just as Jesus had emptied himself, adopted the stance of a slave to others, became obedient, and suffered in order to be faithful to God's call and commission, so the early Christians viewed faithfulness in the same light. Thus they adopted Jesus' attitude and intention as a means to faithfulness, following in the footsteps of their Lord. Such thinking is rarely seen today in Western Christianity, with its focus on emotional effervescence as praise of God to the greatest extent possible while erroneously viewing the beneficial results of its syncretistic compromise as divine blessing. The message of the Suffering Servant, however, is that true faithfulness—that which God expects of the people of God—is anything but what is found in modern Christendom. Indeed, the message of the Suffering Servant is that all who are faithful will suffer. Such was the standard set by Jesus, and such is the consistent message of Scripture.[148]

---

144. Lefebure, "Suffering in the Early Christian Church," 36–37.

145. See Lefebure, in which he quoted Ignatius: "Allow me to be an imitator of the suffering of my God." Lefebure, "Suffering in the Early Christian Church," 34.

146. Lefebure, "Suffering in the Early Christian Church," 34.

147. Lefebure, "Suffering in the Early Christian Church," 33.

148. See, for example, 2 Cor 1:5; 4:8–11; Heb 10:32–34; 1 Pet 2:19–21; 4:12–19.

12

Faithfulness: Commitment and Conduct

JESUS' LIFE OF FAITHFULNESS consisted of far more than just his disposition. Attitude and intention composed his inward faithfulness, but his outward commitment and conduct were the natural outgrowth of his character. It is important to realize that Jesus had no executive moral authority by which he could wield power over others, including his followers. He had no official standing, title, or social status that he could leverage against some and for the benefit of others. Such was the situation of the one who had adopted the position of a slave, and who came not to be served, but to serve.

It should not be concluded that Jesus had no moral authority of any kind, however. Indeed, he had great authority, but not of the kind to which most of current Western society responds, for it was not based upon power. We may ask why the authority of power, or executive authority, has become so important in the West. If Jesus' authority was not based upon power, why does power-based authority prevail in modern society, including within the Christian community? Stassen and Gushee reminded us of the argument Yoder made, namely that "the point of discipleship is faithfulness, not effectiveness."[1] The shortcoming of the modern Western church is that, in its syncretistic approach to values and

---

1. Stassen and Gushee, *Kingdom Ethics*, 167.

conduct, it has adopted the broader society's power-based thinking in which effectiveness rather than faithfulness predominates.

Jesus took a different approach. He had the authority of both his teaching and his example.[2] Whereas Jesus' public instruction and actions occurred throughout his ministry, much of what he sought to convey concerning faithfulness is found in the Sermon on the Mount in the Gospel of Matthew. Emphasizing that the Sermon is to be viewed as practical teaching, rather than idealistic, Stassen and Gushee asserted, "Jesus taught practice norms. They are not mere inner attitudes, vague intentions, or moral convictions only, but regular practices to be engaged in."[3] Although a great many practices from Jesus' ministry could be identified, there are a few that stand out as fundamental; many of the others could be associated with them, and some of the more internal practices could be associated with the elements of the previous chapter. The overt ones that Jesus most desired and expected from those who would be his faithful ones can be captured under three broad categories: solidarity with the needy, peace, and fomenting change.

It should be clear that Jesus' conduct was different—quite different—from the moral norms of his social milieu. The prevailing norm of religious righteousness was that displayed by the scribes and Pharisees. Jesus, however, rejected that norm, and taught that his followers must be more righteous than the religious leaders. He also expected them to understand faithfulness as distinctly different from allegiance to the prevailing powers, be they religious, social, or political. The question for us is in what way are Jesus' faithful followers to be different? What does such faithfulness look like? Bonhoeffer proffered an answer when he wrote, "What make the Christian different from other men is the '*peculiar*.'" He followed with an explanation of the peculiar: "It is the life described in the beatitudes, the life of the followers of Jesus."[4]

It is the peculiar, the extraordinary, that we are seeking to articulate as the essential elements of faithfulness. To that end, let us probe Jesus' standard for solidarity with the needy, peace, and fomenting change.

---

2. For a more thorough discussion of the various types of moral authority, including executive, epistemic, and exemplary, see De George, "Authority and Morality," 31–49.

3. Stassen and Gushee, *Kingdom Ethics*, 136.

4. Bonhoeffer, *Cost of Discipleship*, 169–70; italics original.

SOLIDARITY WITH THE NEEDY

Early in his ministry—after his baptism and temptation but before he called any of the twelve disciples—Jesus went to the synagogue in his home town and read a portion of Isa 61. As recorded by Luke, the passage reads:

> The Spirit of the Lord is on me,
> Because he has anointed me
> To proclaim good news to the poor.
> He has sent me to proclaim
> Freedom for the prisoners
> And recovery of sight for the blind,
> To set the oppressed free,
> To proclaim the year of the Lord's favor.[5]

When he finished reading he announced to the synagogue audience, "Today this scripture is fulfilled in your hearing."[6]

What led Jesus to declare that the passage was fulfilled in the hearing of the listeners that very day? Was there something in his background that was driving or directing him? In what sense could it be said that the passage was fulfilled on the day that he read it? To answer these questions it is important—as it has been with other life elements by which Jesus displayed the divine character—to understand the Old Testament background which formed Jesus' perspective on the needy.

For the one familiar with the Old Testament there should be no confusion concerning God's attitude toward the needy, be they the impoverished, those who are sick, foreigners, orphans, widows, the socially outcast, the abused, or victims of injustice. Throughout the Pentateuch, the Psalms and Proverbs, and the Prophets there is found a consistent and clear depiction of how God views any and all included in the broad category of "the needy." In Deut 10:17 we learn that God "shows no partiality and accepts no bribes." Blind impartiality in all matters appears to characterize God. Yet the following verse shows that such is not the case. The prohibited partiality of verse 17 refers to partiality *toward the rich and powerful in matters involving the administration of justice*,[7] as demonstrated by the specific identification of those who feel that somehow they

---

5. Luke 4:18–19.
6. Luke 4:21.
7. Further indication that the scope of impartiality is limited to the administration of justice is found in such verses as Lev 19:15, Deut 1:17, and Deut 16:19, in which the Israelites were instructed to render impartial justice.

can bribe God in such matters. In contrast, verse 18 reveals that God has a clear predilection toward the fatherless, widows, and foreigners, including the fact that he provides for them. We find the same predilection in the Psalms.[8] Particularly revealing is Ps 146:7–9, which shows that the scope of God's special attention to the needy includes the oppressed, the hungry, prisoners, the disabled sick, those who are broken down, foreigners, the fatherless, and widows. The scope of God's perspective appears to entail a wide range of all who are needy, without exception. Indeed, it is evident that God as depicted in the Old Testament is partial toward those who suffer need. We may even assert that partiality toward the needy is an element of God's character.

The Old Testament not only reveals God's heart toward the needy; it also leverages that divine character element to instruct the faithful that they should adopt the same view. This leveraging is a clear substantiation of the notion that faithfulness consists in acquisition and demonstration of the character of God within the social milieu in which the faithful one lives. Regarding the specific subject of how the faithful one should view and approach the needy, reflection of the divine character requires the same predilection toward the needy as that displayed by God. For example, Prov 22:22–23 commanded the Israelites that they were not to exploit the poor or crush the needy in legal matters. Therein follows an affirmation that "the Lord will take up their case." The character of God, then, is linked to the instruction to God's people that they were to view the poor as does he.[9]

The prophets are even more precise on what is expected of God's faithful when engaging the needy. In the eighth century BC Isaiah the prophet reiterated the message he heard from the Lord, addressed to wayward Israel. Early in the book we find that Israel was to "learn to do right; seek justice. Defend the oppressed. Take up the cause of the fatherless; plead the case of the widow."[10] Toward the end of the book we find the list expanded to include eliminating injustice, lightening others' burdens, freeing the oppressed, feeding the hungry, sheltering the poor, clothing the naked, and satisfying the needs of the oppressed.[11] Two centuries after Isaiah the prophet Zechariah also conveyed to Israel the

---

8. See, for example, Pss 9:18, 12:5–7, 35:10, 68:5–6, and 140:12.

9. In this regard see other instances in Proverbs, for example, Prov 16:19, 19:17, 29:7, and 31:8–9.

10. Isa 1:17.

11. See Isa 58:6–7, 10.

message from the Lord: the people were not to "oppress the widow or the fatherless, the foreigner or the poor."[12] This theme is repeated elsewhere throughout the Prophets.[13]

It is this Old Testament perspective—both on God's approach to the needy and that required of God's faithful—that characterized the background and milieu in which Jesus grew up. His convictions regarding the necessary outworking of the divine character in the life of the faithful one were formed by this perspective. If part of the character of God entailed a predilection toward the needy, then Jesus as the perfect *imago Dei* and depiction of that character likewise would embrace the needy as the special objects of divine favor. Yet the significance of the Isa 61 passage that Jesus read goes beyond an affirmation of God's predisposition toward the needy. The last phrase indicated a proclamation of the year of the Lord's favor. Good news for the poor, freedom for prisoners, sight for the blind, and freedom for the oppressed are linked to "the year of the Lord's favor." According to Yoder the term at the time of Isaiah may have referred "to some particular event either at the end of the age or in the immediate future of the Babylonian captives (or both),"[14] but at the time Jesus was quoting it over seven centuries after Isaiah wrote it the term "most likely meant neither of these but rather the jubilee year, the time when the inequities accumulated through the years are to be crossed off and all God's people will begin again at the same point."[15]

The vision of the Jubilee is found in Lev 25:8–55. Largely it dealt with economic matters, and entailed an economic reset throughout the society. Things were not to be as they normally were, but rather a pristine time was to be established. Yet more fundamentally it referenced the work of God in atoning for his people, setting them free, and consecrating them to himself. It was a time when holiness was to prevail. It is in this sense that Jesus proclaimed that the Isa 61 passage was fulfilled the day he read it. In Jesus, as Isaiah's Servant of the Lord, the righteousness of God was to be visited on people, and all things were to be made new. That included complete relief for any and all who were needy. Throughout Jesus' lifetime he was to enact the vision of the Jubilee. Herein was no syncretism with the prevailing society, but very much the opposite. For Jesus faithfulness meant the upending of the normal ways of society,

---

12. Zech 7:10.
13. See, for example, Jer 5:26–29; Amos 2:6, 7; 4:1; Mic 4:6–7; and Mal 3:5.
14. Yoder, *Politics of Jesus*, 36.
15. Yoder, *Politics of Jesus*, 36.

and their replacement by the divine way: a way made concrete in the social milieu by demonstration—and ideally, through the establishment in society—of the character of God in all things.

The notion of upending societal norms and replacing them with the divine way is also reflected in Mary's Magnificat.[16] Although recorded as part of Luke's Gospel, the surrounding events in which Mary visited her cousin Elizabeth took place prior to the birth of either John the Baptist or Jesus. The Magnificat, then, belongs with the time of the Old Testament, prior to the incarnation. Envisioning that the birth of the Messiah signaled a time of social reversal in which the normal forces that drove society would be supplanted by divine values, Mary proclaimed the scattering of the proud, the demise of powerful rulers and the empowerment of the humble, the emptying of the rich, and the meeting of the needs of the hungry. In parallel with Isa 61, the Magnificat anticipates the advent of the kingdom of God in the incarnation of the Son.

Given this background it is simply too narrow a question to ask if Jesus was biased in favor of the needy. His vision was far more extensive than a simple matter of favoritism. In living within a fallen human society Jesus' intent was not to fix that society, but rather to live in such a manner as to work to replace it. He had in mind not only the divine vision for humanity as expressed in the Jubilee, but also his vision of the new humanity he would later make known to John[17] in Revelation: "Look! God's dwelling place is now among the people, and he will dwell with them. They will be his people, and God himself will be with them and be their God. He will wipe every tear from their eyes. There will be no more death or mourning or crying or pain, for the old order of things has passed away.... I am making everything new!"[18] It is in the context of this vision that Jesus, following the divine pattern, gave himself on behalf of the needy: he wiped away their tears, took away death, mourning, crying, and all other sorts of pain. In doing so, he established the standard for faithfulness that he expected his followers to embrace.

Jesus was living in the reality of the vision of Revelation, and calling all humanity to follow him. He was living out what he read from Isa 61 that day early in his ministry in the synagogue, declaring that the passage was seeing its fulfillment that very day. Harold W. Attridge expressed the impact of Jesus' declaration about himself when he wrote,

16. See Luke 1:46–55.
17. See Rev 1:1.
18. Rev 21:3–5.

"Jesus' proclamation of the coming Reign of God (Matt 4:17; Mark 1:15), a change in administration marking a decided shift in the way the world is run, offered a message of hope to widows, orphans, the blind, and lame, those who also received special treatment in the Torah and prophets of ancient Israel."[19] Stassen and Gushee made this same point when discussing Jesus and the inbreaking kingdom of God:

> How could Jesus claim that in himself the reign of God had come, and yet evil had not yet been eradicated? . . . The kingdom had come in God's presence through Jesus, in the justice of feeding the hungry, welcoming the stranger, visiting the sick, paying attention to the children (Mt 19:14) and forgiving debts (Mt 18:23–35); in the peacemaking of forgiveness and of welcoming the tax collectors, harlots and eunuchs (Mt 19:12; cf. Is 56:4), and proclaiming the gospel throughout the whole world as a testimony to the nations (Mt 24:14); in healing the blind, lame and demon-possessed (Mt 12:28); in the joy of the presence of the bridegroom (Mt 13:34; 25:1–13).[20]

Continuing in the same vein, Stassen and Gushee referenced the thought of theologian Gordon D. Fee when leveraging his 1992 article "The Kingdom of God." After citing Fee's argument that the kingdom of God "was present in Jesus as he performed the practices of the kingdom that Isaiah prophesied,"[21] Stassen and Gushee quoted Fee: "What has been 'fulfilled,' according to Jesus, was that *in his own ministry* the time of God's favor toward 'the poor' had come. In his healing the sick, casting out of demons, and eating with sinners—and thereby showing them God's unlimited mercy—the people were to understand that God's great eschatological day had finally dawned."[22] Jesus, then, in the way he ministered to the needy, was bringing the vision of Revelation into the present reality in which he lived, thereby fostering the inbreaking of the kingdom of God.

In his teaching Jesus translated the vision into words, primarily in the Sermon on the Mount (Matt 5–7). The Sermon begins with the Beatitudes, which parallel very closely the message of Isa 61:1, 2, 3, 7, and 11.[23] Jesus brought the Isaiah vision to the people of his day: humility

---

19. Attridge, "Care of the Poor," 14.
20. Stassen and Gushee, *Kingdom Ethics*, 29.
21. Stassen and Gushee, *Kingdom Ethics*, 29.
22. Stassen and Gushee, *Kingdom Ethics*, 29, quoting Fee.
23. See Stassen and Gushee, in which the authors demonstrated the parallelism between Isa 61 and the Beatitudes of Matt 5, and concluded, "This confirms that the

of spirit, mourning, an attitude of meekness, longing for righteousness, demonstration of mercy toward others, moral purity, working toward a peaceful living environment, and suffering for not compromising morally. Much of the rest of the Sermon is a practical depiction of the new eschatological society pictured in the Revelation vision. By making the vision practical, and requiring his followers to live by that vision, Jesus was conveying what faithfulness entailed *as the people of God lived in the moral realm within their respective social milieus.*

At one point in the Sermon Jesus specifically addressed giving to the needy.[24] It is important to realize contextually that the practice at the time Jesus spoke was to conduct acts deemed to be righteous in such a way that they were on display for others to see. As with much of his ministry, Jesus was changing the societal and religious norm, and thus altered the common understanding of what faithfulness entailed. This is seen in the first verse of Matt 6, which consists of overall guidance against "the general character of Pharisaic righteousness,"[25] according to nineteenth-century Scottish theologian Alexander Balmain Bruce. He went on to assert, "The spirit of ostentation Christ here and elsewhere presents as the leading feature of Pharisaism."[26] A century ago British professor of Semitic languages Theodore H. Robinson expanded this notion when commenting upon Jesus, "On the one hand he saw men bestowing charity, praying, and fasting in such a fashion that others might see them and so recognize and applaud their goodness. The object of their action was to be noticed, to say to the world in effect, 'You see how good I am.'"[27] Rather than condone such outward practice of performing righteous acts for public display, Jesus set a different moral standard for the faithful. He taught that they were to do such things in private. Therein follow three examples of such expected private conduct: almsgiving, prayer, and fasting.

Verse 2 references what seems to be an odd practice of playing trumpets at the time righteous deeds were performed. Early in the twentieth century theologian Alan H. McNeile offered a possible explanation of this practice: "There is perhaps a reference to the practice of sounding trumpets on the occasions of public fasting in times of drought. Services

---

prophet Isaiah provides the context for Jesus' proclamation of the coming of the kingdom as deliverance." Stassen and Gushee, *Kingdom Ethics*, 35.

24. See Matt 6:1–4.
25. Bruce, *Synoptic Gospels*, 116.
26. Bruce, *Synoptic Gospels*, 116.
27. Robinson, *Gospel of Matthew*, 46.

were held in the streets (cf. v 5) to pray for rain, fasting was universal (cf. v 16), and almsgiving was understood to be essential for the divine acceptance of the prayers."[28] This may have been the case. An alternative, however, is also possible. McNeile referenced the thinking of fifth-century AD patriarch Cyril of Alexandria when he asserted that Cyril "and others assume that it was a Jewish custom to summon the poor by trumpets to receive alms."[29] Whatever the local understanding may have been of playing trumpets when giving alms, Jesus' basic point is that doing so is not what God expects of his faithful followers. Instead, his expectation of the faithful when showing concern for the needy is not only that they definitely will do so, but also will do so privately, with God alone being the audience.[30] A. B. Bruce captured this notion succinctly when he wrote, "The meaning is that theatrical virtue does not count in the Kingdom of God."[31]

Several times in the passage the language of "reward" for performing righteous deeds, including giving to the needy, is mentioned. Those who do so ostentatiously are said not to receive a reward from the Father, for they already have received their full reward. Presumably the accolades of the observers are the reward. However, at the end of verse 4 it indicates that the one who gives in secret will be rewarded by the Father. Can it be that the faithful who give according to the standard set by Jesus would be motivated to do so in order to be rewarded by God? If the reward consisted in some sort of personal benefit or gain for the giver, then it perhaps could be said that care for the needy was motivated by the anticipated advantage due to the giver. This would be quite inconsistent with all that Jesus had demonstrated and taught up to that point regarding faithfulness. However, personal gain need not be the Father's reward, nor the motive behind the conduct of the faithful. Stott addressed this concern when he wrote, "What, then, is the 'reward' which the heavenly Father gives the secret giver? It is neither public nor necessarily future. It is probably the only reward which genuine love wants when making a gift to the needy, namely to see the need relieved. When through his gifts the hungry are fed, the naked clothed, the sick healed, the oppressed freed and the lost saved, the love which prompted the gift is satisfied."[32]

28. McNeile, *Gospel According to St. Matthew*, 74.
29. McNeile, *Gospel According to St. Matthew*, 74.
30. See Matt 6:3–4.
31. Bruce, *Synoptic Gospels*, 116.
32. Stott, *Sermon on the Mount*, 132.

Stott's explanation is completely consistent with what we have learned thus far about the character of God expressed in the teaching and conduct of Jesus: self-emptying, sacrifice, and giving for the benefit of others are necessarily characteristics of the faithful.

It should not be surprising to see elsewhere Jesus taught that his followers were to align themselves with the needy. We would expect such to be the case, and hope to find evidence of such alignment among the early Christians. Appealing to concepts similar to those found in the Matt 6 passage, Jesus at one point[33] addressed his Pharisee host, telling him that when he gives a banquet the invitees should not be friends, relatives or the rich; such people had the ability to repay, in a manner not unlike the accolades the observers would give to those who gave alms with public display. Jesus' call was that those who had the ability to give a banquet should "invite the poor, the crippled, the lame, the blind."[34] In a similar incident[35] Jesus called out a Pharisee host for focusing on outward, observable cleanliness, and admonished him to focus instead on cleansing the inward, moral self, stating "be generous to the poor, and everything will be clean for you."[36]

In what is likely the most striking and sobering passage in which Jesus taught the essential nature of care for the needy on the part of God's faithful,[37] the single determining factor upon which one either is invited to eternal life in the kingdom of God or is condemned to eternal punishment of fire with the devil and his angels is how one responded to the hungry, thirsty, stranger, naked, sick, and prisoners. Caring for or ignoring even one needy person appears to be crucial.[38] This vision of the day of judgment at which all the nations stand before the exalted, glorified Son of Man is chronologically prior to the Revelation vision of God's new society, and is a precursor to its establishment. The clear message is that solidarity with the needy is absolutely essential to faithfulness, for without it one cannot be regarded as faithful.

In these three incidents, as well as others, Jesus was challenging the established societal and religious norm, just as he had done throughout the Sermon on the Mount. He was replacing the old standard with the

33. See Luke 14:12–14.
34. Luke 14:13.
35. See Luke 11:37–41.
36. Luke 11:41.
37. See Matt 25:31–46.
38. See Matt 25:40, 45.

moral norm of the new society of—in what would later be revealed in, and recorded as—the Revelation vision. As was the case with the Sermon, the call to the faithful was to live according to that vision in the specific social situations in which they found themselves.

The Christians of the first century appear to have understood and adopted the practical call of Jesus to live out their acquired divine character through predisposition toward the needy, *irrespective of their own social realties*. In the earliest New Testament writing James, the half-brother of Jesus, admonished the early Christians scattered among the gentiles against favoritism toward the rich, which was tantamount to abuse of the poor.[39] The author of the Epistle to the Hebrews recognized the conduct of the letter's readers, and encouraged them not to forget to show hospitality toward strangers and to continue their practice of ministering to those in prison and those being mistreated.[40] In his second letter to the Corinthian Christians Paul told of the impoverished Christians of Macedonia, who excelled in generosity[41] by giving to the impoverished in Jerusalem.[42]

The practice of showing special concern for the needy as a depiction of faithfulness, and thus of the divine character and the *imago Dei*, continued into subsequent centuries. In the early second century—just prior to his martyrdom—Bishop Ignatius of Antioch wrote a letter from Troas to the Christians of Smyrna, a prominent city of Western Asia. After affirming the strength of their faith he heartily endorsed the historicity and physical reality of the events of Christ's life, death, resurrection, and post-resurrection period as recorded in the Gospels. His intent was to counter those he termed "unbelievers" for their denial of the reality of the events of Jesus' life. Later in the letter he further characterized the unbelievers by writing, "Observe those who hold erroneous opinions concerning the grace of Jesus Christ which has come to us, and see how they run counter to the mind of God! They concern themselves with neither works of charity, nor widows, nor orphans, nor the distressed, nor those in prison or out of it, nor the hungry or thirsty."[43] This is a clear example that endorsement of this essential element of faithfulness—concern for

---

39. See Jas 2:1–7.
40. See Heb 13:1–3.
41. See 2 Cor 8:1–4.
42. See Rom 15:26.
43. Ignatius, *Smyrnaeans*, para. 6.

the needy of all types—continued into the post-Apostolic period of the church's history.

Evidence of the early Christians' acceptance not only of the New Testament writings but also of Ignatius's argument, and practical implementation of it within their social surroundings, is found in such writings as Justin Martyr's First Apology, chapter 67. Making the point that the predisposition toward the needy expressed in Acts and the writings of Paul continued, Attridge cited Justin:

> In the middle of the second century Justin Martyr in *1 Apol.* 67, tells of such efforts in the Roman community at their weekly assembly: "And they who are well-to-do, and willing, give what each thinks fit; and what is collected is deposited with the president, who succors the orphans and widows and those who, through sickness or any other cause, are in want, and those who are in bonds and the strangers sojourning among us, and in a word takes care of all who are in need."[44]

Notice that the extent of the care embraced not just one or a few who could be categorized as needy. Rather, it accommodated all who could somehow be described as needy, be they poor, ill, from another country, the fatherless, or any others who were suffering within the society. This, for early Christians, was the practical form of faithfulness in the context of their social milieu.

Faithfulness expressed as solidarity with the needy did not die out as the early centuries of Christian history passed. It did, however, take various forms. One revealing story was captured in the fifth-century work *The Lausiac History of Palladius*. Chapter 14 concerns two brothers named Paesius and Isaias, whose father was a Spanish merchant. The story was included by Placher as part of what Christian calling meant during the first four centuries of the church.[45] After inheriting their father's wealth, the brothers determined to adopt the monastic life. However, they took two different approaches to ministering to the poor. Paesius gave away his money to "the monasteries, churches, and prisons; he learned a trade so that he might provide bread for himself."[46] Isaias, however, kept the money, built a monastery, and "took in every stranger, every invalid, every old

---

44. Attridge, "Care of the Poor," 17.
45. See Placher, *Callings*, 76–77, for the text of the entire story.
46. Placher, *Callings*, 77.

man, and every poor one as well."⁴⁷ Subsequent to their deaths a controversy arose concerning which had chosen the better way. Fourth-century Desert Father Pambo settled the matter when he announced, "I saw both of them standing in paradise in the presence of God."⁴⁸

Solidarity with the needy does not have to take a particular form. It is not the *structure* of such ministry that is crucial for faithfulness, but rather the *fact* of the solidarity. It was essential in the life of Jesus as he brought the reality of Isa 61 and his vision—later recorded in Rev 21—to the lives of the suffering within his local context, since to embrace the needy is to express tangibly the character of God. The early Christians adopted the Jesus example of solidarity with the needy as an indispensable exemplification of faithfulness, living out the *imago Dei*. That indispensability is equally essential to faithfulness today.

PEACE

The seventh beatitude reads, "Blessed are the peacemakers, for they will be called children of God."⁴⁹ In addition to raising questions concerning the nature of peace and the complexion of a peacemaker, the beatitude calls us to wonder about the character of the children of God. First, however, it is important to understand what the Scripture means by the word "peace."

The Greek word for peace is *eirēnē*. It "does not primarily denote a relationship between several people, or an attitude, but a state, i.e., 'time of peace' or 'state of peace,' originally conceived of purely as an interlude in the everlasting state of war."⁵⁰ It was the word used when asking for terms of peace.⁵¹ From such peace "flow all blessings for both the land and people and which is extolled by Philemon as the supreme good."⁵² It can also refer to an attitude of peace, but in a negative sense as "more of the absence of hostile feelings than of the presence of kindly feelings to others."⁵³

---

47. Placher, *Callings*, 77.
48. Placher, *Callings*, 77.
49. Matt 5:9.
50. Kittel and Friedrich, *TDNT*, 2:400–401.
51. Bauer, *Greek-English Lexicon*, 226.
52. Kittel and Friedrich, *TDNT*, 2:401.
53. Kittel and Friedrich, *TDNT*, 2:401.

The Jewish sense of peace, captured in the word *shalom*, is significantly different from that of the Greek word *eirēnē*. "If the main sense of the Gk. word [*eirēnē*] is a state of rest, the Heb. [*shalom*] contains the thought of well-being or salvation."[54] Instead of referring to a state, such as an interlude between hostilities, *shalom* captures the ideal situation of the individual, or community.

> We constrict the term [*shalom*] if we equate it strictly with "peace." At root it means "well-being," with strong emphasis on the material side. In meetings or letters well-being is wished to others, and in conversations one asks about their well-being. . . . Here and in many other instances [*shalom*] really signifies bodily health or well-being and the related satisfaction. More commonly [*shalom*] is referred to a group, e.g., a nation enjoying prosperity. This brings us closer to the thought of peace.[55]

Mid-twentieth-century Scottish theologian William Barclay captured the New Testament notion of peace when he wrote, "Now in the NT sense 'peace' is not just the absence of trouble; it is everything that makes for our highest good."[56]

Why is the difference between *eirēnē* and *shalom* important for our purposes? The reason lies in the fact that even though the New Testament was written in Greek, the prevailing sense of peace throughout the New Testament is that of the Hebrew word *shalom*, rather than the Greek word *eirēnē*.[57] As such, the notion of what constitutes a peacemaker is greatly determined by the sense and extent of *shalom*. When, for example, the seventh beatitude speaks of the peacemakers, it is not simply referencing those who broker the cessation of hostilities; rather, it is speaking not only of that, but also of something far more encompassing.

Living as a Peacemaker

What, then, is involved in peacemaking? The term occurs only once in the New Testament, in the Matt 5:9 beatitude we have been considering.

---

54. Kittel and Friedrich, *TDNT*, 2:406.
55. Kittel and Friedrich, *TDNT*, 2:402.
56. Barclay, *New Testament Words*, 148.
57. See *TDNT*: "That it is not the Gk. sense which predominates in the NT is particularly plain when we consider that the principal meaning is salvation in a deeper sense. We are also brought into the Rabbinic sphere by its frequent use for accord between men." Kittel and Friedrich, *TDNT*, 2:411.

Following the typical understanding of peace—that is, the Hebrew rather than the Greek understanding—it "denotes the establishment of peace and concord between men."[58] It is not simply brokering a truce between combatants, but rather the promotion of harmony among people, be they those engaging in violence or not. Of particular applicability to the current Western church is the fact that "it is thus a mistake to refer with Dausch to those who promote human happiness and well-being. Nor is it a matter of helping others to peace with God, as Brouwer suggests."[59] In the West the beatitude is easily and often understood to refer to something experiential within the individual, such as personal happiness or a sense of peace between the individual and God. To understand the beatitude in this way is to abuse it. Peacemaking is not fundamentally concerned with the individual's emotions or mental state—even though the scope of *shalom* includes well-being, albeit primarily in reference to the well-being and prosperity of the group or nation. Rather, peacemaking concerns bringing together—and creating harmony among—two parties that formerly were at odds.

We may ask about the scope of the beatitude. How far is peacemaking to extend? Are there limits to the subjects between whom the faithful is to broker peace? Political analyst Tod Lindberg weighed in on Jesus' intention in proclaiming the seventh beatitude. He began by observing, "After the 'pure in heart' come 'the peacemakers.' Jesus' intention here is clearly broad, encompassing not only relations between nations and peoples but also all subsets of conflict, down to those between two people."[60] He went on to expand this thought, asserting that "Jesus does not say specifically whether he refers to peace between and among individuals, families, tribes, societies, nations, or some other grouping. His lack of specificity invites the conclusion that he is referring to all of these levels of peacemaking."[61] One strives in vain to proffer an argument against Lindberg's reasoning, not because he is inherently correct, but because any such argument would be grossly inconsistent with the corpus of Jesus' teaching.

The Western church does not apply the beatitude in this way, but rather misappropriates it in order to bring inner comfort to the individual and thereby avoids the difficult peacemaking work to which Jesus calls

---

58. Kittel and Friedrich, *TDNT*, 2:419.
59. Kittel and Friedrich, *TDNT*, 2:419.
60. Lindberg, *Political Teachings*, 23.
61. Lindberg, *Political Teachings*, 24.

the faithful. It also seeks to impose limits on the scope of the beatitude as a means to sustain its erroneous syncretistic conviction that at some point the use of violence in the service of justice is warranted. A corrective within the church is necessary if faithfulness is to prevail.

The end of the beatitude indicates that the peacemakers will be called the children of God. Why is this? How is it that peacemaking and Godlikeness are linked? Several have expressed perspectives on the association. One has to do with the definition of peacemaking itself, indicating that peacemakers are "those who disinterestedly come between two contending parties and try to make peace. These God calls His sons because they are like Him."[62] The linkage has to do with the same concept we have been investigating for some time; that faithfulness entails adoption and reflection of the character of God.[63] In the specific case of the beatitude, the peacemaker is the one who acts like God, who is the peacemaker between himself and the whole of sinful humanity. As such, the peacemaker reflects the divine character.

Stassen and Gushee expanded on this notion of the peacemaker being the reflector of the divine character in the specific sense of how enemies are treated. They argued that "being a peacemaker is part of being surrendered to God, for God brings peace. We abandon the effort to get our needs met through the destruction of enemies. God comes to us in Christ to make peace with us; and we participate in God's grace as we go to our enemies to make peace. This is why the peacemakers 'will be called the children of God.' In a nutshell, *blessed are those who make peace with their enemies, as God shows love to God's enemies.*"[64] Here we see that peacemaking is part of what it means to be faithful, or as Stassen and Gushee put it, "part of being surrendered to God." We also see in their assertion the stark distinction between how God requires his followers to treat enemies compared with—and in clear contrast to—the common way enemies are viewed. The Christian, by virtue of being one of God's faithful, is no longer permitted to seek the destruction of enemies, but

---

62. Kittel and Friedrich, *TDNT*, 2:419.

63. See Lindberg, in which he correctly argued that achieving peace by any means is not what Jesus meant: "Clearly, the Jesusian instruction here will not be fulfilled through the imposition of the peace of the victor upon the vanquished. Nor will it be fulfilled by the purchase of peace at the cost of surrendering what is right. Neither 'I win' nor 'I surrender' will do." Lindberg, *Political Teachings*, 23. Correctly understood, the peacemaker can achieve peace between parties only when reflecting the character of God.

64. Stassen and Gushee, *Kingdom Ethics*, 45; italics original.

rather is to make peace with them (in the sense of *shalom*, not simply *eirēnē*). It is only in doing such that the believer acts as God acts toward enemies, and thus can be called God's child.

Some may object that in the Old Testament narrative not all of God's enemies were treated by God in the peacemaking manner just described. However, as we have observed elsewhere, Jesus—while leveraging and being faithful to his Old Testament heritage—brought a new understanding to the notion of faithfulness. Thus we see in the Sermon on the Mount his phrase, "You have heard it said to the people long ago . . . But I tell you . . ."[65] In bringing the new understanding of faithfulness Jesus also brought a new perspective on the Old Testament narrative. "Jesus showed how to interpret that rich narrative. He never quoted passages that favor killing, war or national supremacy. He quoted only the passages that favor peacemaking."[66] In so doing Jesus negated the oft-used appeal to Old Testament violence as justification of the use of violence against enemies by those who claim to be God's faithful.

Stott also engaged with the beatitude's assertion that the peacemakers will be called the children of God. His approach was to look objectively at what he saw in Jesus' teaching, as well as that of the apostles. "It is clear beyond question throughout the teaching of Jesus and his apostles . . . that we should never ourselves seek conflict or be responsible for it. On the contrary, we are called to peace, we are actively to 'pursue' peace, we are to 'strive for peace with all men,'[67] and so far as it depends on us, we are to 'live peaceably with all.'"[68] Stott was expressing the beatitude's overall expectation that the faithful one will live a peacemaking lifestyle in all respects, adopting the attitude and character of God. As such, "It is hardly surprising, therefore, that the particular blessing which attaches to peacemakers is that 'they shall be called sons of God.' For they are seeking to do what their Father has done, loving people with his love, as Jesus is soon to make explicit."[69]

---

65. See, for example, Matt 5:21–22, and similar phrases in Matt 5:27–28, 31–32, and 33–34.

66. Stassen and Gushee, *Kingdom Ethics*, 154.

67. As we have seen elsewhere, this is an unfortunate use of a gender-specific word to reference all people. Perhaps the reader will be able to look beyond this shortcoming and appreciate the value of the broader point the author is making.

68. Stott, *Sermon on the Mount*, 50.

69. Stott, *Sermon on the Mount*, 50.

Responding to Evil Persons

Concerning peace, Jesus did not leave us with only the beatitude about peacemakers. Later in the Sermon he specifically addressed the matter of retaliation.[70] He began with the common understanding that retaliation was to be in kind—"eye for eye, and tooth for tooth"—followed by his common corrective, "But I tell you . . ." What follows is a prohibition against retaliation: "do not resist an evil person." The subsequent verses present three examples of the form such non-resistance was to take in practice.

It is important to point out that Jesus was not saying that evil should not be resisted. Indeed, Jesus strongly resisted evil throughout his ministry.[71] The old KJV translation "resist not evil" is erroneous, but the background for such a translation is well-understood,[72] and many modern translations are more accurate.

What, then, did Jesus mean when instructing his followers not to resist an evil person? Stott argued:

> But what exactly is the meaning of this call to non-resistance? The Greek verb (*anthistēmi*) is plain: it is to resist, oppose, withstand or set oneself against someone or something. So whom or what are we forbidden to resist? . . . What we are forbidden to resist is not evil as such, evil in the abstract, nor "the evil one" meaning the devil, but an evil person, *one who is evil* (as RSV rightly translates) or "the man who wrongs you" (NEB). Jesus does not deny that he is evil. . . . What he does not allow is that we retaliate.[73]

Early in the twenty-first-century theologian Walter Wink brought clarity to the kind of non-resistance that Jesus was referencing by offering an accurate rendering of Matt 5:39: "A proper translation of Jesus' teaching would then be, 'Don't strike back at evil (or, one who has done you evil) in kind.' 'Do not retaliate against violence with violence.'"[74] Avoid-

---

70. See Matt 5:38–41.

71. See Wink, who asserted, "Jesus was no less committed to opposing evil than the anti-Roman resistance fighters. The only difference was over the means to be used: *how* one should fight evil." Wink, *Jesus and Nonviolence*, 11–12; italics original.

72. See, for example, Wink, in which he pointed out "now we are in a better position to see why King James' faithful scholars translated *antistēnai* as 'resist not.' The king would not want people concluding that they had any recourse against his or any other sovereign's unjust policies." Wink, *Jesus and Nonviolence*, 13.

73. Stott, *Sermon on the Mount*, 105; italics original.

74. Wink, *Jesus and Nonviolence*, 11.

ing the use of violence when responding to an evil person is the incontrovertible instruction being given by Jesus. Opposing evil, as did Jesus many times, certainly is not only permitted, but encouraged. Responding thoughtfully to the evil one who is harming the believer is the point of the three examples given immediately after the instruction not to "resist an evil person." Retaliating by means of violence, however, is strictly forbidden by Jesus. There is no latitude in this regard.[75] Stott captured the heart of Jesus' teaching when he asserted Jesus' "purpose was to forbid revenge . . . He teaches not the irresponsibility which encourages evil but the forbearance which renounces revenge. Authentic Christian non-resistance is non-retaliation."[76] He explained further Jesus' requirement of his faithful: "Instead, what Jesus here demands of all of his followers is a personal attitude to evildoers which is prompted by mercy not justice, which renounces retaliation so completely as to risk further costly suffering, which is governed never by the desire to cause them harm but always by the determination to serve their highest good."[77] The extent to which a believer endorses violence as a legitimate means by which to respond when harmed by another is the extent to which that believer fails both to follow the teaching of Jesus and to live faithfully.

Engaging with Enemies

Having given clear instruction on how his followers were to respond when harmed by someone evil, Jesus immediately moved to how they were to engage with actual enemies. He started once again by rehearsing the common attitude and understanding about engagement with them. In Matt 5:43 he quoted the prevailing viewpoint: "You have heard it was said, 'Love your neighbor and hate your enemy.'"[78] In his typical manner he also offered an update and a corrective: "Love your enemies and pray

---

75. In this regard see Yoder: "By 'nonresistant' here, as in this entire study, is not meant compliance or acquiescence in evil, but what Paul means in [Rom 12:17] and Jesus in Matt. 5:39, the suffering renunciation of retaliation in kind." Yoder, *Politics of Jesus*, 204n13.

76. Stott, *Sermon on the Mount*, 108.

77. Stott, *Sermon on the Mount*, 113.

78. See Bonhoeffer, in which he noted that the prevailing attitude was not reflective of Old Testament teaching: "the Old Testament never explicitly bids us hate our enemies. On the contrary, it tells us more than once that we must love them (Ex. 23.4 f; Prov. 25.21 f; Gen. 45.1 ff; I Sam. 24.7; II Kings 6.22, etc.)." Bonhoeffer, *Cost of Discipleship*, 163.

for those who persecute you, that you may be children of your Father in heaven."[79] Luke's version of this passage adds specificity: "Love your enemies, do good to those who hate you, bless those who curse you, pray for those who mistreat you . . . But love your enemies, do good to them, and lend to them without expecting to get anything back."[80]

Bonhoeffer's insight into this teaching is instructive for the one seeking to be faithful, but it also is sobering and challenging. Our natural tendency, and that which our social milieu has instilled within us from infancy, is that enemies are to be met with power—even violence—and conquered so that they no longer pose a threat. In his teaching, however, Jesus completely rejected such thinking and endorsed an approach radically different from that of the prevailing society. His teaching was both a challenge to and rejection of the syncretistic mindset that dominated the religious thinking of his day, as it still does today within our Western mindset. Bonhoeffer accurately argued that in the Sermon on the Mount "Love is defined in uncompromising terms as the love of our enemies."[81]

Who, we may ask, are our enemies? Who are those to be included in our love response, seeking the best for those who abuse and harm us? We have become accustomed to thinking that enemies are limited to those who are *personal* enemies: those with whom we have constant and ongoing differences, those who annoy or somehow target our good name and reputation, etc. In our syncretistic value system we reject the notion that our enemies—the ones we are to love—include those who are political or social, for those we feel we need to vanquish in order to sustain the society whose values we have adopted and endorse. Such was not the case, however, in the context in which Jesus lived. His reference to enemies was not limited to those who could be regarded as "personal." Rather, as Bonhoeffer observed, "And then there was the enemy which would immediately occur to every Jew, the political enemy in Rome."[82] In the context in which Jesus was teaching the enemies included Rome's political, military, and police functionaries who dominated and harmed Israel.[83] Jesus' unambiguous charge to those who would be God's faithful

---

79. Matt 5:44–45. Note that the reference to being children of the Father is a direct reflection of the seventh beatitude we investigated earlier. Jesus was drawing a direct link between being a peacemaker and the requirement to love one's enemies.

80. Luke 6:27–28, 35.

81. Bonhoeffer, *Cost of Discipleship*, 162.

82. Bonhoeffer, *Cost of Discipleship*, 163.

83. In this regard see Hays, in which theologian Richard B. Hays convincingly

was that all enemies—be they personal or representatives of either the religious or political powers—are to be treated with love, for irrespective of the nature of the enemy, "he has nothing to expect from a follower of Jesus but unqualified love. In such love there is no inner discord between private person and official capacity. In both we are disciples of Christ, or we are not Christians at all."[84]

The reasoning behind Jesus' teaching was made clear by Stott when he argued that "our enemy is seeking our harm; we must seek his good. For this is now God has treated us. It is 'while we were enemies' that Christ died for us to reconcile us to God. If he gave himself for his enemies, we must give ourselves for ours."[85] Once again Jesus was calling his followers to adopt and demonstrate the character of God, acting toward their enemies as God acted toward his (that is, all of us as sinners). To do otherwise is to abandon the quest to be Godlike in the moral realm in which we live our lives.[86]

Conduct Regarding Peacemaking, Retaliation, and Enemies

What shall we conclude from Jesus' teaching concerning peacemaking, retaliation against evil persons, and response to enemies? It simply is that the faithful, as we have seen many times and in many contexts, are to be like God, displaying God's character and reflecting the *imago Dei*. At its most base form the teaching means promoting and creating harmony among people who are at odds, both those who have resorted to violence and those who have not. Even though resisting evil is a fundamental responsibility of faithfulness, following the pattern set by Jesus, when engaging with an individual who has caused harm—be it to an individual, the

---

argued against Richard Horsley's contention that the enemies Jesus referred to in Matt 5:44 were limited to personal enemies. Hays then quoted Heinz-Wolfgang Kuhn to conclude that there is no limit to the range of enemies to be included in Jesus' teaching: "The term *echthroi* is generic. It is often used in biblical Greek of national or military enemies. . . . 'The religious, the political, and the personal enemy are all meant.'" Hays, *Moral Vision*, 327–28.

84. Bonhoeffer, *Cost of Discipleship*, 164–65.
85. Stott, *Sermon on the Mount*, 118.
86. See Stott, in which he concluded, "Having indicated that our love for our enemies will express itself in deeds, words and prayers, Jesus goes on to declare that only then shall we prove conclusively whose sons we are, for only then shall we be exhibiting a love like the love of our heavenly Father's. . . . This, then, is to be the standard of Christian love. We are to love like God, not men." Stott, *Sermon on the Mount*, 120.

collective, or a social/political entity in which the Christian participates—the believer is to be driven by the goal of seeking the offender's highest good, *even if it means that the risk the offender poses remains unchecked.* Retaliation is not a tool at the faithful one's disposal, and responding to violence in kind—with an attitude and commensurate conduct that carries the potential of causing harm—is strictly forbidden by Jesus. He offered no qualifications to this teaching; it applies to his faithful followers at all times, in all places, and in all circumstances. This is difficult to accept, particularly when one is driven by a desire for accountability and justice. Yet the human urge to require an eye for an eye and a tooth for a tooth is the very mindset that Jesus' teaching is intended to correct.

We saw that Jesus' reference to enemies was not limited to those who could be regarded as personal. Rather, it included all who do harm within the believer's social milieu, be they individuals, power groups, or political entities. Unlike the prevailing attitude that sought to engage with enemies with the very tools of power and violence that they employed, Jesus taught that enemies are to be met with love, for that is how God responded to his enemies (us). Just as God's love extends to all of us without discrimination, so the faithful one is called upon not to distinguish between enemies or to choose a response based upon the nature of the enemy. Rather, all enemies are to receive the same response: love. This, too, is hard to accept, particularly by those who see themselves as being on the side of good and enemies as being on the side of evil.

The upshot of Jesus' teaching concerning peace is that his faithful one—be it the individual or the church collective—has been given quite limited options for attitude and conduct. In order to reflect the divine character and display the *imago Dei* within society, promotion of harmony is foundational. Responding in kind by employing violent force is not an alternative the faithful one may choose. The believer's quiver of tools includes only love, nothing else. This means that the Christian is not at liberty to respond as does the broader society in which tools of response include options other than love. Specifically, the faithful one may not engage in any conduct that carries the potential of harming another entity, and thus may not endorse corporal or capital punishment, participate in any sort of police force, or join the military of any country. The reason and justification are simple: Jesus forbids it.

That this approach was not limited to the time of Jesus or his immediate followers was made clear by Hays in his investigation of Paul's letter to the Romans, chapters 12 and 13. Having referenced Rom 12:14–21 regarding how Jesus' followers are to treat those who harm them, those who do them evil, and their enemies,[87] Hays commented on both chapters: "Though the governing authority bears the sword to execute God's wrath (13:4), that is not the role of believers. Those who are members of the one body in Christ (12:5) are never to take vengeance (12:19); they are to bless their persecutors and minister to their enemies, returning good for evil."[88] He went on to conclude, "Thus, from Matthew to Revelation we find a consistent witness against violence and a calling to the community to follow the example of Jesus in *accepting* suffering rather than *inflicting* it."[89]

There remains only one element of the characteristic of peace to be investigated. Jesus' requirement of his followers is clear, unequivocal, and absolute. However, accepting it is difficult for those of us who desire to be faithful, for the society in which we are steeped—the kingdom of this world as opposed to the kingdom of God that Jesus brings—and the leaven of syncretism that thoroughly infiltrates our beings drive us to resist the moral standards of Jesus' new kingdom. He—just as we—lived within a very secular and fallen society; that being the case, he was constrained by virtue of his humanity to conduct himself within it. How, then, did Jesus actually act within his social milieu, as a peacemaker who engaged with very real enemies?

Several incidents from Jesus' life are commonly used by those seeking to justify the use of violence by Christians, and thus to endorse Christian participation in societal violence (e.g., joining a police force or the military). Chief among these is the incident in which Jesus cleansed the temple, an incident recorded in all four Gospels.[90] The proponents of this

---

87. Hays, *Moral Vision*, 330.
88. Hays, *Moral Vision*, 331.
89. Hays, *Moral Vision*, 332; italics original.
90. See Matt 21:12–16, Mark 11:15–18, Luke 19:45–47, and John 2:13–17. The issue of the sequencing of the cleansing within the Gospel narrative, with John's account at the beginning of Jesus' ministry and the other Gospel authors' accounts at the end, is not of concern for our purposes. Meyer, for one, provided a reasonable explanation of the chronological difference in his nineteenth-century critical commentary on the text of Matthew: "This cleansing of the temple is, with Chrysostom, Paulus, Kuinoel, Tholuck, Olshausen, Kern, Ebrard, Baumgarten-Crusius, Schleiermacher, Hengstenberg, Wieseler, to be regarded as the *second* that took place, the first being that recorded in John ii. 13 ff., and which occurred on the occasion of the first visit to Jerusalem. The abuse having been repeated, there is no reason why Jesus should not have repeated this purifying process, and that (in answer to Hofmann, Luthardt, Hengstenberg) without any essential difference. The absence in the synoptical account, of any allusion to a

position are particularly fond of John's account, in which Jesus "made a whip out of cords."⁹¹ Appeal is made to this phrase as incontrovertible proof that Jesus both employed and justified the use of violence in the pursuit of what is understood by the proponents to be a just cause.

It should be noted that Jesus made the whip in haste, with material that was readily available to him at the temple. The term translated "cords" refers to reeds or rushes—as opposed to something like leather thongs—similar to what today we know as binder twine. The resultant product cannot accurately be viewed as a weapon Jesus used in a violent manner. Furthermore, careful reading of the text reveals that Jesus used his device not on people, but on the sheep and cattle with the intent of moving them, not doing them harm.⁹²

We ask ourselves, if Jesus did not use his device with violence, and did not use it on people, then how did he engage with those either selling animals or changing money in the temple courts? The text indicates that he scattered the coins, overturned tables, and spoke to those doing the selling. There is no conduct on the part of Jesus intended to injure or harm anyone, only to get their attention and teach them the way of God.⁹³

Some may assert that the text can be viewed in various manners, and that to conclude that Jesus was not violent is only one perspective among several. Yet careful textual analysis reveals that such is not the case; it can only be understood as a demonstration of divine power, but

---

previous occasion, is sufficiently explicable from the length of time that intervened, and from the fact that the Synoptists take no notice generally of what took place during the earlier visit to Judea." Meyer, *Matthew*, 364; italics original.

91. John 2:15.

92. See Yoder, in which he argued, "Ever since the early Christian centuries, the whip in the temple has been considered the one act in the life of Jesus which could be appealed to as precedent for the Christian's violence. The older versions gave room for such an understanding, as if the whip had been used against the merchants. . . . Yet, ever since the earliest centuries careful analysis of the text has excluded this interpretation, and supported the trend of the newer translations: '. . . drove all the animals out of the temple, both the sheep and the cattle.'" Yoder, *Politics of Jesus*, 51.

93. Many authors have shown how Jesus' conduct in the temple cleansing incident cannot in any way be associated with violence, and thus cannot be argued as a justification for Christians to engage in violence. See, for example, Hays's argument in which he concluded, "The incident is . . . a sign that Jesus intends to bring about a new order in accordance with Isaiah's vision of eschatological peace. It is difficult to see how such a story can serve as a warrant for Christians to wage war and kill." Hays, *Moral Vision*, 334–35. See also Yoder's argument in which he concluded regarding Jesus' conduct, "had the cleansing of the temple been in any way disorderly or illegal, this would have provided a clear legal pretext for action against him, which, however, we are told the adversaries could not find." Yoder, *Politics of Jesus*, 48–52.

not the use of violence on the part of Jesus. To draw any other conclusion or to argue that there are other valid perspectives is either to abuse the text or demonstrate ignorance of it.

Appeal to other texts to justify the use of violence or participation in war on the part of the Christian is less common than appeal to the cleansing of the temple texts. These arguments also have been sufficiently debunked,[94] and do not require further analysis here.

Where do we find Jesus actually engaging with enemies within his social context, and to what extent did his conduct comport with his teaching? The most authoritative incident was the set of events associated with Jesus' arrest.

The first of those events occurred in the Garden of Gethsemane on the night of Jesus' arrest.[95] The Gospel accounts all tell of Jesus' struggle to yield to the Father's will, and to accept the way by which he not only would provide for salvation for humankind, but also the means by which he would engage with the enemies who were out to kill him. We may think of his struggle as Jesus being tugged in opposite directions: one direction was that of the kingdom of the world, including its way of responding to abusive people and its typical response of resorting to violence when dealing with enemies. The other direction was that of the kingdom of God in which the faithful one is to act as a peacemaker, not retaliate in kind to evil people, and seeking the best welfare of enemies. At the end of the struggle Jesus clearly had chosen the latter, in submission to the will of God.

In each of the synoptic accounts of the Gethsemane struggle Jesus says, "watch and pray so that you will not fall into temptation."[96] The accounts differ slightly concerning the target of Jesus' directive, be it Peter alone, Peter as a representative of the disciples, or all of the disciples. Irrespective of the target of the instruction, the question for us is, what is meant by the "temptation" to which Jesus referred? Given the immediate context of Jesus' struggle, as well as the subsequent events surrounding Jesus' arrest, it is quite reasonable to understand the temptation against

---

94. See for example Hays's argument in which he dealt with Jesus' statements, "I have not come to bring peace, but a sword" and "The one who has no sword must sell his cloak and buy one." His conclusion regarding the first—"To read this verse as a warrant for the use of violence by Christians is to commit an act of extraordinary hermeneutical violence against the text." Hays, *Moral Vision*, 332-34—can legitimately also be applied to the second.

95. See Matt 26:36-46, Mark 14:32-42, and Luke 22:39-46.

96. In Luke's account "watch and" was left out.

which Jesus warns the disciples as the same temptation with which Jesus was struggling: the temptation to adopt the way of the kingdom of the world, as opposed to the way of the kingdom of God. Jesus was warning the disciples against responding to those who soon would arrest him in the way the world would dictate. We know from the arrest narrative that the disciples had yielded to the temptation, adopting the way of the kingdom of the world.

In his Gospel Luke recorded a conversation between Jesus and the disciples that occurred just prior to the struggle in the Garden of Gethsemane. In that conversation Jesus spoke of the impending fulfillment of the Scripture concerning Jesus' death, and mentioned "if you don't have a sword, sell your cloak and buy one."[97] Hays explained that Jesus' point was that the disciples were soon to encounter not those who would welcome them, but rather stiff opposition. His instruction regarding a sword, as well as taking "a purse and a bag," was that henceforth they would need to take their own provisions. He was not telling them to engage in armed insurrection.[98] The disciples, as was often the case, misunderstood Jesus' message; they responded that they already had two swords, to which Jesus had to retort with "That's enough!" The disciples, then, were somewhat armed at the time of Jesus' praying in Gethsemane and his subsequent arrest. They had already chosen the way of the kingdom of the world at the time Jesus warned them to "watch and pray so that you will not fall into temptation."

A crowd appeared in Gethsemane to arrest Jesus. The narrative is recorded by all four Gospel writers.[99] They were well-armed, bearing both swords and clubs (John's account indicates "torches, lanterns, and weapons"); they also were well-trained, being both soldiers and officials of the Jewish leadership. After the betrayal by Judas Iscariot the disciples asked Jesus if they should strike with their swords, and at once Peter did so. Jesus' response was to stop the violence immediately, commanding "No more of this!" and to order Peter to put back his sword. He then healed his wounded enemy, and reminded the disciples that by choosing to respond to an enemy with violence they had chosen the way of the kingdom of the world, rather than the kingdom of God: "all who draw the sword will die by the sword."

---

97. Luke 22:36b.
98. See Hays, *Moral Vision*, 333.
99. See Matt 26:47–56, Mark 14:43–52, Luke 22:47–53, and John 18:2–14.

What followed next is the most clear demonstration from the life of Jesus that his conduct in fact aligned with his teaching, even in the most difficult of circumstances. Jesus told all within hearing distance that he had a powerful army at his immediate disposal: 72,000 angels. He chose, however, not to respond to his enemies by seeking their harm and destruction, but by seeking their good (witness that he did not leave the wounded man wounded, but healed him). This he did *even though it meant that the risk to his own well-being remained.* Why, we may ask, did Jesus conduct himself in this way? It was because he was displaying the character of God. He promoted harmony in an explosive situation, and refused to retaliate in kind. He strictly forbade the use of violent force—intended to inflict harm—against his enemies: both the religious officials who may be thought of as his personal enemies, and the soldiers who clearly were impersonal agents of the state charged with using violence to impose the state's will.

There is one more event from Jesus' passion that demonstrates not only his reflection of the *imago Dei*, but also his commitment to the way of the kingdom of God. While being crucified he prayed for the very enemies who were crucifying him: "Father, forgive them, for they do not know what they are doing."[100] The legions of angels were still at his disposal even while he was on the cross. He could have called on them to destroy the Roman soldiers who were crucifying him, as well as the Jewish leaders who were standing by supporting the execution. Yet, even when dying at their hands, Jesus sought his enemies' best, rather than wishing them harm. Indeed, his conduct regarding evil persons and enemies aligned completely with his teaching.

Peace and the Early Christians

How was Jesus' teaching and conduct received by the early Christians? It appears that they, indeed, did embrace and endorse Jesus' teaching and conduct about peace, retaliation, and treatment of enemies. Recall that in part 1 we saw they yielded to Jesus' epistemic and exemplary moral authority. Thus, for example, they did not participate in government-sanctioned work. They realized that they were confronted by two kingdoms—that of the world and that of God—and had to choose between the two. They could not serve both, and so refused to participate in the

---

100. Luke 23:34

secular collective, the government, in order to focus on the life of the Christian collective, the church.

Specifically relating to government-sanctioned killing, the early Christians repudiated any and all such conduct, as well as the social institutions that promoted it. Thus, they refused to be officials in the judicial system as well as the military. To them war could not be reconciled with Jesus' requirement that his faithful love their enemies and seek their best, rather than killing them. At his arrest, when Jesus both stopped Peter from continuing his violent conduct and refused to engage the army of thousands of angels that was at his disposal, he once and forever declared that his followers not participate in retaliation or seek to harm either personal or official state enemies, for such was not the way of the kingdom of God. For the early Christians the extent to which one did not follow Jesus' teaching and example in this regard was the extent to which he or she was lacking in faithfulness.

The early Christians understood what Jesus required of them, and adjusted their thinking and conduct accordingly. Much of the church in subsequent centuries, however—since the time of Constantine—has drifted far afield from Jesus' peace standards, and the vast majority of the modern Western church has rejected them altogether. In their place it has succumbed to the temptation of which Jesus warned his disciples in the Garden of Gethsemane: it has embraced the standard of the kingdom of the world, and thus endorses retaliation in kind, violence as a means of defense, and the slaughter of enemies as a means to maintain its social status quo. It even asserts that such deviation from Jesus' standards can be employed in a manner that can be called "just." The modern church needs to return to faithfulness and learn from the example of the early Christians what it means to follow Jesus in the way of peace.

FOMENTING CHANGE

The final outward element of Jesus' standard of faithfulness has to do with fomenting change. In the last two chapters we have seen that Jesus' attitude, intention, commitment, and conduct were consistently distinct and different from that of the social milieu and moral realm in which he lived. One of the broad descriptors that most characterizes Jesus' life as depicted in the Gospel narratives is "change." In all that he both taught and did he brought the ways of the kingdom of God into the kingdom of the world, pursuing the vision captured in Revelation in which the enthroned, exalted, and victorious Son declared, "Behold, I make all things new."[101]

The word *foment* suggests that Jesus was neither quietly passive nor forcefully domineering in his approach; rather, in bringing the kingdom of God he effectively introduced and actively promoted the inevitable eschatological future, while refraining from immediately overthrowing his worldly social milieu with it. His expectation of the faithful is that they will adopt his paradigm as they seek to live within the environments in which they find themselves.[102] As such, believers—as well as the church—are expected not to adopt a preservationist or conservative stance vis-à-vis the moral standards and values of their dominant social milieu, but rather are to follow Jesus in introducing and promoting God's virtuous alternative—one that reflects the divine character.

Jesus as the bringer of change was active far before the incarnation. Prior to the beginning of time he was the Creator Son.[103] As such he created "all things," and thus brought change everywhere. Inherent to his place as the eternal Son is the function of bringing change. It is a role he played from before the beginning of time, and one that he will continue to play at least into the eschaton. It should not, therefore, surprise us that he was an agent of change during his incarnation.

Elsewhere I made the point that the incarnate Son, being the agent of moral change within his earthly environment (after the standards of the kingdom of God), was not something he evolved into as his ministry progressed. Rather, from before his birth his foundational identity as the bringer of God's social vision was firmly established as an essential element of his persona, and thus was fundamental to who he was:

> In the Magnificat[104] Mary gave us a hint at a proper understanding of her yet-to-be-born son. For those of us who prefer life in a comfortable and predictable social setting Mary's message is quite disturbing, for it envisions social upheaval at the hands of God, who has blessed her with the task of carrying the savior. A simple reading of the text indicates that among God's mighty

---

101. Rev 21:5 RSV.

102. In this regard recall the words of Yoder: "Jesus was, in his divinely mandated (i.e. promised, anointed, messianic) prophethood, priesthood, and kingship, the bearer of a new possibility of human, social, and therefore political relationships. His baptism is the inauguration and his cross is the culmination of that new regime in which his disciples are called to share." Yoder, *Politics of Jesus*, 62–63.

103. See Heb 1:1–2 and Col 1:15–17.

104. See Luke 1:46–55.

deeds is the scattering of the proud, the downfall of political leaders, exaltation of the humble, filling those who are hungry, and rejection of the rich who simultaneously are sent away empty. It reflects a radical destabilization of social conventions. Yoder expresses the message of the Magnificat this way: "In the present testimony of the gospel we are being told that the one whose birth is now being announced is to be an agent of radical social change."[105] . . . Thus at the outset of the Gospels, even before Jesus' birth, he is couched in the context of significant change throughout the society—something quite different from the spiritualized understanding of Jesus that dominates the thinking of many of those of orthodox faith in Western cultures today.[106]

Jesus, as the incarnate, eternal Son, was fundamentally a change agent throughout his ministry because that is what he was as both the perfect *imago Dei* displayed on earth and as the paradigm for the faithful to emulate.

Immediately after his baptism and temptation Jesus went to the synagogue in his home town and read from Isaiah.[107] His first comment on the reading was, "Today this scripture is fulfilled in your hearing."[108] This passage of Luke's Gospel was treated in the section on "Solidarity with the Needy," but one additional observation is apropos for this section: just as was the case with the Magnificat, the content of Jesus' declaration of his purpose represented social upheaval of a type that happened only during the Year of Jubilee (referred to in the passage as "the year of the Lord's favor"). Jesus was announcing that he was bringing something new into the kingdom of the world, and that "something new" involved fundamental change to the social sphere where he had influence.

Plummer commented on the meaning of the original during the time of Isaiah: "In the original the Prophet puts into the mouth of Jehovah's ideal Servant a gracious message to those in captivity, promising them release and a return to the restored Jerusalem, the joy of which is compared to the joy of the Year of Jubilee. It is obvious that both figures, the return from exile and the release at the Jubilee, admirably express Christ's work of redemption."[109] Meyer, however, suggested that

---

105. Yoder, *Politics of Jesus*, 26–27.
106. Wozniak, *Living as the Living Jesus*, 94–95.
107. See Luke 4:16–19 and Isa 61:1–2.
108. Luke 4:21.
109. Plummer, *Luke*, 121.

the change brought by Jesus was superior to that of the Year of Jubilee: "The *year* is an allusion to the *year of jubilee* (Lev. xxv. 9), as an inferior prefigurative type of the Messianic redemption."[110] The benefits to the captives at the time of the captivity indeed included change to their social milieu; however the change Jesus brought by introducing the kingdom of God into the kingdom of the world was significantly greater. It was not a return to a former state, as was the case with Isaiah's vision, but the inbreaking of the eschatological "Behold, I make all things new."

The Sermon on the Mount, which occurred early in Jesus' ministry, not only set out Jesus' moral standards for the faithful. It also introduced a fundamental change in the expected thinking of God's people. Throughout the Sermon the words "You have heard that it was said . . . But I tell you," or very similar words, were used to introduce the notion that moral uprightness involved the internalization of moral attitudes, thoughts, and intentions rather than just external conduct. However, they also were used to bring fundamental change to what it meant to be faithful. This was seen most vividly during our review of Jesus' standards for the treatment of enemies compared with the common notion within the society. Twentieth-century theologian David McKenna captured this notion of change as a characteristic of Jesus' ministry when he wrote, "He extended the Law from its letter to its spirit; he challenged the Sabbath rules when his disciples were hungry; and he kept religious scholars on the defensive by pointing out the conflicts of their tradition."[111]

There are several characteristics of Jesus' change that permeated his ministry. Each can be illustrated by a brief review of a select incident from Jesus' life. Others could be chosen to illustrate and reinforce the characteristics, but the following will suffice for our purposes. During his encounter with Nicodemus Jesus' point was that what he brings is something new, and that Nicodemus had to embrace that change because it was fundamental to faithfulness. Jesus' declaration, "You should not be surprised at my saying, 'You must be born again'"[112] speaks of the *foundational* nature of the change that Jesus brought. It was not tangential to his ministry; rather, it was at the heart of his message.

The authors of the three Synoptics all included an incident in which Jesus responded to a challenge in which the disciples of John the Baptist complained that Jesus' disciples did not fast as did John's disciples and

110. Meyer, *Mark and Luke*, 310; italics original.
111. McKenna, *Jesus Model*, 159–60.
112. John 3:7.

those of the Pharisees.[113] After responding that no one repairs an old garment with a piece of new, unshrunk cloth since the repair will not take and the tear will be made worse, Jesus argued, "And no one pours new wine into old wineskins. Otherwise, the wine will burst the skins, and both the wine and the wineskins will be ruined. No, they pour new wine into new wineskins."[114] New Testament scholar Larry Hurtado explained the meaning of the imagery Jesus used in his response:

> The imagery of 2:21-22 seems intended to show how inappropriate the beliefs and practices of the past are now when the Kingdom of God is already approaching. . . . The two things common in this imagery are the contrast between **new** and **old** or **used**, (the same word in the Greek here) and the fact that both new cloth and new wine possess "life," that is, dynamism or power. They are fitting symbols, not only of the newness of the present moment, which marks the approach of the Kingdom of God, but also of the dynamic effect of the Kingdom of God upon the structure of established religious practice.[115]

Hurtado accurately perceived what Jesus was trying to convey in the use of the cloth and wineskin illustrations. Jesus had brought the kingdom of God into the kingdom of the world (including the religious world), but the two could not be mixed. Syncretism was not a possibility. A bit of the old could not be intertwined with a bit of the new, for the two were completely incompatible. The change Jesus introduced by bringing the kingdom of God was a *comprehensive* one: the faithful had to adopt the new completely, and totally jettison the old.

Once, when Jesus was in the temple courts, the religious leaders brought him a woman who had been caught in the act of adultery.[116] They proclaimed that the law of Moses commanded them, as God's faithful, to stone her. Seeking to trap—and ultimately accuse—Jesus, they then asked for Jesus' judgment on the matter. Jesus started writing on the ground with his finger, then told them, "Let any one of you who is without sin be the first to throw a stone at her," and continued his writing. One by one all of the religious leaders left, with no one remaining to accuse her.

---

113. See Matt 9:14–17, Mark 2:18–22, and Luke 5:33–39.
114. Mark 2:22.
115. Hurtado, *Mark*, 31–32; bold original.
116. John 7:53—8:11. It is curious that the religious leaders brought only the woman to Jesus and not also the man, since the law required that both be executed (Lev 20:10, Deut 22:22).

What followed is the most fascinating part of the incident. Jesus told her to leave her sinful life, but did not condemn her. In fact, he meted out no punishment whatsoever. There is no doubt that the woman was guilty, but the result of the kingdom of God that Jesus brought into her life was mercy and an abrogation of what the law of Moses required. Jesus brought the new into the arena of the old, and in a way that was not slight but *extreme*.

The Jesus change was not launched mildly, a bit at a time, but rather in its full-orbed expression for the benefit of the suffering, the outcast, the confused, the abused, and the sinful. It was instituted as *foundational*, *comprehensive*, and *extreme*, and demonstrated that the work of the Creator Son begun at creation continues.

One more example from Scripture—this one from the Epistle to the Hebrews—will serve to depict both the nature of the change that Jesus brought and his expectation that his followers will embrace that change as they live out their lives faithfully in their respective social situations. It is found in the eighth chapter of the Epistle to the Hebrews, a chapter that views Jesus as the new high priest and compares his ministry to that of Moses. Central to the comparison is the relative value of the two covenants, the old one that took effect under Moses and the new one introduced by the salvific work of Jesus.

The best benefits that could be realized under the old covenant included a reminder to the Israelites that they were sinful, but there was no assuaging their guilt, removal of their sins, or moral cleansing.[117] Furthermore, the benefits only applied to sins committed unknowingly.[118] There was no solution for willful sins. In addition, there were significant shortcomings associated with the Mosaic covenant. Fundamentally, the covenant rendered God inaccessible. Only one Israelite—the high priest—could approach God, and that only once a year. Other than that, God was not approachable, which meant that for all other than the high priest they had no sense of ever being able to come into the presence of God. In addition, as already hinted, under the Mosaic covenant there was no way to deal with volitional, intentional sins; the animal blood the high priest brought before God annually only applied to sins of which the guilty were unaware. As such, it delayed God's response to willful disobedience, but did not deal with the sin itself.

---

117. See Heb 10:1–4.
118. See Heb 9:7.

The author of Hebrews argued that the Mosaic covenant was insufficient, and therefore the need for a new covenant emerged: the one of which Jesus is the mediator.[119] In chapter 7 it even is described as being "set aside because it was weak and useless (for the law made nothing perfect)."[120] Anticipation of a new covenant, however did not begin with Jesus. Six centuries prior to the incarnation the prophet Jeremiah foresaw the need of a replacement covenant, and described its superiority over the old.[121] At its root the new covenant would address the shortcomings of the old: all wickedness would be forgiven and God would be approachable.[122]

Consistent with Jesus' change elsewhere, such as we saw in the Sermon on the Mount, the new covenant that Jesus brought was not external, but internal. It was written on the hearts and minds of the faithful, rather than on tablets of stone. It also had superior benefits, including complete moral cleansing and ongoing fellowship directly with God. This is the change Jesus brought in mediating a new covenant—one that not only was different from that of Moses, but one that was sufficient to meet the most fundamental needs of the human soul.

For those who seek to be faithful to God, embracing and promoting the vast array of changes Jesus brought through the inbreaking of the kingdom of God is essential—both those that impact the social situation and those that meet the most basic moral needs of the individual. Faithfulness to Jesus means being like him, in what he taught and what he did. In doing so, the faithful declare and exhibit that they, indeed, bear the character of God.

---

119. See Heb 8:6–7.
120. Heb 7:18b–19a.
121. See Jer 31:31–34.
122. The author of Hebrews expressed this as "a better hope is introduced, by which we draw near to God" (7:19b).

13

Faithfulness, Love, and the Kingdom of God

FAITHFULNESS IN THE CHRISTIAN life is not limited to the six characteristics outlined in the last two chapters. One cannot conclude that she or he is faithful simply by virtue of displaying those characteristics. To do so would be far too simplistic, reductionistic, and mechanical. Self-emptying, obedience, suffering, solidarity with the needy, pursuit of peace, and fomenting change are necessary evidences of faithfulness—and without them faithfulness is severely lacking—but they alone are not the sum and substance of faithfulness. Rather, they are the result of faithfulness at work, the outcome of the appropriated divine character and *imago Dei de facto* applied to the moral realm in which the believer lives.

We may ask how faithfulness can be put to work, and how the character of God acquired by the faithful one can be applied to the believer's social sphere. What is the means by which the characteristics of faithfulness can be displayed in the believer's life? What moves one from simply having acquired the divine character to leveraging and applying it in a tangible way to the social milieu?

LOVE

There is wide variation among Christian ethicists concerning the nature and scope of ethics itself, but one foundational notion upon which all agree—with extremely rare exception—is that Christian ethics entails love.[1] After asking "What is the chief distinguishing mark of a Christian? What is the hallmark which authenticates people as the children of God?"[2] Stott claimed, "Love is the principal, the paramount, the preeminent, the distinguishing characteristic of the people of God. Nothing can dislodge or replace it. Love is supreme."[3] Regarding ethics in particular, Wogaman asserted that the Christian tradition "has always affirmed the centrality of love in the nature of God and in the character of human life. Christian understanding of the meaning of that love has varied, but the importance of love has almost always been affirmed by Christian ethics. Christians have not always been loving in their actions and decisions, but usually they have known that that is what, as Christians, they are called to be."[4] It is not surprising, then, that when treating the *imago Dei* not merely as a fact of human creation, but as the ideal outworking of the human purpose, Grenz concluded, "We fulfill our purpose as those designed to be the *imago Dei* as we love after the manner of God, that is, as our relationships are likewise characterized by *agapē*. No wonder Christian ethicists have consistently spoken about the centrality of this kind of love."[5]

Considering the preeminent place of love in moral discourse as well as the practical outworking of faithfulness, it is tempting to conclude that love is the *only* standard in the moral sphere and that all else is relative, contingent, or situational. This was the position espoused by ethicist Joseph Fletcher. In the mid-twentieth century Fletcher proposed

---

1. See, for example, Gustafson: "Perhaps the feature of Christian ethics that is cited most often as its distinctive note is the centrality or primacy of love. The fact that love, *hesed*, is an abiding theme in Jewish Scripture is recognized, but it seems for various exegetical and other reasons to take on unique importance in Christian ethics. The New Testament is the source of ample evidence of its importance in Jesus' teachings, of his life being acts of love, of his life and death being revelations of God's love. Particularly I John 4 is a combination of theological and moral connections between God as love, the particularities of the Christian story, and the conduct expected of the Christian community." Gustafson, *Moral Discernment*, 203.

2. Stott, *Contemporary Christian*, 147.
3. Stott, *Contemporary Christian*, 148.
4. Wogaman, *Christian Ethics*, 270.
5. Grenz, *Moral Quest*, 285.

a situationist approach to ethics, asserting that "we are always, that is to say, commanded to act lovingly, but how to do it depends on our own *responsible* estimate of the situation. Only love is a constant; everything else is a variable."[6] For Fletcher there were no moral norms except love; all else could serve as guidance, but determining morally upright conduct in any situation depended entirely upon the individual's judgment *in situ*.[7] He went on to argue that "in *Christian* situationism the ultimate criterion is, as we shall be seeing, 'agapeic love.' It relativizes the absolute . . ."[8]

Later Fletcher opined about the great difficulties that result from his "love only" ethic. He questioned:

> Here is precisely the serious difficulty of love. How are its favors to be distributed among so many beneficiaries? We never have one neighbor at a time. How are we to love justice, how are we to be just about love, how are love and justice related? If to love is to seek the neighbor's welfare, and justice is being fair as between neighbors, then how do we put these two things together in our *acts*, in the situation? The answer is that in the Christian ethic the twain become one. Even if we define justice as giving to others what is their due, we must redefine it Christianly. For what is it that is due to our neighbors? It is love that is due—*only* love. ("Owe no man anything except to love.") Love is justice, justice is love.[9]

Herein we see precisely the difficulty with Fletcher's position. By jettisoning all but love as morally normative he painted himself into a corner in which there is nothing that determines how love is to be applied. He left himself morally adrift; his only way out was to propose the dubious position that love and justice are identical (something not supported by the preponderance of Scripture), and even so did not answer the question of how love works out the divine character and essential faithfulness characteristics in the Christian life. It is important, then, not to focus on love

---

6. Fletcher, *Situation Ethics*, 45; italics original.

7. See Wogaman: "Joseph Fletcher gave popular expression to an ethic of intuition based upon love. Moral principles can be helpful as 'rules of thumb,' but there are no intrinsically binding moral norms other than the general norm of love. Love decided 'then and there,' in the situation, what is the most loving thing to do. The work did not draw heavily upon theological resources other than the broad commitment to Christian love." Wogaman, *Christian Ethics*, 230.

8. Fletcher, *Situation Ethics*, 45; italics original.

9. Fletcher, *Situation Ethics*, 88–89; italics original.

alone—in isolation from all other moral maxims—as the only element of Christian ethics.[10]

The Nature of Love

Acknowledging the foundational place of love in Christian ethics—essential as that may be—does not yield any understanding about its function in the living out of faithfulness in the moral realm of human experience. Thus far we have learned that God's essence is love, and that love is at the heart of God's being. It is not so much an attribute he possesses—distinct from the divine nature—but is the divine nature itself. Yet love is not exclusive to God; rather, it can be conveyed to human beings, and can be appropriated and experienced by them. When this occurs, the divine character—at least in some respect—has been communicated to humans.

Recall that Grenz pointed out that love, as found in God, finds its expression as reciprocal self-dedication between and among the members of the Trinity. It is more fundamental to who God is than anything else, being not only his essence, but also his will. It is the foundation of his moral attributes, as well as his character. The relationship between God as Creator and all of creation is characterized by love, and as expressed through Jesus as the incarnate Son was demonstrated by outgoing concern for others. Emulation of love as found in God is what it means to be faithful. Both the individual believer and the believing collective—the church—are obligated to demonstrate love after the divine pattern.

Love has been characterized in many ways. When considering how love is related to faithfulness, the New Testament word *agapē* captures most closely both the expected attitude of the faithful and how they are to conduct themselves within the society, engaging others.[11] *Agapē* love

---

10. In this regard, see Gustafson: "Consistent with, or congruent with, belief in the proposition 'God is love' are loving attitudes, a disposition to be loving, a commandment to love, and even rules of conduct. But the relationship is not just one of congruence between religious propositions and moral statements. The relation of the religious man to God is one of confidence in him, of faithfulness to him; it is believing with passionate assent. This relationship, analogous to personal relationships with others, enables and requires certain moral beliefs, dispositions and attitudes, sensibilities, motives, and intentions." Gustafson, *Theology and Christian Ethics*, 71.

11. See Grenz: "As we come to see how God has acted toward us—that is, as we understand the biblical narrative—we discover what love truly is. . . . This grand narrative of the One who freely sacrificed for our sakes led the biblical writers to the previously obscure Greek word *agapē*, for this term expresses the self-giving attitude that characterizes the God of the salvation narrative. The New Testament writers, following the

itself has been described by various terms. Objectively it has been labeled as a law, a command, a principle, a characteristic, a trait, and self-sacrifice. Subjectively love has been seen as a drive, an essence, a motivator, an emotion, and a Christian grace.

To understand the fundamental meaning of *agapē* it is best to contrast it with the other three Greek words for love, since *agapē* is rare in pre-biblical Greek[12] and its meaning therein is imprecise.[13] Barclay mentioned that "*Erōs* had quite definite associations with the lower side of love; it had much more to do with passion than with love."[14] "*Storgē* was very definitely tied up with family affection,"[15] and "*Philia* . . . was definitely a word of warmth and closeness and affection; it could only properly be used of the near and the dear."[16] In defining *agapē*, however, Barclay wrote:

> Let a man be a saint or let a man be a sinner, God's only desire is for that man's highest good. Now, that is what *agapē* is. *Agapē* is the spirit which says: "No matter what any man does to me, I will never seek to do harm to him; I will never set out for revenge; I will always seek nothing but his highest good." That is to say, Christian love, *agapē*, is *unconquerable benevolence, invincible good will*.[17]

We have already seen the implication of *agapē* for the moral life of the believer, and the requirement it makes of the faithful. It fundamentally entails an intent—and the commensurate commitment and conduct—in the direction of another. The exercise of the will for the good of another is foundational to the faithful one's quest to exhibit the divine character

---

path charted by the Hebrew Scriptures, take the grand biblical narrative one additional step. God's glorious love for us leads us to love also." Grenz, *Moral Quest*, 282.

12. See *TDNT*: "It is indeed striking that the substantive [*agapē*] is almost completely lacking in pre-biblical Greek." Kittel and Friedrich, *TDNT*, 1:37. See also Barclay, in which he pointed out that in the New Testament "*agapē* occurs almost 120 times and *agapan* more than 130 times." Barclay, *New Testament Words*, 20.

13. Kittel and Friedrich, *TDNT*, 1:37.

14. Barclay, *New Testament Words*, 20. See also *TDNT*, which adds that the word group indicates "passionate love which desires the other for itself." Kittel and Friedrich, *TDNT*, 1:35.

15. Barclay, *New Testament Words*, 20.

16. Barclay, *New Testament Words*, 20. See also *TDNT*, which indicates that the word group "signifies for the most part the inclination or solicitous love of gods for men, or friends for friends. It means the love which embraces everything that bears a human countenance." Kittel and Friedrich, *TDNT*, 1:36.

17. Barclay, *New Testament Words*, 21–22; italics original.

and the *imago Dei* in her or his social milieu. Barclay concluded, "*Agapē* has to do with the *mind*: it is not simply an emotion which rises unbidden in our hearts; it is a principle by which we deliberately live. *Agapē* has supremely to do with the *will*. It is a conquest, a victory, and achievement. No one ever naturally loved his enemies. To love one's enemies is a conquest of all our natural inclinations and emotions."[18]

Recently scholars have questioned if this meaning of Christian love alone is sufficient,[19] and if *agapē* by itself is broad enough to accommodate the expectation of the faithful one. Grenz suggested that in addition to *agapē*, the notions of warmth and friendship associated with *philia* may also be part of the overall concept of Christian love found in the New Testament, since Jesus referred to his disciples as "friends."[20] Furthermore, stories such as the parable of the prodigal son[21] suggest that the familial elements of *storgē* love perhaps are part of Jesus' overall understanding of the love Christians should display.[22] Although acknowledging the dangers associated with suggesting that Christian love should include some sort of concept of *eros*,[23] Grenz went on to assert that it is appropriate to do so "if we understand *eros* in its deeper sense of a desire for communion with the beloved."[24] While reaffirming the primacy of *agapē*, he argued that without the concepts associated with the other words for love, "our conception of the God who is *agapē* can easily degenerate into a distant, austere, 'Stoic' deity."[25]

Thinking in terms of love as the expression of faithfulness within the moral realm of human experience, Grenz concluded:

---

18. Barclay, *New Testament Words*, 21; italics original.

19. See Gustafson for an example of how the understanding of love varies among scholars: "Indeed, the literature has come to view *agape* as a distinctively Christian term for love, and has interpreted its meaning in various ways. Is it always self-sacrificial and self-denying, or is it mutuality and self- and community-affirming? Does it direct our natural desire, *eros*, or does it run counter to nature in the name of an independently authorized norm? Is it a rule term, or a motive term? Is it a general principle which has to be applied in ways to, e.g., issues of justice? Or is it a power that informs intuitions about what is the neighbor's need?" Gustafson, *Moral Discernment*, 203.

20. See Grenz, *Moral Quest*, 287.

21. See Luke 15:11–32.

22. Grenz, *Moral Quest*, 288.

23. See Grenz, *Moral Quest*, 288.

24. Grenz, *Moral Quest*, 289.

25. Grenz, *Moral Quest*, 290.

Putting the matter in Christian theological terms, the kind of love that lies at the heart of the Christian agapeic ethic is an *agapē* informed by a "sensing with" others as those whom God has created with the goal of participating in an eternal community. As the Holy Spirit mixes the self-giving impulse (*agapē*) with a compassionate familial concern for (*storgē*), plus a sincere desire to enjoy the friendship of (*philia*) and true communion with (*eros*) each other in God's eternal fellowship, the Spirit of the relation between the Father and the Son leads us into the fullness of the Christian love ethic. It is this kind of comprehensive love that characterizes truly *Christian* caregiving relationships, not only in the medical realm but in every context.[26]

Grenz has made it clear that the moral obligation of the faithful to love is far broader than what *agapē* alone suggests. It entails the exercise of the will and the resolve to seek the best for the one loved, but it also includes the full range of relational concepts, particularly within the Christian community. It also has in view all people in all situations, including the ones the kingdom of the world asserts should be treated not with love, but with violence. This is the way Jesus loved all, including his enemies. His expectation of the faithful is that they will follow him in the way of love—if necessary, all the way to the cross.

Love as a Moral Instrument

To understand how faithfulness can be put to work, displayed in the believer's life, and how the divine character can be applied to the social milieu, we need to view love instrumentally. This is not to deny any of the other understandings of love's nature, but in the moral realm we are considering love not ontologically, but rather love as a functionary—as the means by which faithfulness achieves expression. Gustafson drew from John 13:1 when he observed that love was instrumental in Jesus' life as he gave tangible expression to his loving character.[27] Yet conveying love tangibly was not a trait reserved for Jesus alone. Rather, just as Jesus demonstrated his divine character and expressed the *imago Dei* through specific actions, the collective of the faithful—the church—is called upon to do the same in imitation of its Lord.[28]

---

26. Grenz, *Moral Quest*, 293; italics original.
27. See Gustafson, *Theology and Christian Ethics*, 158.
28. See Grenz: "Our calling as [God's] holy people is to show forth the divine reality,

Love can act instrumentally in a number of different ways, giving rise to moral conduct that can only be labeled as love-made-tangible. Grenz, for example, held that love can function as an inspiration and motivator. Offering some specifics, he wrote, "In whatever relational contexts we find ourselves—marriage (Eph 5:22–32), the Christian community (e.g., Rom 14:15) or even in a hostile world in which people mistreat or persecute us (1 Pet 2:20–24; 3:9)—believers are to draw from the narrative of the loving God and the self-giving example of Christ the model for living."[29]

Gustafson saw in Jesus' crucifixion love working as a paradigm that is to be emulated by the church in mercy and self-sacrifice.[30] He also saw that love can function as a justifier of the choice to affirm certain moral conduct as upright:

> One finds in the fourth Gospel a reason for being moral that is present throughout the scriptures, namely, that in response to the love of God for his creation and redemption, the people ought to be grateful and ought to walk in his way, follow him, and, indeed, imitate his loving deeds in their actions toward one another. The ultimate reason for being moral is that God has shown his love toward man, and thus man, both out of joyous gratitude and out of obligation to God, is to be concerned for the well-being of others.[31]

In Stott's thinking, love functioned as a driver of conduct loyal to the expectation of Jesus: "Jesus Christ calls us to obedience.... The way to prove our love for Christ is neither by loud protestations of loyalty like Peter, nor by singing sentimental ditties in church, but by obeying his commandments. The test of love is obedience."[32]

Love, then, has a specific role to play in the life of the faithful believer. It serves in an instrumental capacity to guide, spur, and encourage the conduct of the faithful as they strive to live like Jesus in the moral milieu of society. However, in addition to speaking of love, and demonstrating love at work tangibly in his environment, Jesus spoke of the kingdom of

---

that is, to be the image of God. The church reflects God's character in that it lives as a genuine community—as it lives in love—for only as the community of love can the church mirror the nature of the triune God." Grenz, *Moral Quest*, 295–96.

29. Grenz, *Moral Quest*, 282.
30. See Gustafson, *Theology and Christian Ethics*, 158.
31. Gustafson, *Moral Discernment*, 41.
32. Stott, *Contemporary Christian*, 92–93.

God. From the early days of his ministry[33] through his passion[34] and even after his resurrection,[35] the kingdom of God was a constant theme of Jesus' teaching. How, then, are love and the kingdom of God related, and how should the faithful one consider and participate in the kingdom?

THE KINGDOM OF GOD

Earlier we explored the nature of the kingdom of God, and reviewed a number of its characteristics. The image that emerged was of the kingdom viewed *objectively*, including how the prevailing understanding of the kingdom changed from the Old Testament perspective to the one promulgated by Jesus. Recall that the fundamental notion of the kingdom was God's rule over all, both created and uncreated. The kingdom society was one in which God reigned supreme, and the subjects of the kingdom enjoyed fellowship with God. In this view there would be no blending of the kingdom with the broader society; rather the two were in constant conflict with each other. The people of the kingdom were distinct from and in opposition to the rest of the populace. There was antagonism between the kingdom of God and the kingdom of the world; compromise between them was not possible. The characteristic that distinguished the kingdom of God and its participants from the kingdom of the world was absolute righteousness in all things.

When the people of Israel considered the possibility of establishing the kingdom of God within their present social milieu, they soon judged that such an achievement was not possible since it would require a total rebuilding of the existing society—something that Israel could not accomplish. They concluded that God had ruled supreme in the past, and would once again in the eschatological future, but they enjoyed no notion of the kingdom of God in the present.

Jesus' message of the kingdom was different. He announced that it had arrived *in the present*. Furthermore, it was not ancillary to his overall message, but rather formed its heart. Unlike the former understanding, which focused on God's *power*, Jesus' teaching on the kingdom gave preeminence to God's *presence*. That presence was both ubiquitous and abiding. Not only was God present within and throughout the current

---

33. See Matt 4:17.
34. See Luke 22:30 and John 18:36.
35. See Acts 1:3.

social environment, there was the potential for God to be present in the lives of people. Jesus' message of the kingdom indeed affirmed its present reality, but also introduced an understanding of the kingdom vastly different from the one assumed by his audience.

Participation in the kingdom of God would not come without danger. Thus Jesus included in the Sermon on the Mount the eighth beatitude: "Blessed are those who are persecuted because of righteousness, for theirs is the kingdom of heaven."[36] Participating in the kingdom of God did not free one from risk; rather, it increased it. The reason is the kingdom of God and the kingdom of the world were in direct conflict, and that conflict demonstrated itself through the suffering of the kingdom participants at the hands of those who were loyal members of the kingdom of the world. In such a situation faithfulness took on a new meaning: it not only included ascription to the values of Jesus' message and the divine righteousness it portrays, it necessitated endurance when that message and its adherents were opposed by those who affirm the values of the kingdom of the world. Such faithfulness was all-consuming, requiring not only participation in the kingdom of God, but immersion in it. One could not be partially faithful or faithful part of the time.

A key notion of the kingdom of God is that it entails a fundamental reversal of the present social order: one in which egalitarianism reigns, the ingrained "haves" are demoted, and the abused "have-nots" are elevated. Jesus' practical outworking and demonstration of the kingdom of God not only helped needy individuals, it challenged the accepted social conventions. Confrontation between the partakers of the kingdom of God and those of the kingdom of the world was an inevitable result of the kingdom of God in the present, for the two kingdoms hold to vastly different virtues and values. They have two different sources, and are sustained by two different instigators who themselves are in absolute conflict. There is no middle ground, and any attempt at syncretism—be it conscious or subconscious—is foreign to the concept of faithfulness, serving as its enemy. Whereas at the time of Jesus the kingdom he proclaimed did not engage in aggression against Rome[37] (for such would be a violation of Jesus' teaching concerning treatment of enemies), it was in direct conflict in the moral sphere—both individual and social. Jesus

---

36. Matt 5:10.

37. See Thompson: "Jesus' message of the kingdom addressed the deep longings of an oppressed people. However, the Gospels contain no record of a confrontation with Roman rule." Thompson, *Christ and Culture in the New Testament*, 33.

bore the inevitable result of that conflict; the faithful can expect to have to do the same.

Such is the nature of the kingdom of God *objectively*. What, however, is the kingdom like from a *subjective* perspective? How does it function? What are its dynamics?

It is important to realize that Jesus' entire view of righteousness, virtues, attitudes, intentions, commitments, values, justice, and conduct was tied up with his notion of the kingdom of God. His ideal moral milieu—and that of his disciples—was the ethic of the kingdom present in his social situation.[38] Moral uprightness took tangible form through life in the kingdom: God's reign on earth. The implication was that God's faithful—which eventually would become the church—was, as Stott put it, "supposed to be God's new society, the living embodiment of the gospel, a sign of the kingdom of God, a demonstration of what human community looks like when it comes under his gracious rule."[39] It is within that divine rule—the kingdom of God—that faithfulness can find its complete and integrated expression.

For the one seeking to be faithful to Jesus, the kingdom was not something to be built, such as was the case with the former thinking of Israel in which God's people were to rebuild the existing society according to God's prescriptions. Rather, the kingdom was something that already existed. In the incarnation of Jesus the kingdom *in situ* had arrived,[40] and thus when asked when the kingdom of God would come Jesus replied, "the kingdom of God is in your midst."[41] It was something that "has come upon you."[42] For those just learning what it meant to be faithful, the kingdom was not something they were to build, but rather something into which they entered.[43] Grenz captured this reality when he concluded, "For Jesus the good life is not the quest for happiness but the pursuit of God's kingdom (Mt 6:33). The good life is life under God's reign."[44] For those who actually had entered the kingdom, that transition involved a gracious

---

38. See Grenz: "At the center of Jesus' ministry lay his announcement of God's reign ... whatever else it may have been, the ethic our Lord set forth was an ethic of the kingdom." Grenz, *Moral Quest*, 110.

39. Stott, *Contemporary Christian*, 253.

40. See Mark 1:15.

41. Luke 17:21.

42. Luke 11:20.

43. See Mark 9:47.

44. Grenz, *Moral Quest*, 110.

act of God, described by Paul as follows: "For he has rescued us from the dominion of darkness and brought us into the kingdom of the Son he loves."[45] Here we see in subjective terms the reality we formerly observed, that the kingdom of the world and the kingdom of God are not only completely distinct but reflect the age-old conflict between evil and good.

Perhaps the most surprising aspect of the kingdom is that it is enduring violent attack. Jesus, in speaking to a crowd about John the Baptist, said, "From the days of John the Baptist until now, the kingdom of heaven has been subjected to violence, and violent people have been raiding it."[46] Jesus was emphasizing what we saw when viewing the kingdom objectively: it exists in conflict with the kingdom of the world, even to the extent that it exists within a violent reality. The present reign of God is not embraced by all; rather, there are those who seek to destroy it by force. As was the case with John the Baptist, those who live in God's kingdom will not escape this reality. This notion was further explained by Jesus in the parable of the weeds,[47] in which he told of an enemy who sowed weeds in a field that had just been planted with wheat (the kingdom of God). The enemy's intent was to destroy. The evil was tolerated for a while, just as God tolerates the kingdom of the world in the present age, but eventually the kingdom of God will prevail and the enemy will be destroyed.

I suggest that the best way of seeing how the kingdom of God actually functions is to delve into some of Jesus' other kingdom parables, for in them he described the kingdom's dynamics. For this purpose we can group the parables under three headings: those that describe the kingdom's movement, the ones that reveal the surprising nature of the kingdom, and parables focused on the kingdom's immensity.

The first group—which describes the kingdom's movement—begins with the parable of the growing seed,[48] in which planted seed inevitably grows irrespective of human intervention. Just so, the kingdom of God inevitably will grow. The parable of the mustard seed[49] illustrates that although the kingdom started very small—simply with Jesus' announcement of its presence—it will grow to be huge. Lastly, the parable of the yeast[50] is a picture of how the kingdom of God will permeate everywhere.

45. Col 1:13.
46. Matt 11:12.
47. See Matt 13:24–30.
48. See Mark 4:26–29.
49. See Matt 13:31–32, Mark 4:30–32, Luke 13:18–19.
50. See Matt 13:33, Luke 13:20.

The surprising nature of the kingdom is captured in the next group of parables. After declaring that children are the possessors of the kingdom[51] and that the rich have difficulty entering it,[52] Jesus told the parable of the workers in the vineyard.[53] In the end all workers are paid the same amount, irrespective of how long they worked in the vineyard. The social convention in Jesus' context was that pay was determined by the length of service. The generosity shown by the vineyard owner to those who worked less was Jesus' way of teaching that the dynamics of the kingdom of God are vastly different from those of the kingdom of the world, determined only by God but enjoyed by those on whom he pours out his generosity. As such, it was a significant challenge to the kingdom of the world, and clearly in opposition to it.

We have already investigated the parable of the wedding feast;[54] the surprising point about the kingdom that the parable illustrates is that those not expected to be invited are, but also are required to have the necessary credentials to remain. Invitation into the kingdom by itself, although unexpected, welcome, and broad, is not sufficient for entry into the kingdom.

Two other parables complete this group. The parable of the virgins[55] and that of the gold[56] both have a wealth of content, but the surprising teaching of both is that the kingdom comes unexpectedly, or perhaps comes with unforeseen expectations. The ones who anticipate the kingdom's arrival, as well as its requirements, are those who enter it: those who do not will suffer the consequences of not being prepared.

The kingdom's immensity is the common theme of the final group. Five parables depict different aspect of immensity. The first two, the parable of the treasure in the field[57] and the parable of the pearl,[58] both teach that the kingdom is more valuable than anything else—worth any sacrifice—and brings great joy to all who find it. The parable of the net[59] shows that the kingdom is vast enough to accommodate all; it also warns

---

51. See Matt 19:14.
52. See Matt 19:23.
53. See Matt 20:1–16.
54. See Matt 22:1–14.
55. See Matt 25:1–13.
56. See Matt 25:14–30.
57. See Matt 13:44.
58. See Matt 13:45–46.
59. See Matt 13:47–50.

that only the righteous will remain in the kingdom. Endless treasures of the kingdom is the point of the parable of the teaching disciple,[60] and the boundless mercy of the kingdom is illustrated by the parable of the unmerciful servant.[61] It comes with a caveat, however: the one to whom mercy has been shown must in turn show mercy to others.

The kingdom of God viewed experientially, or subjectively, includes an ethic by which the faithful enter into and live in the kingdom. This is what Jesus termed "the secret of the kingdom of God."[62] The kingdom is not something to be built, for it already has arrived; rather, the faithful who enter it must focus not on expanding it, but on inculcating within themselves the requirements for entry. It is in the kingdom that full-orbed faithfulness can be expressed in all of its aspects, for the kingdom is the milieu in which all elements of faithfulness can be integrated into a single articulation.

Although the kingdom has arrived, it inevitably will grow to be huge, and eventually will permeate everything. It is characterized by the unexpected, and those who appear to the world not to be candidates for the kingdom are, in fact, its best candidates. Their entry is not automatic, but their invitation is. Upon entering the kingdom, they find it to be more valuable than anything and everything else, full of vast treasures and endless mercy to enjoy. They must, however, enter prepared and ready.

The kingdom's dynamics are thoroughly different from those of the kingdom of the world. They appear to the world's residents as a threat, and thus the kingdom of God incurs the wrath of the world. The world seeks to destroy God's kingdom, and thus subjects it to violence, once again reviving the ages-old conflict between evil and good. In this environment the members of the kingdom—God's faithful—live; they, just like Jesus, can expect to endure the inevitable consequences.

LOVE AND THE KINGDOM OF GOD

We have explored love instrumentally—as the driver of faithfulness in the believer's social milieu—as well as the kingdom of God as the environment in which the faithful one enters in order, in fact, to be faithful. How, though, are love and the kingdom of God related? The most challenging

---

60. See Matt 13:52.
61. See Matt 18:23–35.
62. Mark 4:11.

expression for the faithful one was articulated by Jesus in the Sermon on the Mount when he altered the common understanding of how enemies are to be treated. They are not to be treated with viciousness or violence or even in-kind conduct. Rather, they are to be treated with love, and the enemy's best is to be sought by the one seeking to be faithful. Such an expression of love would not come without cost to the one who lives as Jesus required, as witnessed by Jesus' own experience of crucifixion by those who opposed him. However, Jesus allowed for no alternative or exception to his demand for love on the part of his followers, and in his own life conducted himself in no other way than the way of love.

Why did Jesus make such a demand, and why was it so absolute? What was his goal in doing so? It appears that the kind of love Jesus required was necessarily instrumental as the means of introducing the kingdom of God into the social domain of his earthly environment:

> Here speaks the One who without illusion or sentimentality has introduced the ideal of neighbourly love into reality. He speaks of these impossible demands with the same tone of steady seriousness and sense of reality as of that which every man should and can do.... Jesus knows this world and He thus calls for a life within it wholly grounded in love. He does so with sober realism and certainty.... The fact that His demand for love is now so self-evident is an indication that He has more to proclaim than a new demand. He proclaims and creates a new world situation.[63]

The new world situation that Jesus creates—the kingdom of God—is one in which love is an essential requirement of those who aspire to be kingdom participants. Without it, entry is not possible, and without entry faithfulness is not possible. Love is the vitality of the kingdom. Through it "He creates a new people of God which renounces all hatred and force and with an unconquerable resolve to love treads the way of sacrifice in face of all opposition. And He Himself dies, as the ancient traditions [sic] tells us, with a request for the hostile world (Lk. 23:34)."[64] Grenz reflected this link between love and the kingdom when he contended that for Jesus "the central ethical principle of the ethic of the kingdom is heartfelt love for God and others. The citizens of the kingdom are those who love God from their heart and who love others as themselves. Such love, however,

---

63. Kittel and Friedrich, *TDNT*, 1:46–47.
64. Kittel and Friedrich, *TDNT*, 1:48.

is no mere inward affection. Instead it involves humble service to God and the neighbor."[65]

A few weeks after the resurrection, but before his ascension, Jesus met Simon Peter and asked him three times in quick succession, "Do you love me?" Peter was no novice in his experience with Jesus, and had spent the past three years learning from Jesus about the kingdom of God. At the point Jesus asked, "Do you love me?" Peter had encountered Jesus four times since the resurrection. Why, then—with all Peter's experience of Jesus—was it so important to Jesus to ask if Peter loved him?

We have seen that love is the instrument by which the realities of the kingdom of God are brought to impinge upon people. It was true in the life of Jesus, and it is the required motivator of the faithful who live in the milieu of the kingdom. In asking Peter if he loved him, Jesus was impressing upon Peter that he had to express love—first for Jesus as Peter's motivator, and then as Peter's attitude toward those he would encounter in fulfilling the commission Jesus gave him: "feed my sheep." In doing so Peter would care for those Jesus claimed as his own, just as Jesus had done. He also would follow Jesus in losing his life, but would be functioning faithfully within the kingdom.

FAITHFUL POSITIONING WITHIN THE SOCIAL MILIEU

The kingdom of God in the present announced by Jesus is the reality through which Godlikeness is expressed in the social sphere, both by faithful individuals and by the Christian collective. Believers participate *de jure* in the kingdom of God by virtue of salvation, but they participate *de facto* by having acquired and cultivated the divine character and the *imago Dei*. Love, as the character of God revealed, is the vehicle for actuating faithfulness within the social environment and realizing the kingdom of God's impingement upon the broader social and moral milieu. Yet how are the faithful—both individual and collective—to establish themselves as kingdom representatives within the local social domain? This was the question faced by the early Christians as they considered how to live within the Roman society in which they found themselves.

---

65. Grenz, *Moral Quest*, 111.

Forming a Perspective on Society

A helpful exercise to think through this matter is to consider options for Christian engagement with society developed throughout the history of Christianity. A range of alternatives was articulated in the mid-twentieth century by H. Richard Niebuhr in *Christ and Culture*, mentioned at the beginning of part 1. The book has had such a great impact that it needs to be mentioned. Niebuhr's approach was to assume a certain notion of Christ, and position it in various ways against a static and generic notion of culture. In doing so, the *relationship* between the two was the focus. The book has significant shortcomings;[66] for example, the charge leveled by Hauerwas and William Willimon that Niebuhr had formulated his argument in such a way that the book is repressive toward churches that are not significantly broad in their approach: "Niebuhr ensured that the most inclusive ecclesiology would be viewed as the most truthful, that any church becoming too concerned about its identity and the formation of its young would be rejected by American culture as incipiently 'sectarian,' as irresponsible in a state that had given us the political tools to transform the world. *Christ and Culture* thus stands as a prime example of repressive tolerance."[67]

In addition, the book has been the subject of scholarly criticism[68] for over seventy years, such as Craig Carter's criticism of Niebuhr's

---

66. See, for example, Hauerwas and Willimon: The authors point out that Niebuhr failed to be prescriptive, to the detriment of the church: "Niebuhr failed to describe the various historical or contemporary options for the church. He merely justified what was already there—a church that had ceased to ask the right questions as it went about congratulating itself for transforming the world, not noticing, that in fact the world had tamed the church." Hauerwas and Willimon, *Resident Aliens*, 41. See also Carter, in which he referenced Yoder's criticism of the entire approach Niebuhr took to *Christ and Culture*: "Yoder is correct to see that, fundamentally, the relationship between Christ and culture is not the place to start. One must start with the question of the relationship between the church and its surrounding society." Carter, "Inadequate Christology," para. 22.

67. Hauerwas and Willimon, *Resident Aliens*, 40–41.

68. A general and scathing criticism of *Christ and Culture* was leveled by Hauerwas and Willimon: "We have come to believe that few books have been a greater hindrance to an accurate assessment of our situation than *Christ and Culture*. Niebuhr rightly saw that our politics determines our theology. . . . But his call to Christians to accept 'culture' (where is this monolithic 'culture' Niebuhr describes?) and politics in the name of the unity of God's creating and redeeming activity had the effect of endorsing a Constantinian social strategy. 'Culture' became a blanket term to underwrite Christian involvement with the world without providing any discriminating modes for discerning how Christians should see the good or the bad in 'culture.'" Hauerwas and Willimon, *Resident Aliens*, 40. For a more specific criticism of Niebuhr's view of culture, see

theology: "Niebuhr's position is vitiated by a weak Christology and a misuse of the doctrine of the Trinity. Niebuhr has introduced great confusion into the debate by treating the 'Christ Against Culture' approach as doctrinally deficient, whereas it is his own position that departs from Nicene orthodoxy."[69] Later he added detail: "Niebuhr's portrait of Christ ignores his teaching, his example, his call to discipleship, his promise of the Spirit, his atoning death and resurrection, and his Great Commission to his disciples who live under that Lordship in joyous anticipation of the full coming of the reign of God."[70]

Yet, in spite of its shortcomings and the critique it has engendered, it still is highly influential[71] and has helped many Christians adopt the challenge of how the faithful are to engage with the society in which they find themselves. It is still beneficial to consider Niebuhr's approach to dealing with the issue of faith and society. Even Yoder, a severe critic of Niebuhr, encouraged the reading of *Christ and Culture*: "It continues to be worthwhile to read Niebuhr carefully, even a near half-century after he wrote. Niebuhr taught more than a generation of mainstream American ethical thinkers. . . . His pupils have led the Christian social ethics guild in North America ever since."[72]

Although the alternatives presented by Niebuhr may initially appear to be actual options for social involvement, none of them should be seen as representative of the stance of any specific individual, church, or Christian tradition. Rather, they are best viewed as logical approaches that help clarify the distinctiveness of each and the differences between them. In this limited regard they may be helpful; however, our objective is different.

Yoder: "Culture for Niebuhr is first of all *monolithic*. In the course of the argument, we observed that each position was measured by Niebuhr according to the *consistency* with which a thinker responds to the entire realm of values called 'the world' or 'culture.'" Yoder, "How H. Richard Niebuhr Reasoned," 54; italics original. Also see Yoder: "What for H. R. Niebuhr is the definition of 'culture' in its essence is for the New Testament the definition of perdition and demonic self-glorification." Yoder, "How H. Richard Niebuhr Reasoned," 69.

69. Carter, "Inadequate Christology," para. 1.

70. Carter, "Inadequate Christology," para. 11.

71. See, for example, Carter regarding the impact of *Christ and Culture*: "It has had enormous impact on the way theology students, pastors and college and seminary professors, as well as scholars from other academic disciplines, think about how culture should be engaged today by thoughtful Christians." Carter, "Inadequate Christology," para. 2.

72. Yoder, "How H. Richard Niebuhr Reasoned," 31.

We are seeking to determine an *actual* social stance the believer can adopt as an expression of faithfulness. To that end both Niebuhr's nebulous understanding of Christ[73] and his monolithic understanding of culture[74]—essential concepts within his presentation—are not of benefit to us, thus rendering the articulation significantly flawed for our purposes.

The world in which Christians live—and it could be argued the local social context in which *any* individual Christian lives—consists of a plethora of cultural elements and even many cultures. In such a social milieu it is the Jesus of the Scripture, not a social construct developed in such a way as to foster the building of a typology, that should drive the concept of social engagement adopted by the faithful one. The challenge is to ascertain what notion should form the concept: fusion, amalgamation, confrontation, metamorphosis, antagonism, withdrawal, or some other notion.

The proper perspective to determine the appropriate social/moral stance is to appreciate the challenge Jesus conveyed to his followers. At the heart of that challenge was that Jesus' followers are to live faithfully under the lordship of Christ *as they live in society*. Instead of asking how Christ should relate to culture, the faithful Christian as well as the Christian community should concentrate on how the individual and the church living faithfully in the kingdom of God should engage the kingdom of the world. To that matter we now turn.

---

73. Although writing at some length about Christ, Niebuhr never articulated a clear definition and actually admitted as much: "If we cannot point to the heart and essence of this Christ, we can at least point to some of the phenomena in which his essence appears. Though every description is an interpretation, it can be an interpretation of the objective reality. Jesus Christ who is the Christian's authority can be described, though every description falls short of completeness and must fail to satisfy others who have encountered him." Niebuhr, *Christ and Culture*, 14. He went on to assert that "other approaches besides the moral one must be taken if Jesus Christ is to be described adequately." Niebuhr, *Christ and Culture*, 29.

74. Niebuhr adopted an overly simplistic, and thus unrealistic, understanding of culture: "What we have in mind when we deal with Christ and culture is that total process of human activity and that total result of such activity to which now the name *culture*, now the name *civilization*, is applied in common speech. Culture is the 'artificial, secondary environment' which man superimposes on the natural. It comprises language, habits, ideas, beliefs, customs, social organization, inherited artifacts, technical processes, and values. This 'social heritage' . . . is what we mean when we speak of culture." Niebuhr, *Christ and Culture*, 32.

The Kingdom of God and the Kingdom of the World

We have explored the nature of the kingdom of God, both objectively and subjectively, but what is the kingdom of the world? It is not a singular concept, and it cannot be judged to be wholly evil, all good, or some mediating concept such as generally good but flawed. Rather, the kingdom of the world is the environment—the social and moral milieu—in which both the Christian and the local Christian collective find themselves. Its characteristics will vary depending upon its constituent elements: historical tradition, religious makeup, cultural elements, values, priorities, political realities, and the like. The reason a single term—kingdom of the world—can be used as an umbrella for the infinite number of its variations is not that they all share a common suite of characteristics, but that one characteristic is common to them all: they have not submitted to the lordship of Christ, and thus are wholly distinct from the kingdom of God.

This does not mean that no good can be seen in the kingdom of the world. Education, health care, supporting the needy, and many other similar efforts can be found in great abundance in many places throughout the world. So can the great evils that plague the world's population. The failure is not the degree to which a particular social and moral milieu harbors and fosters good; it is the fact that Christ is not lord over that environment, and thus it warrants being labeled the kingdom of the world.

The question facing Christians living within their particular variation of the kingdom of the world is how to find direction for living within it faithfully. The answer is not to make an arbitrary selection, based upon emotion or perhaps what makes one comfortable. We are not simply to choose a stance that appeals to us. Instead, direction is found by appealing to three entities: the moral hermeneutic for interpreting Scripture, the moral authority of Jesus, and (as a foil, or check-and-balance, against the other two entities) historical precedent.

The first guide to which we may turn is the appropriate moral hermeneutic for using Scripture to direct us. Accurate appropriation of Scripture—without abusing it—for direction in the moral realm is the goal. In this regard, we need first to affirm the progressive nature of God's revelation in Scripture. There is moral development in Scripture, and whereas all of Scripture is authoritative the moral guidance provided therein evolves from the beginning of the Decalogue through the end of the New Testament. We derive the most accurate direction for establishing a social stance by interpreting Scripture after the pattern set by Jesus.[75] When using Scripture Jesus presented a proper approach to values, and thus to the moral obligation incumbent upon the faithful.

God's involvement with humanity is presented as a story that grows as Scripture progresses. Jesus is the overarching figure throughout the story. In the part of the story that depicts Jesus' earthly life—the Gospels—we see Jesus at work using the Old Testament not only to announce the arrival of the kingdom of God in his social sphere, but also to give authority to his teaching and conduct. The means by which Jesus used the Old Testament is the hermeneutic he established for his followers. It forms the interpretive grid by which Scripture is appropriated for application in the moral realm. Primarily that hermeneutic entailed a prophetic mindset, calling the one seeking to be faithful from living according to the moral norms of the prevailing social milieu to the redemptive sphere where the ways of God prevail. Scripture, when interpreted according to the hermeneutic of Jesus, envisions an arc of transport that carries God's aspiring faithful from the social realm not yielded to God's rule to the one where God's rule prevails—movement from Egypt to the promised land, from the magi authoritative in the east to the same magi kneeling before the infant Savior, from the kingdom of the world to the kingdom of God.

The hermeneutic of Jesus, when applied to God's story not only in the Old Testament but also in the New, summons the faithful to a moral milieu distinct from that of the prevailing society. Yielding to that summons is, according to Paul, the merciful work of "the Father, who has qualified you to share in the inheritance of his holy people in the kingdom of light. For he has rescued us from the dominion of darkness and brought us into the kingdom of the Son he loves."[76]

Turning to the second element, it was through Jesus' moral authority—both his teaching (epistemic moral authority) and his example (exemplary moral authority)—that he gave guidance concerning how the one seeking to be faithful should live within the society. After his early ministry announcement of the presence of the kingdom of God within the present social and moral milieu, he went on to teach of the kingdom and demonstrate its presence. He made it clear that the kingdom of God is a reality into which one enters and lives *in contradistinction from the*

---

75. For a more extensive presentation of the appropriate hermeneutic for the moral realm, see Wozniak, *Living as the Living Jesus*, 62–69.

76. Col 1:12–13.

kingdom of the world.[77] There is no blending of the two, and the two cannot be reconciled short of the eschaton. Thus the rich ruler had a very difficult time leaving the kingdom of the world in which he lived in order to enter the kingdom of God—and, it appears, ultimately failed to do so.[78] Children, however, are the ideal of those who live in God's kingdom,[79] and serve as the example for those who would enter. There were those who participated in the kingdom, and those who were "on the outside."[80] Others were merely close, but not yet in the kingdom.[81] What we take from Jesus' teaching and example is that the kingdom of God that he announced, explained, and demonstrated is a distinct entity—already present, but qualitatively different from the kingdom of the world because it holds to different values. Indeed, the kingdom of God is presented by Jesus as an *alternative* to the kingdom of the world.[82]

How, though, is the kingdom of God different from the kingdom of the world? It may be an alternative, but what does it entail that is unique from all of the various expressions of the kingdom of the world in which Christians may find themselves? The thought of New Testament scholar James W. Thompson is particularly helpful in this regard. He saw that Jesus' message of the kingdom was, fundamentally, in conflict with that of the surrounding social and political environment: "While the Gospels do not record a direct challenge to Roman power by Jesus, the message of the kingdom inevitably led to a conflict with Roman power . . . Thus the Gospels report a conflict between Jesus and both the Jewish leadership and the Roman rulers."[83] Thompson expanded on this thought, explaining, "As the arrest and execution of Jesus indicate, his message of

---

77. In this regard, see Thompson: "Jesus made his announcement in the context of political, religious, cultural, and social institutions that already existed and would be challenged by his message. . . . he did not minister within the established institutions or affiliate with any of the parties within Galilee and Judea." Thompson, *Christ and Culture in the New Testament*, 32.

78. See Matt 19:16–24.

79. See Matt 19:14.

80. Mark 4:11.

81. See Mark 12:28–34.

82. See Thompson, who wrote regarding Jesus, "he consistently indicates that the kingdom is already present. . . . Jesus dissociates his message of the kingdom from the common expectations and announces the reversal of values that is already present among his disciples. Jesus presents an alternative world that is already present in his ministry." Thompson, *Christ and Culture in the New Testament*, 36.

83. Thompson, *Christ and Culture in the New Testament*, 34.

FAITHFULNESS, LOVE, AND THE KINGDOM OF GOD

the kingdom was nevertheless subversive, for it relativized political affiliation and undermined the absolute loyalty that Rome demanded."[84]

In such an environment of conflict between the kingdom of God and the kingdom of the world, how is the Christian—as an individual and as a member of the believing community—to live within the social and moral milieu in faithfulness? Once again, Thompson's thinking helps clarify the expectations of Jesus that his followers are to live in their society, but in no manner adopting its values or blending into its conduct. Regarding the Beatitudes, he asserted that they "imply an ethical dimension, signifying the manner of life that distinguishes this community from their society."[85] Indeed, the Christian community lives within the kingdom of God as an alternative to, and a replacement of, the kingdom of the world. Love is to drive the community members in all that they do as a witness to the kingdom of the world of the uniqueness and moral superiority of the divine kingdom. Thompson asserted, "At the heart of the community's existence is love for one another as the community replaced the functions that had belonged to the families from whom they were separated."[86]

The faithful one, then, is called to live in the kingdom of God in clear distinction from life in the kingdom of the world, yet not withdraw from it. Syncretism in any form—so characteristic of and ubiquitous throughout Western Christianity today—is not permitted for the faithful. This not only was the consistent message and example of Jesus, but was adopted by the other New Testament writers as the societal expectation of Christians within their moral milieu.[87]

As the final entity to which we may appeal for guidance, how did the early Christians—those closest to the earthly life of Jesus—establish themselves vis-à-vis their social and moral milieu? This entity is not ultimately authoritative for the believer, but serves to check our judgments against those who have gone before us in the quest for faithfulness. In part 1 we looked into the influences on the early Christians of the first few centuries that guided their thinking regarding the appropriate stance

---

84. Thompson, *Christ and Culture in the New Testament*, 46.
85. Thompson, *Christ and Culture in the New Testament*, 38.
86. Thompson, *Christ and Culture in the New Testament*, 183.

87. In this regard, see Thompson: "The Johannine literature demarcates believers from the world that hates them (John 15:18), and Paul distinguishes between believers and unbelievers, insiders and outsiders. . . . both the authors of Hebrews and 1 Peter describe believers as 'aliens and exiles' (cf. Heb 11:13-16; 13:13-14; 1 Pet 2:11). Thus they knew sharp boundaries between themselves and the world." Thompson, *Christ and Culture in the New Testament*, 183.

vis-à-vis the societies in which they lived. Chief among those was the written Gospel accounts of the life of Jesus, for they painted a more accurate and complete picture of Jesus' teaching and conduct than did the letters from Paul. Upon gaining a clear understanding not only of Jesus' life, but also of what he expected of his followers, the early Christians' convictions regarding the nature of faithfulness changed significantly, along with their commensurate stance within their social and moral milieu. The Gospels served as a corrective to the social and moral lifestyle to which they were accustomed—a corrective that necessitated a dramatically different social stance, including the way they responded to the demands of Rome.

From the Gospels those early Christians learned that the kingdom of God was the overarching concern of Jesus during his time on earth. In his life he demonstrated the character of the kingdom, with particular emphasis on the divine presence among the people of God. Power over enemies was not the focus of Jesus' conveyance of the kingdom, but rather God's present reality: Immanuel—God with us. Jesus' example of living immersed in the reality of the presence of God became exemplary for the early faithful. In Jesus they saw how to establish themselves within their social reality, taking on the role of Jesus' apprentices and learning through imitation.

Through his teachings the first believers learned much about the nature of the kingdom, including the stark reality that the righteous of the kingdom would be persecuted. Their suffering would increase as a result of aligning themselves with Jesus. Since the kingdom of God and the kingdom of the world had different core allegiances, there existed a fundamental conflict between them. That foundational antagonism required one to choose between "Jesus is Lord!" and "We have no king but Caesar!" The faithful could not remain so and compromise their affirmation of the lordship of Christ, irrespective of the cost. Immersion in the kingdom of God necessarily entailed rejection of the demands of Rome—the kingdom of the world. Syncretism was not possible.

We see, then, that the social stance embraced by the early Christians confirms the judgments that resulted from the other two guiding entities: the moral hermeneutic for interpreting Scripture and the moral authority of Jesus. What is incumbent upon the faithful is absolutely clear; there are no alternatives that avoid compromising faithfulness. The individual must choose a stance for participation in the social and moral milieu: faithfulness requires one to choose the kingdom of God in contradistinction from the kingdom of the world. Anything other constitutes unfaithfulness.

Conclusion
Rediscovering Forgotten Faithfulness

EACH OF US LIVES within a social context: a milieu that entails relationships, cultural elements, environmental assumptions and expectations, power realities, groups, beliefs, and other elements characteristic of a common living arena. Our human experience does not occur in isolation, outside of the social context. For the believer, faithfulness before God on the part of both the individual and the Christian collective, the church, is foundational to what it means to be Christian. Without faithfulness the one who professes to be a Christian is not so, irrespective of the theological content to which one ascribes. Whereas faithfulness is made manifest and tangible within the social context, it most certainly does not involve an ostentatious promotion of one's piety or orthodoxy, or even a reserved one. Faithfulness is a moral notion, for it occurs in the moral realm of human experience—in the social milieu in which one finds oneself. It does not exist outside of one's daily, routine life experience. The faithful one cannot be so outside of the collective human context. One does not extract oneself from the social milieu in order to be faithful, but rather becomes immersed in the milieu in faithful living. The expression of faithfulness in its essence, then, entails the world of ethics:

attitudes, intentions, values, virtues, commitments, character, responses, judgments, conduct, and the like.

Faithfulness is not a recent concept, or even one whose origin can be traced back to, for example, the life of Jesus or the giving of the Ten Commandments. Instead, it extends through the eons of human history all the way—it could be argued—to the Garden of Eden in which Adam and Eve were called upon to be faithful to God. Even beyond that, our understanding of God as the archetype of faithfulness is part of eternity itself. The primary challenge for the believer has not been knowing that God expects faithfulness, but rather what it means to be faithful in the social and moral situation in which one finds oneself. Meeting the challenge well requires a sizeable and long-term investment on the part of the believer, and entails effort to understand at least early church history in this regard, studying the Scripture to discern the meaning of faithfulness, and focusing specifically on the significance of the life of Jesus as he lived it faithfully within his social context.

THE FAILURE OF THE MODERN CHURCH

The vast majority of today's Western church has failed to meet the challenge both of understanding faithfulness and uncompromisingly embracing it. In its place the church has substituted a syncretistic social ethic in which the individual believer as well as the Christian collective values such items as comfort, emotional experience, materialism, nationalism, power, secularism, capitalism, civil religion, and the like. These are all included as typical and common elements of the Western church's understanding of true Christianity, its denial of such notwithstanding. Piety, sincerity, commitment, spirituality, and other admirable traits abound in the Western church; yet it has to a great extent—somewhat unwittingly—failed to grasp the essence of what God requires of the faithful. Effectiveness rather than faithfulness drives both the church's and the believer's priorities; the resultant success reinforces the fall into syncretism, with the adherent's predictable affirmation that she or he is experiencing the blessing of God. It is unsurprising that the Western church and its constituents also have adopted as their values the vices of the secular social milieu they have embraced—believing those vices to be consecrated by God—including the use of force as the driver of both domination and achievement, employment of violence as the means not only of defense but also to prevail, and a teleological mindset as the norm for what they believe to be justice and moral uprightness. It thus has succumbed to the temptation about which Jesus warned his followers in the Garden of Gethsemane. Indeed, the preponderance of Western Christianity does not display any distinction from the surrounding society, but rather the full endorsement of it, including its appetite for pleasure, entertainment, self-fulfillment, and affluence. What it believes to be its divinely ordained syncretic social stance has—to a great extent—been adopted without discretion, being devoid of the character of Jesus. It has adopted Aristotle's moral mean as its stance within the society: a heart of moral compromise that is a drastic departure from God's standard of faithfulness. Reminiscent of the moral mediocrity of the Laodicean church's conduct,[1] the Western church is in dire need of a corrective.

THE EARLY CHRISTIANS AND FAITHFULNESS

The early Christians held an extremely different view of what it meant to be called to faithfulness. Their social situation was more similar to ours than at any at any other time since the first few centuries after Christ: they lived in an environment of pluralism in many ways—racial, religious, ethnic, cultural, linguistic, philosophical—and interacted with people and social institutions that held to a wide range of values, priorities, perspectives, and moral commitments. It was in that situation that they worked out what faithfulness required in the context in which they lived. Since their situation was so close to the current one, we should be able to learn a great deal about faithfulness from their struggle with what it means to live faithfully in a specific social context.

The first Christians had the advantage of being the believers closest to Jesus, both temporally and proximally. At the time there was no tradition of interpreting the gospel message, and thus no hermeneutical filter that could blind them to what faithfulness actually meant. They had the gospel story in its most pristine form—which drove their developing concept of faithfulness—and the very earliest of them actually were in contact with those who lived with Jesus. By observing how they approached faithfulness we can construct a basis for how we should as well.

---

1. See Rev 3:15-16, in which Jesus criticized the church in Laodicea: "I know your deeds, that you are neither cold nor hot. I wish you were either one or the other! So, because you are lukewarm—neither hot nor cold—I am about to spit you out of my mouth."

CONCLUSION 259

What, then, were the important elements of faithfulness to them, and how did they meet the challenge to be faithful?

For the early Christians the notion of God's call was fundamental to their understanding of what it meant to be a Christian. For them the call of God was a summons to be faithful, not a plan for the individual's happiness, prosperity, success, and fulfillment as is affirmed by much of Western Christianity today. The divine summons was an invitation to walk in the way of Jesus, and was undergirded by the very authority of God. The summons was common to all and applied equally to all. They shared it in solidarity as God's people distinct from the social and moral milieu in which they found themselves. Its fundamental concept was the invitation to become part of God's new community, in contradistinction from conformity to the ways of the world. Those who responded positively to the summons left their life of adherence to the prevailing ethics of the social milieu in which they found themselves, and joined those who walked in the way of Jesus as aliens and exiles within their social context. For the early Christians, to continue to walk in the way of Jesus, irrespective of the consequences, was what the summons entailed.

The first believers initially suffered from a misperception common at the time: they had a limited Old Testament understanding of the kingdom of God that entailed a past expression and hope for a future one. However, it did not include a concept of the kingdom of God in the present. This shortcoming initially influenced their view of how to make their way in society until the eschatological kingdom arrived. It entailed accommodation of the dominant social milieu as a matter of practicality, with its associated values and expectations. This perspective colored how they viewed the letters from Paul and others with which they may have come in contact. However, when later they were exposed to the gospel oral tradition and eventually the written Synoptic Gospels, they came to understand that the present kingdom of God was central to the message of Jesus; it was his overarching concern during his sojourn on earth. That notion—that they lived within the present reality of the kingdom through God's abiding presence with them—changed drastically their concept of faithfulness. It was the fuller picture of Jesus' life and teachings as found in the Gospels that drove a correction of their former misunderstanding of the kingdom, and required that they—as those who had responded to the summons of God—commit themselves to a social stance far different from that to which they were accustomed. That stance included how they responded to the demands of Rome. No longer engaging in compromising accommodation to the prevailing moral milieu, their former syncretistic social stance had given way to open defiance when pressured by the state.

The new understanding of faithfulness—and the associated social stance—adopted by the early believers carried implications for their daily lives. Since the foundation of faithfulness entailed walking in the way of Jesus, adherence to a set of rules or external demands was not their primary focus. Rather, intense relationship with Christ, and the continual enhancing of that relationship, was at the heart of faithfulness. Just as Jesus had been immersed in the tangible realities of his social environment, so they were to be. At the same time, as the believing community, they were to be morally distinct from their social and political surroundings. Their values were appropriate only for them as members of God's new society. Thus, they broadly repudiated the workings of Rome that violated the moral standards of the kingdom of God. Participation in government-sanctioned killing, including both the justice system and the military, was rejected by the early believers as a violation of the way of Jesus. The result was that they were misaligned with the norms of their social milieu. Rome was intolerant of such challenges, and responded as only a secular government can: with force and violence in order to quell the challenge. As a result the Christians suffered the wrath of Rome, as had Jesus. Yet, even in extreme suffering, they were walking in the way of Jesus, and thus expressing their faithfulness.

What can we, as twenty-first-century Christians, learn about faithfulness from our faithful sisters and brothers who first followed in the Jesus way? Foremost is understanding just that: faithfulness entails following in the way of Jesus, and having a mindset focused on the living Jesus.[2] This concept is what Kierkegaard described as contemporaneousness with Jesus. Although the Jesus of the Gospels is the historical one who is to be our paradigm, he is not to be relegated to the first century.

Of paramount importance to the early Christians seeking to live faithfully was their commitment to the new community of God. The divine call was common to all Christians, and so they could, *as a local collective*, pursue faithfulness. Their shared foundational narratives concerning Jesus gave content to the beliefs of the community members, and drove their values and character as each matured in their common faith. The collective notion of faithfulness is a concept that modern Christians

---

2. Essential to focusing on Jesus as living and exalted is inclusion of the Jesus pictured in the Epistle to the Hebrews.

have generally forgotten but should adopt, rather than each pursuing his or her unique understanding of what it means to be faithful. Since the community's narratives were rooted in God's self-disclosure through both the life of Jesus and the Scripture, the values and character that distinguish faithfulness are those of God himself. The early Christians understood this, and in response pursued Godlikeness; the Western church largely has forgotten to do so.

Finally, suffering after Jesus' pattern was an understood essential element of faithfulness for the first believers. Jesus as the one who announced the present kingdom of God as distinct from the predominant moral milieu—religious, social, and political—incurred the predictable ire of the dominant environment. Not only that, but he promised that all who would follow him likewise would suffer. Christians of our day generally believe that one of God's purposes—and one of their motivators for believing in God—is the expectation that God will save them from suffering. A quid pro quo is at work in the Western church: "we believe in You, and in turn You keep us from suffering." When suffering comes their way, they charge God with failing them. Such was not the way of the Father with his own Son, and we need to learn from the early Christians that such is not the way of those who follow the Son.

FAITHFULNESS: THE ETHIC AFTER GOD'S OWN HEART

Faithfulness rightly conceived involves an ethic: a means by which life in the moral realm of human experience is approached. Since the time of Moses God's people have been charged by God to "be holy, because I am holy."[3] Peter reiterated the charge to the early Christians when he wrote, "But just as he who called you is holy, so be holy in all you do; for it is written: 'Be holy, because I am holy.'"[4] This call to holiness is the heart of what it means to be faithful. It is rooted in the very being of God, and forms the most fundamental element of the believer's ethic. Faithfulness is Godlikeness. Far from being a collective of moral judgments following some structure of moral directives, the ethic of the faithful one is the ongoing, continuous quest to be like God; the heart of the faithful one's

---

3. Lev 11:44, 45; 19:2.
4. 1 Pet 1:15–16.

being is to be the divine character, for the divine character is the moral expression of God's being.

Any truthful examination of human character, however, quickly reveals the truth that human character falls very short of God's character. Becoming Godlike necessitates a *transition* of character from the current state to the character of God. Somehow the one aspiring to be faithful must inculcate the divine character. Since character is not fixed and rigid, but rather fluid and malleable, the transition is possible. One can determine to guide, or form, character in a particular direction through habitual practice, and so the possibility exists to transition the gap between the present state of character and the goal of realizing God's character in the life of the faithful one.

The foundational notion of the divine character is that God's character is love. It is not something ineffable, leaving us without hope for inculcating it within ourselves, but has been disclosed by God through his communicable attributes. Through those attributes the love of God impinges upon humans, and allows for the aspiring faithful to begin the quest of character development after the character of God. Initially God communicated his love through direct engagement with Adam and Eve via the ongoing, direct relationship between the Creator and the Created. Subsequent to the fall the encounters continued at times, such as God's interactions with Abraham and Moses. In time God's self-disclosure of his love character occurred through the giving of the Word of God in written form. The clearest divine self-disclosure, however, was through the incarnation of the second person of the Trinity, the Son, in the person of Jesus. It is in the life of Jesus that we see clearly the character of God. Those who pursue acquisition of God's character are guided in the task by viewing Jesus as the paradigmatic divine character *on display*. Through his teaching and conduct the character of God was given tangible form—the outworking of the divine character—and so observation of Jesus' life is the preeminent means of discerning the character of God. However, rote emulation of Jesus is not the faithful one's first goal; rather, inculcation of the character of God as found in the life of Jesus is what the faithful one is to pursue first. Emulation alone is insufficient to render one faithful. Those who see faithfulness only as mimicking Jesus' conduct risk falling into the category of those who declare, "Lord, Lord, did we not prophesy in your name and in your name drive out demons and in your name perform many miracles?"⁵ Jesus' response to them will be, "I never knew you. Away from me, you evildoers!"⁶ The basis for Jesus' response is not lack of emulation of Jesus' conduct, but failure to "do the will of my Father who is in heaven."⁷ That will is Godlikeness, the inculcation of the character of God.

For the one seeking to be faithful the challenge is not affirming that in Jesus the character of God was on display. Rather, it is how to appropriate the divine character, and thus grow in faithfulness. By what means is one to form one's character after that of God? Key to knowing what is instrumental in this regard is the realization that all human beings are created in the image of God, and by nature are unique among creation. The *imago Dei* is inherent to what humans are *de jure*. Yet that image is fallen; faithfulness requires renewal of the image. Cultivating that image so that the individual's moral experience reflects the image of God *de facto* is the means to inculcate the character of God. God's communicable essence realized within a person equates to acquisition of the divine character, and the *imago Dei* is the actualization of that character in the person's moral expression.

In the incarnation of the divine Son the *imago Dei* was not lost, neither was it obscured or tainted in any way. In Jesus is seen the character of God in its perfection through the display of the divine image in ideal form. The image in Jesus did not require renewal, for its pristine nature remained as the Son's essence, though incarnate. As the visible revelation of the character, being, and will of God, Jesus was the disclosure of God's heart in a form that is comprehensible by human beings. Conformity with that heart is what it means to be faithful, and Jesus' display of that heart was intended to guide the restoration of the tainted *imago Dei* in humans. When this happens, the faithful one is, as Paul expressed it, "being renewed in knowledge in the image of its Creator,"⁸ and the character of God is engraved on the individual.

Renewal of the divine image may be the means by which character is formed, but what is the habitual effort by which the renewal occurs? One is not left alone in this endeavor, for when Jesus left the earth he sent the Holy Spirit as his emissary: the One who would guide the aspiring faithful one in truth while walking in the way of Jesus. Submission to

5. Matt 7:22.
6. Matt 7:23.
7. Matt 7:21.
8. Col 3:10.

the guidance of the Spirit is the core of living in contemporaneity with the exalted Son. Through such submission Christ is formed in us,[9] and his *imago Dei* becomes ours *de facto*. By means of habitual engagement with, and submission to, the Spirit we reappropriate the image of God, and our character is transformed into the character of God. Without equivocation we can affirm that faithfulness is Godlikeness inculcated and demonstrated, following the example of Jesus. As such it is the ethic after God's own heart.

LIVING THE ETHIC

Godlikeness inculcated is only part of what the ethic of faithfulness includes. Demonstrating Godlikeness is the other part. Such demonstration is accomplished when the faithful one—*as a participant in the present kingdom of God announced by Jesus*—lives within the social milieu. *Building* the kingdom is not the task of the one who aspires to faithfulness, for it is God who builds the kingdom. The faithful *enter* it, and become fully immersed in it by following in the Jesus way. This is what Jesus termed "the secret of the kingdom." In the kingdom environment the participant—as one of the Christian collective—is empowered to manifest faithfulness.

The concept of entering the kingdom of God suggests transport from some other realm—the kingdom of the world, a social realm not yielded to the lordship of Christ—to a realm where Jesus reigns. That transport is accomplished when one views the Scripture prophetically, as did Jesus, and internalizes for one's own journey of faithfulness the Gospel story of Jesus' paradigmatic life. This is what the early Christians did, and it forms a core element of the current believer's transport into the kingdom of God.

Such all-consuming immersion in the kingdom of God comes with great risk, since the kingdom of God is at odds with the kingdom of the world. The two hold to vastly different values, have two different masters, and have two distinct sets of followers. This is the reality to which Jesus was referring when he said, "Do you think I came to bring peace on earth? No, I tell you, but division."[10] The infiltrating nature of the kingdom of God into the kingdom of the world inevitably means the two

9. See Gal 4:19.
10. Luke 12:51.

will clash. So the faithful one enters into and lives within the kingdom of God as subversive of the kingdom of the world and in contradistinction from it. The kingdom of God is an alternative to and replacement of the kingdom of the world; any attempt at a syncretistic stance exposes an extreme dearth of faithfulness. The individual must select between the two kingdoms; to choose one is to reject the other.

For the one who chooses to live in her or his social and moral milieu as a participant in the kingdom of God, the root means by which faithfulness is expressed is love. It is the reality by which the kingdom of God impinges upon those of the kingdom of the world. As the character of God revealed, love plays the instrumental role for actuating faithfulness *within a specific social context*. Without it one cannot participate in the kingdom of God; with it the kingdom participant is guided and encouraged in conduct following the Jesus standard. That standard is exercise of the will for the good of another as an exhibition of the divine character and the *imago Dei*.

Love, however, can be expressed in a myriad of ways. It is both futile and shortsighted to attempt to articulate the limits of love's expression. Faithfulness does not necessarily entail all of the possible ways love can be demonstrated, but it does include certain manifestations, for they express most closely the character—and heart—of God and were central to Jesus' introduction of the divine kingdom.

When God expressed love for sinful humanity, he did it by self-giving in the extreme: he gave the Son. Likewise the Son emptied himself of that which he enjoyed as part of the Trinity and took the form of a slave. Throughout his earthly sojourn he was limited in many ways, eventually giving even his life as an expression of divine love for his creation: humanity. These two demonstrations of love exposed the heart of God, and established in tangible form the divine character. Self-emptying in the extreme is divine love at work for the benefit of another, and is the norm by which the faithful are to show love within the social milieu in which they find themselves.

When Jesus expressed divine love through emptying himself he did so as the One obedient to the Father, for such was his commission. Having taken the form of a slave at his incarnation, he was not at liberty to do anything other, and although struggling in the Garden of Gethsemane, he maintained his obedient submission. The implication of his obedience was suffering in the extreme, to the point of a torturous death for the eternal benefit of others. In this he not only followed the prophetic pattern, but he demonstrated that he was the foretold Suffering Servant of God expressing love for those embroiled in the kingdom of the world. Obedience to the point of suffering is what Jesus requires of all who follow in his way. In his final earthly words he spoke of obedience by those who would be faithful. Not only did he expect obedience of them, he commissioned them to teach others to obey what he had commanded. Adherence to Jesus' commands is a moral obligation of the faithful as love incarnated, irrespective of the cost or degree of suffering required. The early Christians understood this very well, embraced the requirement of faithfulness, and willingly followed in the Jesus way; the vast majority of Western Christianity fails to do so.

Jesus' suffering, as well as that of his faithful followers, came at the hands of the participants in the kingdom of the world, both religious and political. The challenge he faced as the perfect expression of God's character and image was how he should respond. For Jesus there was no equivocation regarding how to engage faithfully with such enemies, for engagement with them required the same kingdom instrument as any other social engagement: the tangible expression of love for the benefit of others. To that end Jesus refused to respond in kind to those who sought to do him harm. When some tried to throw him off a cliff he did not seek to do the same to them. When others plotted his death, he did not subsequently plot theirs. At his arrest and trial those who employed violence against him did not experience retaliatory violence on the part of Jesus, even though he had vast heavenly resources at his immediate disposal capable of doing so. Instead, when a friend coming to his defense attacked someone seeking to do Jesus harm, Jesus stopped him in the strongest possible terms, and healed the one Jesus' friend had attacked. This he did even though by doing so the risk of violence to himself remained. Stopping the risk was irrelevant to Jesus; loving the one posing the risk was paramount. In doing so Jesus forever set a standard of faithfulness for his followers: retaliation in kind, particularly the use of force and violence, is never permitted. There are no qualifications on the standard, or mitigating circumstances that invalidate it in any context, be it involving personal or political enemies. Such mitigation or invalidation is not the way of the kingdom of God.

Throughout his life Jesus' teaching was consistent with his conduct toward those who would do him harm. Not only his enemies, but also those of his followers, were to be treated only with love. Retaliation in any form was not permitted in any circumstance, for any reason. Seeking the good of enemies, even at the expense of the faithful one, was the kingdom standard Jesus taught. As we might expect, such a kingdom standard was at odds with the standard of the broader society, for which force and violence in the interest of self—be the self an individual or the state—was assumed and often employed. For the faithful one, however, such violence is not an option, including participating in any sort of state-sponsored use of force. The reason is simple and clear: Jesus forbids it.

Jesus' announcement of the kingdom of God was not intended as a means to fix the society in which he lived, but rather to replace it. The kingdom of God and the kingdom of the world are irreconcilable. The Old Testament vision of the Jubilee as well as the vision of the new humanity in Revelation anticipate a different society, one in which God's character predominates through manifestations of love. In such expressions the needy are afforded preeminence, while those who leverage the benefits of the kingdom of the world for their own advantage—to the detriment of the needy—are brought low. Captives are released, and the mournful are comforted. The needy no longer are excluded, but are brought into the sphere of the great banquet of the kingdom of God. These visions speak of grand societal change; not preservation of the existing social order, but replacement of it by a new one. The introduction of fundamental moral and social change was foundational to the kingdom message of Jesus. His message to social conservatives was that the kingdom of God is not an enhancement or a corrective, but an alternative to the established social reality. The enduring dynamic of the Sermon on the Mount is "You have heard that it was said . . . But I tell you." Fundamental change to what faithfulness entails is the implication of the kingdom that Jesus introduced. As those who walk in the way of Jesus his faithful ones must be agents of change, as was Jesus. In bringing the new kingdom Jesus put the character of God on display through love expressed in the moral and social milieu in which he found himself, and thus put faithfulness on display as well. Those who aspire to follow him in faithfulness can do no less.

Modern-day Christianity struggles with faithfulness, chiefly due to its refusal to reject the kingdom of the world and choose the kingdom of God. Instead, many of those who believe themselves to be God's faithful have embraced that which God requires them to abandon, and have abandoned the essential manifestations of faithfulness that Jesus embraced. As such, they are ruled by a syncretistic mindset that has no place among the faithful, and thus have rejected the tangible kingdom expressions of love in their social milieu. Living faithfully necessitates making choices between alternatives: inculcating the character of God rather than maintaining the character common to humanity; renewing the image of God from *de jure* only to *de facto* in daily experience; walking in the way of Jesus led by the Spirit instead of embracing the enjoyable benefits of society's ways of moral compromise; becoming immersed in the kingdom of God as distinct from the kingdom of the world; living a life of divine love expressed even to enemies rather than responding with the self-aggrandizing values that form society's norms; and becoming an agent of God's eschatological social vision in the present instead of clinging to society's present form. In doing so we will become God's faithful followers, and can proclaim joyfully that "he has rescued us from the dominion of darkness and brought us into the kingdom of the Son he loves."

Bibliography

Albert, Ethel M., et al. *Great Traditions in Ethics*. New York: American, 1953.
Alexander, Loveday. "The Gospels and Acts: Discipleship and the Kingdom." In *The Meanings of Discipleship*, edited by Andrew Hayes and Stephen Cherry, 7–21. Eugene, OR: Wipf & Stock, 2021.
The Analytical Greek Lexicon. Grand Rapids: Zondervan, 1974.
Attridge, Harold W. "Early Christians and the Care of the Poor." *Reflections* (Fall 2010) 14–17. https://reflections.yale.edu/article/no-more-excuses-confronting-poverty/early-christians-and-care-poor.
Bainton, Roland H. *Christendom: A Short History of Christianity and Its Impact on Western Civilization*. Vol 1. 2 vols. New York: Harper & Row, 1966.
Barclay, William. *New Testament Words*. Philadelphia: Westminster, 1974.
Bauer, Walter. *A Greek-English Lexicon of the New Testament and Other Early Christian Literature*. 4th revised and augmented edition, 1952. Translated and edited by William F. Arndt and F. Wilbur Gingrich. Chicago: University of Chicago Press, 1974.
Berkhof, Louis. *Systematic Theology*. 4th ed. Grand Rapids: Eerdmans, 1974.
Bernard, J. H. *A Critical and Exegetical Commentary on The Gospel According to St. John*. Vol 2. Edited by A. H. McNeile. International Critical Commentary, edited by S. R. Driver et al. Edinburgh: T. & T. Clark, 1928.
Bessenecker, Scott. "Through My Lens—American Christian Syncretism." *InterVarsity* (blog), Jan 30, 2020. https://intervarsity.org/blog/through-my-lens-american-christian-syncretism.
Bonhoeffer, Dietrich. *The Cost of Discipleship*. Translated by R. H. Fuller. New York: Macmillan, 1976.
———. *Ethics*. Translated by Neville Horton Smith. New York: Touchstone, 1995.
Boulton, Wayne G., et al., eds. *From Christ to the World: Introductory Readings in Christian Ethics*. Grand Rapids: Eerdmans, 1994.

Boyd, Don. "The Prophets—Suffering Affliction and Of Patience." 2006. https://kc-cofc.org/39th/Lectures/2006_Manuscripts/Boyd_TheProphetsSufferingAffliction.pdf.

Boyd, Greg. "How Reliable Were the Early Church's Oral Traditions?" *Reknew*, Nov 3, 2021. https://reknew.org/2021/11/how-reliable-was-the-early-churchs-oral-traditions/.

Brandon. "John Calvin on the Image of God." *Siris* (blog), Jul 7, 2005. http://branemrys.blogspot.com/2005/07/john-calvin-on-image-of-god.html.

Brawley, Robert L., ed. *Character Ethics and the New Testament: Moral Dimensions of Scripture*. Louisville: Westminster John Knox, 2007.

———. "Generating Ethics from God's Character in Mark." In *Character Ethics and the New Testament: Moral Dimensions of Scripture*, edited by Robert L. Brawley, 57–74. Louisville: Westminster John Knox, 2007.

———. "Identity and Metaethics." In *Character Ethics and the New Testament: Moral Dimensions of Scripture*, edited by Robert L. Brawley, 107–23. Louisville: Westminster John Knox, 2007.

Bredenhof, Ruben. "The Kingdom of God in Jesus and Paul." *ResearchGate*, Feb 2021. https://www.researchgate.net/publication/349052747_The_Kingdom_of_God_in_Jesus_and_Paul.

Brooks, David. *The Road to Character*. New York: Random House, 2016.

Bruce, Alexander Balmain. *The Synoptic Gospels*. Edited by W. Robertson Nicoll. The Expositor's Greek Testament 1. Grand Rapids: Eerdmans, 1956.

Bruce, F. F., ed. *The Epistle to the Hebrews*. The New International Commentary on the New Testament. Grand Rapids: Eerdmans, 1964.

Brueggemann, Walter. "Foreword." In *Character Ethics and the Old Testament*, edited by M. Daniel Carroll R. et al., vii–xi. Louisville: Westminster John Knox, 2007.

Burke, Jonathan. "In the Beginning: The Character of God (1/3)." *Bible Apologetics* (blog). https://bibleapologetics.wordpress.com/in-the-beginning-the-character-of-god/.

Carroll, M. Daniel R. "He Has Told You What Is Good." In *Character Ethics and the Old Testament*, edited by M. Daniel Carroll R. et al., 103–18. Louisville: Westminster John Knox, 2007.

Carroll, M. Daniel R., et al., eds. *Character Ethics and the Old Testament*. Louisville: Westminster John Knox, 2007.

Carter, Craig. "The Legacy of an Inadequate Christology: Yoder's Critique of Niebuhr's *Christ and Culture*." *Mennonite Quarterly Review*, Jul 29, 2003. https://www.goshen.edu/mqr/2003/07/july-2003-carter/.

Challies, Tim. Review of *Lest Innocent Blood Be Shed: The Story of the Village of Le Chambon and How Goodness Happened There*, by Philip Hallie. *Challies*, Jun 4, 2006. https://www.challies.com/book-reviews/lest-innocent-blood-be-shed/.

Character Lab. "Character." https://characterlab.org/.

Cockayne, Joshua. "Imitation and Contemporaneity: Kierkegaard and the Imitation of Christ." The Logos Institute for Analytic and Exegetical Theology, Department of Divinity, University of St. Andrews, 2017. https://research-repository.st-andrews.ac.uk/bitstream/handle/10023/18651/Kierkegaard_on_imitation_AAM.pdf?sequence=1.

De George, Richard T. "Authority and Morality." In *Authority*, edited by Frederick J. Adelmann, 31–49. The Hague: Nijhoff, 1974.

Denio, F. B. "The Kingdom of God in the Old Testament." *The Old Testament Student* 6.2 (Oct 1886) 55–58. Reprinted by The University of Chicago Press.

———. "The Kingdom of God in the Old Testament II." *The Old Testament Student* 6.3 (Nov 1886) 71–76. Reprinted by The University of Chicago Press.

Denney, James. *St. Paul's Epistle to the Romans*. Edited by W. Robertson Nicoll. The Expositor's Greek Testament 2. Grand Rapids: Eerdmans, 1956.

Eastvold, Kory. "The Image of God in Old Testament Theology." *Stone-Campbell Journal* 21 (Fall 2018) 239–51.

Eigenmann, Urs. "The Social Contract and the Kingdom of God: On the Compatibility of Basic Social Conceptions with the Kingdom of God." *International League of Religious Socialists*. Translated by Jean Drummond-Young, Aug 1999. https://ilrs.org/english/reports/eigenmann.html.

Eurnekian, Eduardo, and Tenembaum, Baruch. "Pastor André Trocmé—the Rescuer from Le Chambon-sur-Lignon." *Jerusalem Post*, Apr 6, 2021. https://www.raoulwallenberg.net/general/pastor-andre-trocme-the-rescuer-from-le-chambon-sur-lignon/.

Fee, Gordon D. "The Kingdom of God." In *Called and Empowered: Pentecostal Perspectives on Global Mission*, edited by Murray Dempster et al., 10–11. Peabody, MA: Hendrickson, 1992.

Fletcher, Joseph. *Situation Ethics: The New Morality*. Philadelphia: Westminster, 1966.

Forell, George W., ed. *Christian Social Teachings*. Minneapolis: Augsburg, 1971.

Frankena, William K. *Ethics*. 2nd ed. Englewood Cliffs, NJ: Prentice-Hall, 1973.

Galli, Mark. "Persecution in the Early Church: A Gallery of the Persecuting Emperors." *Christian History* 27 (Jan 1, 1990). https://christianhistoryinstitute.org/magazine/article/persecution-in-early-church-gallery.

Garland, David E. *Mark: From Biblical Text . . . To Contemporary Life*. NIV Application Commentary. Grand Rapids: Zondervan, 1996.

Gentry, Peter J., and Stephen J. Wellum. *God's Kingdom through God's Covenants: A Concise Biblical Theology*. Wheaton: Crossway, 2015.

Gonzalez, Mileidy. "Early Christians in the Roman Empire of the 3rd Century CE: Faith or Family?" *Post Augustum*. http://www.postaugustum.com/en/early-christians-in-the-roman-empire-of-the-3rd-century-ce-faith-or-family-2/.

Gregory, Thomas M. "Obedience." In *The Zondervan Pictorial Encyclopedia of the Bible*. edited by Merrill C. Tenney, 4:482–84. 5 vols. Grand Rapids: Zondervan, 1975.

Grenz, Stanley J. *The Moral Quest: Foundations of Christian Ethics*. Downers Grove, IL: InterVarsity, 1997.

———. *The Social God and the Relational Self: A Trinitarian Theology of the Imago Dei*. Louisville: Westminster John Knox, 2001.

———. *Theology for the Community of God*. Grand Rapids: Eerdmans, 1994.

Gustafson, James. *Moral Discernment in the Christian Life: Essays in Theological Ethics*. Edited by Theo A. Boer and Paul E. Capetz. Louisville: Westminster John Knox, 2007.

———. *Theology and Christian Ethics*. Philadelphia: Pilgrim, 1974.

Hagner, Donald A. *Encountering the Book of Hebrews*. Edited by Walter A. Elwell and Eugene H. Merrill. Encountering Biblical Studies. Grand Rapids: Baker Academic, 2002.

Hallie, Philip. *Lest Innocent Blood Be Shed: The Story of the Village of Le Chambon and How Goodness Happened There*. New York: HarperCollins, 1994.

Hammond, Leslie. "Heroes of the Faith: André Trocmé." *Christians for Social Action*, May 19, 2015. https://christiansforsocialaction.org/resource/heroes-of-the-faith-andre-trocme/.

Hart, Donna. "5 Ways God Calls You!" Biblical Counseling Center (blog), Mar 10, 2016. https://biblicalcounselingcenter.org/5-ways-god-calls-you/.
Hauerwas, Stanley. *Character and the Christian Life: A Study in Theological Ethics.* San Antonio: Trinity University Press, 1979.
———. *A Community of Character: Toward a Constructive Christian Social Ethic.* Notre Dame: University of Notre Dame Press, 1981.
Hauerwas, Stanley, and William H. Willimon. *Resident Aliens: Life in the Christian Colony.* Nashville: Abingdon, 1989.
Hays, Richard B. *The Moral Vision of the New Testament: Community, Cross, New Creation: A Contemporary Introduction to New Testament Ethics.* New York: HarperCollins, 1996.
Heddle, Edmund. "Persecuted Prophets." *Prophecy Today UK*, Nov 6, 2015. https://prophecytoday.uk/study/teaching-articles/item/234-persecuted-prophets.html.
Hodge, Charles. *Commentary on the Epistle to the Romans.* Grand Rapids: Eerdmans, 1974.
———. *An Exposition of 1 and 2 Corinthians.* Wilmington, DE: Sovereign Grace, 1972.
Hoekema, Anthony A. *Created in God's Image.* Grand Rapids: Eerdmans, 1994.
Horsley, Richard A. "Oral and Written Aspects of the Emergence of the Gospel of Mark as Scripture." *Oral Tradition* 25.1 (2010) 93–114.
Hurtado, Larry W. *Mark: A Good News Commentary.* San Francisco: Harper & Row, 1983.
Ignatius of Antioch. *Ignatius to the Smyrnaeans.* https://www.ewtn.com/catholicism/library/ignatius-to-the-smyrnaeans-12519.
International Standard Bible Encyclopedia. 5 vols. Chicago: Howard-Severance, 1915.
Jewish Foundation for the Righteous. "Pastor André Trocmé | France." https://jfr.org/rescuer-stories/trocme-pastor-andre/.
Keil, Carl F., and Franz Delitzsch. *Commentary on the Old Testament.* 10 vols. Translated by Francis Bolton et al. Grand Rapids: Eerdmans, 1975.
Kempis, Thomas à. *The Imitation of Christ.* Edited by Harold C. Gardiner. Garden City, NJ: Doubleday, 1976.
Kierkegaard, Søren. *For Self-Examination and Judge for Yourselves! and Three Discourses 1851.* Princeton: Princeton University, 1968.
———. *The Present Age and Of the Difference between a Genius and an Apostle.* Translated by Alexander Dru. New York: Harper & Row, 1962.
———. *Purity of Heart Is to Will One Thing.* Translated by Douglas V. Steere. New York: Harper & Row, 1956.
———. *Training in Christianity.* Translated by Walter Lowrie. New York: Vintage, 2004.
———. *Works of Love: Some Christian Reflections in the Form of Discourses.* Translated by Howard Hong and Edna Hong. New York: Harper & Row, 1962.
Kirk, Kenneth E. "The Cardinal Virtues." In *From Christ to the World: Introductory Readings in Christian Ethics*, edited by Wayne G. Boulton et al., 238–41. Grand Rapids: Eerdmans, 1994.
Kirkegaard, Brad. "Placing Early Christianity as a Social Movement within Its Greco–Roman Context." *Journal of Lutheran Ethics* 6.1 (Jan 2006). https://www.elca.org/JLE/Articles/619.
Kirsch, Jonathan. "Fourteen Things You Need to Know about King David." *My Jewish Learning.* https://www.myjewishlearning.com/article/fourteen-things-you-need-to-know-about-king-david/.

Kittel, Gerhard, and Gerhard Friedrich, eds. *Theological Dictionary of the New Testament*. Translated by Geoffrey W. Bromiley. 10 vols. Grand Rapids: Eerdmans, 1964–76.

Klein, William W., and Daniel J. Steiner. *What Is My Calling?* Grand Rapids: Baker Academic, 2022.

Kornbluth, Jesse. Review of *Lest Innocent Blood Be Shed: The Story of the Village of Le Chambon and How Goodness Happened There*, by Philip Hallie. *Head Butler*, Mar 23, 2021. https://headbutler.com/reviews/lest-innocent-blood-be-shed-the-story-of-the-village-of-le-chambon-and-how-goodness-happened-there/.

Lane, William L. *Hebrews: A Call to Commitment*. Vancouver, BC: Regent College Press, 2004.

Leaney, A. R. C. *A Commentary on the Gospel According to St. Luke*. New York: Harper & Brothers, 1958.

Lefebure, Leo D. "The Understanding of Suffering in the Early Christian Church." *Journal of Dialogue and Culture* 4.2 (Oct 2015) 29–37.

Leitch, A. H. "Image of God." In *The Zondervan Pictorial Encyclopedia of the Bible*, edited by Merrill C. Tenney, 3:256–58. 5 vols. Grand Rapids: Zondervan, 1975.

Lewis, Gordon R. "Suffering and Anguish." In *The Zondervan Pictorial Encyclopedia of the Bible*, edited by Merrill C. Tenney, 5:530–33. 5 vols. Grand Rapids: Zondervan, 1975.

Lightfoot, J. B. *St. Paul's Epistle to the Philippians*. Grand Rapids: Zondervan, 1974.

Lindberg, Tod. *The Political Teachings of Jesus*. New York: HarperCollins, 2007.

Lints, Richard. *Identity and Idolatry: The Image of God and Its Inversion*. Downers Grove, IL: InterVarsity, 2015.

Loyola Press (blog). "Early Christian Martyrs." https://www.loyolapress.com/catholic-resources/saints/saints-stories-for-all-ages/early-christian-martyrs/.

Marshall, I. H. "Kingdom of God, of Heaven." In *The Zondervan Pictorial Encyclopedia of the Bible*, edited by Merrill C. Tenney, 3:801–9. 5 vols. Grand Rapids: Zondervan, 1975.

McKenna, David. *The Jesus Model*. Waco: Word, 1977.

McNeile, Alan Hugh. *The Gospel According to St. Matthew*. London: Macmillan, 1928.

Meeks, Wayne A. *The Moral World of the First Christians*. Philadelphia: Westminster, 1986.

———. *The Origins of Christian Morality: The First Two Centuries*. New Haven, CT: Yale University Press, 1993.

Meyer, Heinrich August Wilhelm. *Critical and Exegetical Handbook to The Epistles to the Philippians and Colossians, and to Philemon*. Translated by John C. Moore. Meyer's Critical and Exegetical Handbook to the New Testament. New York: Funk & Wagnalls, 1885.

———. *Critical and Exegetical Handbook to The Gospel of Matthew*. Translated by Peter Christie. Meyer's Critical and Exegetical Handbook to the New Testament. New York: Funk & Wagnalls, 1884.

———. *Critical and Exegetical Handbook to The Gospels of Mark and Luke*. Translated by Robert Ernest Wallis. Meyer's Critical and Exegetical Handbook to the New Testament. New York: Funk & Wagnalls, 1884.

Moore, T. V. *The Last Days of Jesus; or, The Appearances of Our Lord during the Forty Days between the Resurrection and Ascension*. Philadelphia: Presbyterian Board of Publication, 1858.

Moule, C. F. D. "Further Reflections on Philippians 2:5–11." In *Apostolic History and the Gospel: Biblical and Historical Essays Presented to F. F. Bruce*, edited by W. Ward Gasque and Ralph P. Martin, 264–76. Exeter: Paternoster, 1970.

Niebuhr, H. Richard. *Christ and Culture*. New York: Harper & Row, 1951.

Nixon, R. E. "Faith, Faithfulness." In *The Zondervan Pictorial Encyclopedia of the Bible*, edited by Merrill C. Tenney, 2:479–91. 5 vols. Grand Rapids: Zondervan, 1975.

O'Brien, Brandon J. "The Social, Economic, and Political Commitments of the Early Church." *Christianity Today*, Sep 6, 2011. https://www.christianitytoday.com/biblestudies/articles/spiritualformation/faithaction.html.

Olson, Dennis T. "Between Humility and Authority." In *Character Ethics and the Old Testament*, edited by M. Daniel Carroll R. et al., 51–61. Louisville: Westminster John Knox, 2007.

Orr, James, ed. "Faithful; Faithfulness." In vol 2, *ISBE*. 5 vols. Chicago: Eerdmans, 1939. https://www.internationalstandardbible.com/F/faithful-faithfulness.html.

Park, Daeun, et al. "A Tripartite Taxonomy of Character: Evidence for Intrapersonal, Interpersonal, and Intellectual Competencies in Children." *Contemporary Educational Psychology* 48 (2017) 16–27.

Paul-Choudhury, Sumit. "Tomorrow's Gods: What Is the Future of Religion?" *Future*, Aug 1, 2019. https://www.bbc.com/future/article/20190801-tomorrows-gods-what-is-the-future-of-religion.

Peppiatt, Lucy. *The Imago Dei: Humanity Made in the Image of God*. Eugene, OR: Cascade, 2022.

Peterson, Ryan S. *The Imago Dei as Human Identity: A Theological Interpretation*. Winona Lake, IN: Eisenbrauns, 2016.

Pittenger, Norman. "God's Nature as Changing or Permanent." In *The Living God: Readings in Christian Theology*, edited by Millard J. Erickson, 393–98. Grand Rapids: Baker, 1973.

Placher, William C., ed. *Callings: Twenty Centuries of Christian Wisdom on Vocation*. Grand Rapids: Eerdmans, 2005.

Plummer, Alfred. *A Critical and Exegetical Commentary on The Gospel According to S. Luke*. International Critical Commentary, edited by S. R. Driver et al. Edinburgh: T. & T. Clark, 1989.

Pozzi, Maura, et al. "(Dis)Obedience in U.S. American Young Adults: A New Way to Describe Authority Relationships." *Europe's Journal of Psychology* 14.2 (Jun 2018) 404–23. https://www.ncbi.nlm.nih.gov/pmc/articles/PMC6016029/.

Read the Spirit. "André Trocmé (1901–1971)." https://readthespirit.com/interfaith-peacemakers/andre-trocme/.

Rees, Paul S. *The Epistles to the Philippians, Colossians, and Philemon*. Grand Rapids: Baker, 1964.

Reid, Jennings B. *Jesus: God's Emptiness, God's Fullness: The Christology of St. Paul*. New York: Paulist, 1990.

Robinson, Theodore H. *The Gospel of Matthew*. Moffatt New Testament Commentary, edited by James Moffatt. London: Hodder and Stoughton, 1937.

Rudd, James B. "American Evangelical Syncretism." *Reverence Journal*, Jan 11, 2020. https://www.reverencejournal.com/journal-enties/2020/2/3/american-evangelical-syncretism.

Ruthruff, Ron. "Creation in Context (Psalm 8)." *The Christian Century*, Jun 2, 2023. https://www.christiancentury.org/sunday-s-coming-creation-in-context.

Sartorius, Ernst Wilhelm C. *The Doctrine of Divine Love; or Outlines of the Moral Theology of the Evangelical Church.* Translated by Sophia Taylor. Edinburgh: T. & T. Clark, 1884.

Severance, Diane. "Blandina: A Faithful Witness." *Christianity.com*, May 3, 2019. https://www.christianity.com/church/church-history/timeline/1-300/blandina-a-faithful-witness-11629606.html.

Smith, C. Drew. "If Any Want to Become My Followers." In *Character Ethics and the New Testament: Moral Dimensions of Scripture*, edited by Robert L. Brawley, 209–23. Louisville: Westminster John Knox, 2007.

Stassen, Glen H., and David P. Gushee. *Kingdom Ethics: Following Jesus in Contemporary Context.* Downers Grove, IL: InterVarsity, 2003.

Stott, John R. W. *The Contemporary Christian.* Downers Grove, IL: InterVarsity, 1992.

———. *The Message of the Sermon on the Mount.* The Bible Speaks Today, edited by J. A. Motyer and John R. W. Stott. Downers Grove, IL: InterVarsity, 1978.

Strong, Augustus Hopkins. *Systematic Theology.* Valley Forge, PA: Judson, 1974.

Swartley, Willard M. "Peacemaking Pillars of Character Formation in the New Testament." In *Character Ethics and the New Testament: Moral Dimensions of Scripture*, edited by Robert L. Brawley, 225–43. Louisville: Westminster John Knox, 2007.

Taylor, Ed. "7 Unique Callings of God." *Ed Taylor* (blog), Feb 6, 2020. https://edtaylor.org/2020/02/06/7-unique-callings-of-god/.

Theology of Work Project. "The Character Approach." https://www.theologyofwork.org/key-topics/ethics/systematic-presentation-of-ethics/different-approaches-to-ethics/the-character-approach.

Thiessen, Henry Clarence. *Introductory Lectures in Systematic Theology.* Grand Rapids: Eerdmans, 1949.

Thompson, Frank H. "Obedience." In *Baker's Dictionary of Christian Ethics*, edited by Carl F. H. Henry, 465–66. Grand Rapids: Baker, 1973.

Thompson, James W. *Christ and Culture in the New Testament.* Eugene, OR: Cascade, 2023.

Timpe, Kevin. "Moral Character." *Internet Encyclopedia of Philosophy*. https://iep.utm.edu/moral-ch/.

Trench, Richard C. *Synonyms of the New Testament.* 9th ed. Grand Rapids: Eerdmans, 1975.

Troeltsch, Ernst. *The Social Teaching of the Christian Churches.* Translated by Olive Wyon. Vol. 1. 2 vols. New York: Harper Torchbooks, 1960.

Tusculum University. "Early Christian Oral Transmission of Gospel Stories Focus of Concluding Session of Theologian Lecture Series." Mar 2, 2017. https://www3.tusculum.edu/news/news/2017/early-christian-oral-transmission-of-gospel-stories-focus-of-concluding-session-of-theologian-lecture-series/.

Van Vliet, Jason P. "Calvin's Teaching on the Image of God." *Christian Study Library*, 2009. https://www.christianstudylibrary.org/article/calvin%E2%80%99s-teaching-image-god.

Verhey, Allen. *Remembering Jesus: Christian Community, Scripture, and the Moral Life.* Grand Rapids: Eerdmans, 2002.

Vlach, Michael J. "The Kingdom of God in Paul's Epistles." *The Master's Seminary Journal* 26.1 (Spring 2015). https://tms.edu/wp-content/uploads/2021/09/tmsj26e.pdf.

Wells, David F. "Persecution." In *The New International Dictionary of the Christian Church*, edited by J. D. Douglas et al., 766–67. Grand Rapids: Zondervan, 1974.

Wheatcroft, G. Richard. "The Kingdom of God: A Domination Free Order." *ProgressiveChristianity.org*, Apr 9, 2006. https://progressivechristianity.org/resources/the-kingdom-of-god-a-domination-free-order/.

Wink, Walter. *Jesus and Nonviolence: A Third Way*. Minneapolis: Fortress, 2003.

Wogaman, J. Philip. *Christian Ethics: A Historical Introduction*. Louisville: Westminster John Knox, 1993.

Wozniak, Kenneth W. M. *Living as the Living Jesus: A Broader Jesus Ethic*. Eugene, OR: Wipf & Stock, 2021.

Wright, D. F. "Ignatius." In *The New International Dictionary of the Christian Church*, edited by J. D. Douglas et al., 498–99. Grand Rapids: Zondervan, 1974.

———. "Perpetua." In *The New International Dictionary of the Christian Church*, edited by J. D. Douglas et al., 765. Grand Rapids: Zondervan, 1974.

———. "Polycarp." In *The New International Dictionary of the Christian Church*, edited by J. D. Douglas et al., 791–92. Grand Rapids: Zondervan, 1974.

Yoder, John Howard. "How H. Richard Niebuhr Reasoned: A Critique of *Christ and Culture*." In *Authentic Transformation: A New Vision of Christ and Culture*, 31–89. Nashville: Abingdon, 1996.

———. *The Politics of Jesus*. Grand Rapids: Eerdmans, 1972.

www.ingramcontent.com/pod-product-compliance
Lightning Source LLC
Chambersburg PA
CBHW071239230426
43668CB00011B/1508